PENGUIN BOOKS

HICKY'S BENGAL GAZETTE

Andrew Otis holds a PhD in Journalism from the University of Maryland. He spent five years researching and writing this book, first as a Joseph P. O'Hern scholar and then as a Fulbright Fellow in Kolkata, India. He lives in Washington D.C. For more about him, you can visit andrewotis.com.

HICKY'S BENGAL GAZETTE

THE UNTOLD STORY OF INDIA'S FIRST NEWSPAPER

ANDREW OTIS

PENGUIN BOOKS

An imprint of Penguin Random House

PENGUIN BOOKS

USA | Canada | UK | Ireland | Australia
New Zealand | India | South Africa | China

Penguin Books is part of the Penguin Random House group of companies
whose addresses can be found at global.penguinrandomhouse.com

Published by Penguin Random House India Pvt. Ltd
4th Floor, Capital Tower 1, MG Road,
Gurugram 122 002, Haryana, India

Penguin
Random House
India

Published by Westland Publications Private Limited in 2018
This edition published in Penguin Books by Penguin Random House India in 2022

ISBN 9780143459330

Typeset by Jojy Philip
Printed at Replika Press Pvt. Ltd, India

www.penguin.co.in

MIX
Paper from
responsible sources
FSC
www.fsc.org   FSC® C016779

Contents

Part III
Perseverance

Preface

Eight years ago, I visited Kolkata, India, for the first time. For more than 200 years, from the end of the seventeenth century to the beginning of the twentieth, Kolkata had been the centre of British India, an unbroken territory stretching from Pakistan in the west to Myanmar in the east, from the Himalayas in the north to the Indian Ocean in the south. The city's stately stone-gray Victoria Memorial, perched on the green Maidan, complemented the history I saw percolating through its crowded streets. Everywhere were physical reminders of the city's past. While I left the city with respect for its heritage and institutions, never did I expect I would come back, nor dedicate the next six years of my life to one period of its history.

A few months later, while looking for resources to write a paper, I saw an unmarked brown-covered book deep in the basement of my university's library stacks, in Rochester, New York. I stood transfixed. I had never come across something like it before. I knew I had found something special as soon as I flipped through its dusty pages in the dim light.

Inside I found a copy of the *Memoirs* of William Hickey, lawyer for journalist James Augustus Hicky. As a member of England's upper class in the eighteenth century, Hickey represented clients in India, the West Indies and England, all of which he had documented in vibrant detail in the diary. His descriptions of Kolkata (then Calcutta) caught my attention, with their colourful characters, complaints of a deleterious climate, and details of entanglements between the Indians and British. Much like a travel guide, he pointed me to my subsequent research.

Through the memoirs, I learned about James Augustus Hicky's story. I learned he had founded a newspaper and tried to expose corruption in the British East India Company and embezzlement in the Christian Church. I learned Hicky was sued for libel for his reporting. Up against both Church and State, Hicky fought for the freedom of the Press, but his newspaper was shut down. His campaign against corruption and tyranny came to an end, and the East India Company would rule much of India with an iron fist for many years to come. It was an interesting story, I thought, but at the time I did not see myself pursuing it further.

Later that year, I found myself in the airy reading rooms of the British Library in London on a scholarship to investigate early Indian newspapers. For a month, I travelled daily to the British Library's newspaper holdings and lost myself in lives from two hundred years ago. The dry paper in my hands conjured up romantic visions of the past. There was heat, a mixing of cultures, and an incredible richness of life. There was also desperation, poverty, and a deep divide between the British and those they ruled. Like all romantic visions, what I imagined was based only on a fragment of truth.

As I pored through the newspapers of Kolkata's past, I wondered: what had started it all? Why and how had India's press become so vibrant? What had been that first spark of free expression? These questions led me back to James Augustus Hicky and his publication, the first printed newspaper in Asia. I found that there had been no exhaustive investigation of his life or his paper. For centuries he had been ridiculed as a scurrilous muckraker who insulted his social betters, not worthy of the title 'journalist'. No one had placed him properly in his time or considered his true importance. I realised that here was my chance. I began thinking of a book on *Hicky's Bengal Gazette*. And I began thinking of ways to return to Kolkata.

Two years later, I got my chance when I was awarded a Fulbright Fellowship to study the origins of journalism in India. It was the height of the monsoon when I returned to Kolkata, with Bengal's humid air hanging over the city like a sticky mango. I was eager to begin, and started compiling a list of the archives and institutions I would need to visit. The first was the Victoria Memorial.

I had only been in Kolkata a few days when I met the Victoria Memorial's director. I had heard before, from professors in the US, that the Memorial held notebooks written by one of the first Supreme Court justices of Bengal, John Hyde. These notebooks, written over a twenty-year span, and comprising over 20,000 pages, are the best legal records from eighteenth century Bengal. If I wanted to write about Hicky and his gazette, I would have to understand more about the place and context in which he lived. I would also have to understand more about his conflict with the East India Company, and why he was sued for libel in the Supreme Court of Bengal. Hyde's Notebooks would be a good place to start.

Two colleagues and I walked into the Victoria Memorial unannounced, with no plan in mind. We were ushered into the director's office, where I introduced myself and explained my project. In that meeting, I learned that the Memorial had initiated a project to digitise Hyde's Notebooks, a project estimated to take six months. Digitisation would mean the notebooks would be preserved indefinitely, but it also meant the original notebooks would be unavailable during much of my stay.

Over the next six months, I spent much of my time at the National Library of India, which had an incomplete and partially damaged microfilm copy of Hyde's Notebooks. As I was wheeling through the microfilm, I came across what looked like secret code written throughout the notebooks. At first I ignored these incomprehensible symbols, not knowing what they were. But I kept seeing the symbols. Hyde had written many of them around Hicky's trials. He had obviously wanted to conceal something. What was he hiding?

I teamed up with Carol Johnson, an expert in ancient shorthand at the New Jersey Institute of Technology, in the US. But the project was not so simple. I needed to get Carol photocopies of the microfilm. At first, the National Library allowed me to make digital copies. Then they allowed only paper copies. Then they allowed only one-third of the number of pages I requested. So if Hyde wrote six pages on any given date, I could only copy two of the pages. Much later, after my time in India, Carol broke Hyde's code. She discovered that Hyde had been secretly recording the corruption of his fellow judges in the Supreme Court.

When I checked in at the Victoria Memorial six months later, digitisation had not yet started, and the original notebooks were still unavailable. Finally, the last place where there might be records, the High Court of Calcutta, had rejected my request to research in its archives.

As if matters could not get more complex, the Foreigner's Regional Registration Office, where all foreigners must register in order to live in India, had postponed my visa extension. The rumour was that a diplomatic spat between the Indian and American governments had resulted in backlash against Americans. An Indian diplomat had been arrested for visa fraud in the US, and had been strip-searched by suspicious American law enforcement staff, enraging Indian government officials. I spent many frustrating days at the Registration Office, filling endless paperwork and satisfying byzantine requirements to get an extension.

Eventually I received my visa extension. Also, the Victoria Memorial kindly let me have an advanced look at its digitisation of Hyde's Notebooks. Lastly, with the help of a lawyer, the High Court of Calcutta let me research in its archives. Things, finally, began to go as planned.

Although the High Court of Calcutta has long since moved into a new building, I imagined its workings were similar to what Hicky would have encountered 200 years ago. Staff swarmed in vast cluttered halls. Construction crews actively remodelled, lawyers congregated in deadly hot side-rooms. And judges yelled in barely audible courtrooms over the din of rustling papers.

I learned that the Court had not one, but six archives. I visited them all. Invariably, I found mustachioed men drinking chai and frowning over stacks of yellowing records. Sometimes I was entreated to come back another time. Other times I would be waved in to investigate floors upon floors of records at my leisure. At one point a staff member even told me that the records for the whole Court had been moved to another office, on the other side of the city. I followed this unbelievable lead too, even though little came of it.

Eventually, I reached the archive I was looking for, where tens of thousands of old records, dating back to Hicky's time, reside in varying degrees of decay. Some records were organised in bundles by year, wrapped in twine between wood slats, looking like accordions overstuffed with crinkling paper. These were placed along the edges of the room. The majority of the records were stacked across the room, unindexed and uncatalogued, rendering them inaccessible to scholars.

I was told I would need permission for each individual trial I wanted to see. Yet, conspicuously missing was a catalogue for the time period I was researching. Without a catalogue, it would be impossible to know which records existed, and without knowing which records existed, it would be impossible to know what to ask permission for. The Catch-22, though unintentional, was frustrating.

Armed with my best educated guesswork, I came back a week later with a stack of request letters in my arm, hoping that I had requested records that actually existed.

I grew used to haggling for time.

'*Konta baje bondo?*' What time will you close, I would ask.

'*Duita baje bondo.*' Two o'clock close, a staffer would reply.

Eventually we would come to an agreement where I would push for more time, and they would push to get back to their other duties. (The archive would only open when I was there.)

The archive was remarkable. The difficulty in accessing it means few scholars have seen its records. I found a copy of *Hicky's Bengal Gazette* that had been lost to time for over 230 years.[1] It was in this extraordinary issue, printed only days before his trials, that Hicky exhorted his readers to stand up for the freedom of the Press in the face of tyranny. I also found records of Hicky's earlier life before he became a printer, when he worked as a doctor and surgeon. I learned that he had spent nearly two years in prison before becoming a journalist, and I found clues to why he had become a printer: it was an attempt to pay his debts and get out of jail.

After Kolkata, I set my sights on Delhi. I had been told that important documents had been moved to Delhi decades ago. I spent many weeks on a fruitless search in India's Supreme Court for records last seen in 1911.[2] I never managed to find those records, but I did find other useful documents. At the National Archives of India, I found many of Hicky's original letters. I saw, for the first time, his handwriting and his signature. I learned what happened to him after his trials, and I learned much of the time in which he lived.

After over a year of research, I left India on Christmas eve 2014, and landed in the drizzling cold of Germany. There, in the orderly rows of the Franckesche Stiftungen in Halle—the institute that trained many missionaries who went to India—I read the letters of Johann Zacharias Kiernander, the missionary who sued Hicky for libel. I came to realise I might have become too sympathetic to Hicky at the expense of others. Now I saw Kiernander's pain, his despair, and his isolation after Hicky's allegations of corruption and embezzlement caused his fellow missionaries to abandon him. The tormenting fall-out would haunt him for the rest of his life.

Finally, I found myself back at the British Library, where my research had begun. There—after two more trips—I finished my research. Through the letters of the British Governor-General Warren Hastings, Supreme Court Chief Justice Elijah Impey, and Colonel Thomas Deane Pearse, I saw how the upper echelon of Company servants dreaded Hicky. I saw how they viewed him, too: as a pitiful scoundrel, a panderer of filth, and a purveyor of insolent abuse against his social betters. I saw how Hastings, trying to protect the Company from criticism, shut down Hicky's newspaper. And I saw how Hastings eventually paid the price for his absolute power, suffering through eight years of impeachment proceedings for abuse of office.

History has long misrepresented the founder of India's first newspaper. Scholars during the British imperial era characterised Hicky as a rogue and scoundrel, a man who undermined the British Empire. Some recent historians have gone too far in the other direction, claiming Hicky's newspaper was a 'gem of journalism', unmatched and unparalleled.[3] Small errors have compounded over time into serious mistakes. Modern historians have misspelled Hicky's name, or gotten basic facts wrong. Some have incorrectly stated that he was deported from India. Others have misstated his place of birth. Yet others have included fanciful, wholly imaginative drawings of him.[4]

Only recently have scholars challenged simplistic narratives and offered nuanced interpretations. Tarun Kumar Mukhopadhyay has suggested that Hicky was not uneducated or 'uncultivated' as his contemporaries would have us believe, but was instead a diehard moralist who refused to accept the corruption of his countrymen. Most recently, Partha Chatterjee has pondered Hicky's greater implications: suggesting both that he was the first in India to publicly assert that British subjects had inalienable rights, and that he was the first in India to create a public platform to criticise British rule.[5]

In this book, I call for further interpretation of Hicky. He saw himself as the voice of the poor and those of lower status. He also articulated that the means of imperialism must match the ends, that the East India Company should not launch wars of conquest. Perhaps this is why, for centuries, he was dismissed as a scoundrel. British imperial historians, mired in class-based attitudes, focused on his interest in scandal, ignoring that he was concerned with more serious issues, such as questioning the moral right of Britain to an empire.

It is important to note that news dissemination in Asia was complex long before Hicky's paper. Chinese officials founded bulletins thousands of years before him. Korean officials distributed government newsletters. Japanese printers block-printed handbills. Mughal leaders spread news by handwritten newsletters known as akhbarats, distributed by networks of thousands of hircarrahs, runners.

Colonists, as well, distributed news. Portuguese Jesuits introduced the first printing press in India in the 1550s. The Dutch East India Company printed a newsletter in 1615; the Spanish printed their own twenty years later. Printing spread through missionary settlements in South India through the next century.[6]

Despite this long history of printing in Asia, Hicky was the first to found a newspaper, something that was printed on a regular basis and intended to convey information. He was part of a greater struggle for Enlightenment ideals of inalienable rights, ending taxation without representation, and the freedom of the Press. The fact that four near-complete copies of *Hicky's Bengal Gazette* have survived to this day, while other newspapers of his time often exist only in fragments, if at all, is a testament to how important his paper was. He became part of India. His children grew up and died in India.[7] His legacy remains.

Main Characters

James Augustus Hicky, founder of *Hicky's Bengal Gazette*, the first newspaper in India.

Warren Hastings, Governor-General of British India and first in command of the Supreme Council.

Johann Zacharias Kiernander, first missionary sent by the Society for the Promotion of Christian Knowledge.

Johann Christian Diemer, second missionary sent by the Society for the Promotion of Christian Knowledge.

Philip Francis, second in command of the Supreme Council.

William Hickey, lawyer at the Supreme Court.

Elijah Impey, Chief Justice of the Supreme Court.

Thomas Deane Pearse, Colonel of Artillery in the Company's Army.

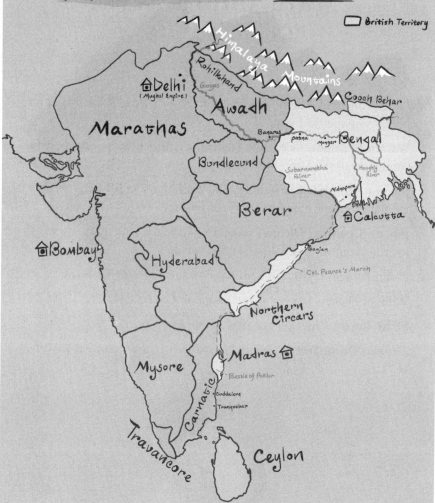

Prologue
The *Ajax*

What unrepented Sins of mine
Or stranger destiny of Time
Doom'd us to linger here
Where broiling sun and scorching Wind
And overwhelming Floods combined
Alternate mark the year.
— *Hicky's Bengal Gazette*, 19 August 1780.

October 1802. En Route to China.

'Ship's company! Off hats,' came the yell from the *Ajax*'s deck.

An old man coughed in the ship's dark holds. For months at a time he had been unable to move from his bed. His handwriting shook. His body was unsteady. He feared he would be carried out of this world in convulsions at any moment.

The old man had stepped aboard the *Ajax* in May 1802. His ultimate destination was Canton, China, to join a mission to bring hemp and nutmeg back to India.[8] His role on this ship is unknown. He may have gone as a surgeon; he kept silver-plated surgical tools, medicines, and anatomy books at home. Or, he may have gone to trade, to bring items like porcelain and tea back to India.[9]

But he was neither truly a trader nor a surgeon. He had been many things in his life, but there was one thing above all for which he had found purpose. He was a journalist.

Leaving Calcutta was a dangerous decision. But poverty had made him desperate. He had lived in the city for over a generation but had seen little work for years and had a large family to feed. He had sacrificed everything, even degraded himself to provide for them, blackmailing old colleagues, calling in old debts, and even begging old political enemies for favours or work.[10] Amid it all, he had struggled to put his children through school—he had even contemplated sending them to London to be placed with a charity. By 1799 he had sold, mortgaged and peddled almost everything he owned. Still it was not enough.[11]

The *Ajax* peacefully passed the Straits of Malacca, a narrow strip of water separating the Indian and Pacific Oceans, and sailed up the South China Sea before approaching Canton. It was a hazardous route. Islands, ill-charted reefs, and unpredictable monsoons made the voyage treacherous. Pirates and hostile Dutch and French ships—it was the midst of the Napoleonic wars— made the passage yet more perilous.[12] Two British warships, the *Intrepid* and the *Comet,* had recently gone missing in their search for another missing ship, the *Talbot,* last seen at the eastern entrance of the Straits.[13] But the *Ajax*, strong, teak-built and newly sheathed and coppered, passed uneventfully.[14]

Somewhere along the route, the old man collapsed. When his best-mates found him, they wrapped his hammock gently around his frame. They sewed it shut, starting at his feet and working their way up his torso, putting the last stitch through his nose to be sure he was dead. Then they heaved his body on their shoulders and carried him up to the deck, tying cannon balls to his feet and placing him on the mess table.

The captain prepared his last rites.

'Ashes to ashes. Dust to dust. The Lord bless him and keep him. The Lord make his face to shine upon him and be gracious unto him. The Lord lift up his countenance upon him, and give him peace. Amen.'

'Amen,' the crew echoed.

The captain nodded. And with one swift movement, the crew tipped the table. The shrouded white-as-cotton form slid into the inky deep.

'On hats. Dismissed,' came the captain's call.[15]

Back in Calcutta, the wheels of fate moved quickly. The old man's creditors began to call in his debts within days of news of his death, eager to cement their claims before anyone else.[16] The East India Company placed a guard at his house and began to inventory his estate, and in May 1803 it twice advertised that what little he owned would be auctioned to pay his debts: 'A beautiful Eight-light lustre (chandelier)', 'Forty Cases of Holland's GIN', 'Thirty-five Dozen Pale Ale', 'A variety of OTHER LIQUORS', and his 'Gold Watch, capped and jewelled'. All this was for sale.[17]

But what they did not advertise were the tools that had made him famous. The ink and type that for two years, from 1780 to 1782, made him prominent, notorious, feared even. His types were so worn, and his printing press so decayed that the estate administrators did not think they were even worth advertising.[18]

In those two years, he had uncovered corruption in the East India Company, challenged the tyranny of a despotic government, and exposed embezzlement in the Christian Church. He had fought for the freedom of the Press against a company eager to eliminate dissent, and against a missionary eager to profit under the facade of faith. He had defied both the Church and State, and had demonstrated the power of the Press to protect the people and to expose tyranny, injustice and corruption.

He had done this all through a process that had changed little in centuries, a process of inking type and pressing paper hundreds of times over. It was slow, tedious work, but the final product was powerful enough to challenge an empire.

His name was James Augustus Hicky.

PART I

THE JOURNALIST

The Wild Irishman

I ... found a most eccentric creature apparently possessed of considerable natural talents, but entirely uncultivated. Never before had I beheld a mortal who so completely came up to what I had often heard described as 'a wild Irishman'!

– William Hickey, in his memoirs.[19]

November 1777, Lal Bazar (The Red Market)

William Hickey had only been in Calcutta for a few days when a man in the common jail sent him a letter begging for help.[20] He was curious to meet this Irishman whose last name was almost the same as his.

Everything William saw shocked him. Everything, even people, were for sale. Bathhouses offered their services and taverns sold cheap arrack. On one side of the square, elite society held lavish balls and banquets in the Harmonic House, Calcutta's most fashionable club. On the other, prisoners fought for daily survival in Calcutta's common jail.[21]

Nooses were on display outside for those sentenced to death. Pillories were prepared for perjurers, nails ready to be hammered into their ears to mark them as criminals for life.[22] Thieves were whipped up and down the square to the beat of a tom-tom drum, while prisoners were brought to and from jail in a device that looked like a giant birdcage with perforated air holes, suspended fourteen feet in the air on wheels, so the whole city could see their shame.[23]

William entered the jail through a deep gateway leading into a small courtyard. The smell of rot, faeces and decay assaulted him.

He peered into the rooms surrounding him, where small cells held hundreds of prisoners.[24] There were almost no windows, and the few openings were too small to let much air pass through. 'The stench is dreadful,' he later recalled, 'more offensive than any [I] ever experienced in this country.'[25]

The jail was horrific on a level he had never seen before. It brought him back to when he visited the King's Bench prison in London as a young lawyer. While it had been overcrowded, Calcutta's was so much worse. 'They will not bear a comparison,' he said of the two jails.[26]

William moved deeper into the jail. He could feel the despair in the humid heat. Hindus, Muslims, Europeans, men and women, all lived in the same space. Felons, debtors, and fettered prisoners intermingled, their iron chains clinking as they moved. Many were deathly ill. There was no hospital or infirmary, so the sick had to fend for themselves. Prisoners also had to pay for their own food, water and lodging, trapping them in an impossible cycle of debt. Their situation was made worse by the British East India Company's refusals to forgive their debts.[27]

William headed to the prison yard at the back where he saw many living in the open, and where some Europeans had erected small bamboo huts. Open drains of excrement and urine ran into the water tank nearby, the jail's only water source, where the prisoners drank, washed, and bathed. If prisoners were fortunate, the jailor allowed their family, servants or friends to bring them food or water. But not all were so fortunate.

An old woman approached and begged him for money. She said she only wanted to buy water, otherwise she would have none.

Then William spotted the bamboo shed he had been looking for, and greeted the man inside. The man, more than anything in this jail, would shock him most of all.

Inside was James Augustus Hicky, the man who would found the first newspaper in India. James told him his tale.

The City of Palaces

A moderate share of attention, and your being not quite an idiot are (in the present situation of things) ample qualities for the attainment of riches.

> – Richard Barwell to his father, 1765.[28]

Nine o'clock Thursday evening, 4 April 1772. Off the coast of England.

A small rowboat sidled up to the *Marquis of Rockingham*. The soft yellow glow of a lantern glimmered in the night, casting a thin sheen of light against the black waves. The captain lowered the ship's gangplank into the calm waters in greeting. Stooped in the darkness, grasping the gangplank's rope handrails, the surgeon's mate, James Augustus Hicky, made his way on deck.[29]

He knew the crew were anxious to leave. They had sailed from London over a month ago, yet still were not ready for open ocean. The skies were gray and wet like morning mist. Good weather, it seemed, was always out of reach. They had washed the deck, cleaned the rigging and loaded more supplies than they could count. A contingent of soldiers bound for the Company army muddled nervously about with their guns, swords, and munitions. Finally, on April 9, under squally skies and light rain, they weighed anchor and set off.[30]

Almost nothing is known about Hicky's early life. What is known is that he was probably born in Ireland around 1739 or 1740. His father, a linen weaver, died when he was young. As a young man, he had found a job as a clerk for an attorney in Dublin.

But he had wanted more in life than to be someone's assistant, so he travelled to London and apprenticed with a Scottish printer, hoping to begin his own career.[31]

Yet, instead of taking his freedom from the printers' guild and starting his own shop, he joined the British Navy, where he served on a Man o' War and was nicknamed 'the Captain'.

Before long, he changed his career again, returning to London to clerk for one of England's most famous lawyers, Serjeant Davy, the lawyer responsible for a trial that banned slavery in England.[32] But he grew bored. While he waited in Davy's office, receiving briefs of cases, he passed his time by reading books on surgery that he found lying around. Then the idea struck him to try his hand as a surgeon.

But few people were willing to employ him as a surgeon in London, so he went back to sea again, and was hired as a surgeon's mate on a slave ship trading to Guinea, in west Africa. Despite his hopes, this path did not bring success either. After three or four voyages in the slave trade he had not gained a shilling.

So, he decided to change his path one final time: he would go to India.[33]

The *Rockingham* followed a route to India formed from hundreds of years of trade. They sailed past Europe's contours, landing in the Canary Islands, before heading around Africa and the tortuous waters of the Cape of Good Hope.[34] With the aid of the monsoon winds, they passed Madagascar and the Comoros Islands and reached Bombay. After two months, they set sail again, traversing India's southern tip, their path tracing a wide arc around Sri Lanka, the Andaman Islands, and the coast of Burma, before approaching Bengal from the east.[35]

The journey was as dangerous as it was monotonous. The endless blue waters gave Hicky freedom. But they also spoke to the unyielding fears of all those who sailed. Every voyage was a prayer that violent storms or hidden shoals would not beget a dark watery doom or shipwreck on a forlorn coast. One of the *Rockingham's* passengers reminisced that on the high seas, 'the waves rose mountains high, the winds roared, the sailors vied with the elements in noise [while] I betook myself quietly to my shelf, where I meditated on past follies, and formed aerial schemes of future wealth and magnificence.'[36] Hicky, too, took time to think about his future and why he had made this journey.

Hicky also faced the boredom that came with long months in the doldrums, where the ship sat in still silence under the hot sun and the crew fell to drinking. The Captain used corporal punishment to keep them in line, demoting one for drunkenness and giving another a dozen lashes.[37] And then there was the threat of scurvy, brought by a diet of hardtack and gruel. Starting with bleeding gums, and ending with organ failure, scurvy was a disease that, if it did not kill, could lay someone low for months.

It was a journey that many would take, but few would live to return. Those who travelled might survive the voyage, but they might not survive what came next. With little resistance to local disease, Europeans suffered from frequent illnesses, tropical fevers, and venereal disease.[38] India was indeed fatal for many Europeans. Only 10 per cent of Company cadets survived long enough to draw their pensions, while roughly a quarter of European soldiers sent to India died every year.[39] For Hicky, who had neither the money nor privileges of his richer peers, his most likely outcome was death. But for Hicky, like many others, the potential for fortune made it all worthwhile.

On December 16, the *Rockingham* docked at the mouth of the Hooghly river, one hundred kilometres from Calcutta. Two weeks later they reached the city.[40] Ships of all sizes glided by, from single-sailed ketches and budgerows, to East Indiamen merchant ships, and even majestic Men o' War. On both sides of the river, white mansions with green lawns, as fine as the best palaces in Europe, descended to the water's edge. They gave the impression that, here, anyone could find their fortune.[41]

The *Rockingham* continued north, past Fort William, an under-construction mess of yellow bricks and mortar, and the huge grassy plain known as the Maidan, cleared to provide a field of fire against invading armies.[42] The Maidan was once covered in jungle. But much had changed in only a few years. Now, white colonnaded mansions were being constructed nearby with reckless abandon, while wealthy Company servants—as

Company employees were known—paraded through the streets in coaches and palanquins.

Hicky jumped ship on 1 February 1773, abandoning his position as surgeon's mate, and stepped onto the streets of Calcutta.[43] Those first steps could be a bewildering, terrifying experience. Many met with disappointment, expecting easy fortune, but finding hard toil instead.[44] Scams were a serious concern. Touts at the docks would lead travellers to taverns, where they would be told that anyone they knew was out of town, but they were welcome to stay a few days. After which, they would be presented with huge and unannounced bills for their food, entertainment and lodging. New arrivals sometimes never recovered from these scams, floundering in impossible debt until they died in Calcutta's notorious jails.[45]

Scams were an unfortunate entry into a city quickly rising as the star of British India. Calcutta grew with little planning and little order. The wealthy built their mansions where they pleased. The East India Company, which ruled British India, saw little need to provide services like city planning, police, hospitals, or road construction. In Calcutta, private individuals were expected to provide for society, if they were expected to provide at all.

Hicky soon discovered that the many mansions belied Calcutta's seedier side. Opium dens, whore houses, and taverns in dingy lanes hosted a shadowy multi-ethnic underground. Gangs up to 200-strong roamed the streets, while rowdy bands of sailors traversed the taverns, arrack stalls, and punch houses, coercing any man they could find into the navy.[46] Packs of mangy dogs bathed in the city's main drinking water supply. Corpses could be seen protruding from one of the cemeteries' shallow graves. Bodies were carried naked to the ghats at all hours to be burned. The poor dumped theirs directly in the river. The destitute were left to decompose for days.[47]

As Hicky moved away from the river, away from the European 'White Town', he entered neighbourhoods where Armenians, Anglo-Indians, Portuguese, Jews, and Parsis formed the city's crucial glue, interlocuting between British and Indians. The building boom meant opportunity for those who could turn British dreams into reality. Furthest was 'Black Town', where Indians lived. Here the streets were the most crowded, but also the most vibrant and diverse. Hindus and Muslims, potters, tanners, oil pressers, tailors, blacksmiths and lower class Europeans all lived together.[48] It was still a city of palaces, but one where a merchant's lofty mansion could stand next to a peasant's thatched hovel.[49]

This was where Hicky settled, a place where no respectable European lived. But Hicky belonged to a different class of people looking for adventure and advancement. Often without the Company's sanction to stay in India, their lives have often gone unrecorded in history. They fought and languished in the bottom ranks of the Company army. They frequented punch shops and arrack stalls. They set up trading ventures or worked as shopkeepers and assistants. While they are not remembered individually, as a class, they were tremendously important in shaping India. They are known as the subalterns, meaning those below every other.[50]

It was the ever-increasing opportunity for riches that drew a subaltern like Hicky to Calcutta. If India was the jewel in the Empire's crown, Calcutta was its shining star. The 'City of Palaces' made men rich. In a time when the average man in England made £17 a year, the average Company servant earned well over £800 a year. Fortunes were greatest at the highest ranks. One General John Carnac took home £50,000 in two years. A Lt. Colonel Mark Wood took home £200,000 after five years.[51] Richard Barwell was believed to have made £400,000 while in India.[52] This was wealth beyond the wildest dreams of many. Hicky thought he, too, could find his place in this land of plenty.

Yet only a select few could achieve this wealth. They were the Company servants, appointed by the Company's directors back in England. Company servants had many ways to make money. The most common was skirting the Company's monopoly, a practice known as private trade. Although officially forbidden, private trade was ubiquitous, countenanced, and even encouraged by all ranks, its volume so great that in some places it may have even exceeded the Company's trade. This trade greased the wheels of the Company's business.[53]

Company servants had other illegal means to increase their income. Servants embezzled resources, rigged deals, doctored their accounting, marked up the cost of goods they sent back to Europe, or even gave themselves contracts under fictitious names.[54] For instance, Richard Barwell made thousands giving himself contracts to run the Company's salt farms under false names, while the men on Calcutta's Board of Trade talked openly in public about how they rigged their contracts.[55] The military was rife with such schemes. One officer encouraged his troops to drink arrack because he made a profit on every bottle sold. Another authorised two officers, one of them his son, to recruit two battalions for the Nawab of Awadh. Neither battalion existed anywhere other than on paper.[56]

Bribes, euphemistically called 'presents', were another means of wealth. Company servants took home an estimated £15 million in presents between 1757 and 1784, draining wealth from India to Britain like a giant sucking straw.[57] This stream of money allowed top Company servants to come home wealthy beyond belief. The most notorious was the governor of Madras, Sir Thomas Rumbold. In two years he amassed a £750,000 fortune. Rumbold even had the audacity to commandeer three Company ships to transport his riches home. Although subjected to Parliamentary and Company inquiries, he defeated all attempts to make him disgorge his loot, and even purchased a seat in Parliament.[58] Despotism, corruption, bribery, nepotism, embezzlement, impunity, and the flagrant abuse of rights were the result of a monopoly, run by servants whose first goal was profit, and whose first loyalty was to their pockets.

A man could go with nothing and come back to England as rich as a nawab, a prince. Hicky may have left England as a surgeon's mate, but he was determined to secure himself a bright future. If Calcutta was the warm heart of the British Empire, then profit was the intoxicating blood on which it flowed.[59] And Hicky was determined to have a part of that profit. Unlike the sons of Britain's upper class, he was responsible for making his own fortune. And his path would be fraught with obstacles unknown to those who had the connections to propel them to the top. For here was the beckoning, shining star of wealth, whispering in his ear, that he could make his fortune.

This reckless abandon would not last forever. And, although Hicky did not know it yet, he would have a hand in its end. It would be because of him that this impunity, corruption, and arbitrary power would be known to the world.

A Plan of Industry

[Instead of] giving himself up to mellancholly reflections and Indolence, he strikes out upon a plan of industry to maintain his family and to work for his freedom.

– James Augustus Hicky, *Hicky's Bengal Gazette*,
4 November 1780.

Spring 1778, Calcutta's Common Jail

William came back again and again to hear Hicky's story.

Hicky told him that he practised as a surgeon when he landed in Calcutta, prescribing medicines, attending and bleeding patients, and removing abscesses.[60]

But he had his hopes set on greater things. He borrowed money to begin a business, purchasing a small vessel to trade along the coast of India between Calcutta and Madras. But in 1775 or 1776, his vessel returned to harbour, its cargo damaged after two months at sea in bad weather. At the same time, many of his debts came due. He pleaded with his bankers, saying that his vessel would be ready to sail again soon, but the bankers refused.[61]

He was now without hope, and saw only one thing to do. He secretly gave all the money he had left—Rs 2,000 (a rupee was roughly one-tenth the value of a British pound)—to a man he trusted, hoping this money would be beyond the reach of the bankers, knowing he might one day need it. And, on 20 October 1776, for the first time in his life, he entered jail as a debtor.[62] The bankers seized everything he had: his ship, his house, even his furniture.

But he refused to give up, he told William. He had an idea to put the skills he learned as a young man to use. He asked for his Rs 2,000 from his trusted friend. With it, he bought types and hired carpenters to make a printing press, smuggling these tools inside jail. He began working from his hut, often from six in the morning to one or two at night, printing handbills, advertisements, almanacs, paraphernalia, documents for the Supreme Court, and even insurance forms. Since prisoners had to pay for their own food and water, it was not uncommon for them to find ways to make money.

Soon, people began to go to him to print items that cost too much to copy by hand, or were too short to send to Europe to complete. After many long months, he scraped together a few hundred rupees, enough to order a proper set of printing supplies from England.[63] Finally, he was back on track.

William had doubts about Hicky. What he learned concerned him. Hicky's conduct in Court was so notorious that he actually remained in jail because no lawyer dared represent him. 'Upon enquiring particularly into the character and conduct of my namesake,' William wrote, 'I learnt that he was extremely violent, yielding so much to sudden gusts of passion and so grossly abusing whoever acted for him that at length not a professional man could be found.'[64]

Yet he was drawn to Hicky. He respected him for enduring Calcutta's common jail.

'It would be impossible for any European to exist for any length of time within the prison,' he later said. 'Even in that shed, it was at times scarcely to be endured.'[65]

William saw himself as the bringer of justice to unjust causes. And Hicky's cause seemed so unjust that he felt compelled to help.

'I could not help feeling for the unfortunate man,' he wrote.[66]

If no one else would represent Hicky, he would. But he would do so only on his own terms. Hicky would have to promise to let him conduct the trial as he saw fit, and 'not, as I understood had thentofore been the case, bounce up in Court every five minutes to complain of his lawyers to the Judges.'[67] After Hicky promised, William began to prepare the case.

But the wheels of justice moved slowly. It was not until the summer of 1778 that Hicky finally stood trial for his debts.

After gathering evidence and witnesses, William and his partners prepared Hicky's case. Their first trial was to remove Hicky's debts to Rammody Bysack, a member of a powerful banking family. Bysack had sued Hicky for Rs 8,955 in upaid loans.[68]

The trial immediately went awry. In the middle of a cross-examination of a witness by William's legal partner, Tilghman, Hicky 'suddenly started from his seat like a maniac, swearing he (Tilghman) did not know how to probe the conscience of a rascally native of Bengal and he would question him himself.' Tilghman threw up his brief in indignation, and threatened to walk out, accusing William of breaching his word that he would be responsible for Hicky's conduct.

William was furious at Hicky for this outburst. 'I told him he was a lying vagabond scoundrel, who ought, and should for me, rot in jail,' he wrote in his memoirs. 'The poor devil burst into a violent flood of tears, threw himself upon his knees, entreating the Judges to plead for him with me, and that if I would forgive him and continue to manage his business he would leave the Court and in future be guided solely by me.'

In the end, the Court ruled for Hicky, cancelling his debts to Bysack. The judges even expressed their opinion that one of Bysack's witnesses should be indicted for perjury, presumably for lying about the terms of one of Hicky's loans.[69]

Hicky's suit to remove his debts to the estate of John Hester came next. Hester, who had been Hicky's tenant and also the chief mate of a 'large country ship', had lent Hicky money two or three times.[70] Hester was also Hicky's patient and had been suffering from a slow, painful, and debilitating stomach disease. When Hester died, his estate claimed Hicky owed Rs 3,000 in unpaid loans.[71]

They went to trial on 29 July 1778. William argued that Hester actually owed Hicky more than Hicky owed Hester. Hicky's witnesses proved that he had fed Hester good dinners and had given him medical care, all of which Hester had not paid for. Hester's former enslaved person, Pompey, testified for

Hicky, saying that Hicky gave Hester anything he needed. 'I lived in the house of Mr Hicky, ate and drank there and I lived well,' Pompey said.[72]

But Hicky still made a scene. When one of Hester's witnesses claimed that Hester owed Hicky nothing, Hicky could be heard whispering to himself, 'Auch, the thief! The villain! The perjured villain, how he lies! Auch, Jasus (Jesus), sweet Jasus, how am I persecuted and torn to paces (pieces).'[73]

Still, Hicky won this trial. The judges ruled that the difference between what Hicky owed Hester and what Hester owed Hicky was so great that they not only cleared all Hicky's debts, but they also ordered Hester's estate to pay Hicky Rs 600 to make up the difference.[74]

By the time these cases were resolved, William had gotten rid of all of Hicky's debts. With his new freedom, Hicky would begin a business that would enter him into posterity.

Coote's Contract

To Print—or not to Print—that is the Question. Whether it is nobler for a man to suffer the threats and anger of the S–p–e C–n–L or to defy them ... The Pangs of weekly toil sorting Types. – laws array, the damn'd Post Office, and the spurns a patient Printer of the unworthy takes, when he himself might his quietus make by breaking up his Press, – Who wou'd bow, and cringe, and fawne obsequious at a Great Man's Breakfast, but that the dread of this same cursed starving, that land of Famine from whose fell Grips no Victime'er returns, – Puzzels the will, and makes the Printer bear his present ills, and induces him to continue to Print his Original Bengal Gazette than fly to projects that he knows not yet. – Thus Famine doth make Cowards of us all.

– James Augustus Hicky, 'The Printer's Soliloqui',
Hicky's Bengal Gazette, 23 December 1780.

August 1779. Breakfast with General Coote, Calcutta.

James Augustus Hicky spread an array of his past work in front of the Commander-in-Chief of the Company army, Sir Eyre Coote. He told Coote that he could print the army's new regulations faster and cheaper than anything that could be done by hand.

Just sitting across from Coote, discussing the army's largest printing contract, was a sign of how far he had come since leaving jail, only one year ago.

He pointed to his first contract with the Company, a job in 1777 to print the army's pay and batta, extra-duty, bills. Although he had been in jail at the time, he had been Calcutta's only printer, so the Council had chosen him. He was proud that he had saved the Company hundreds of rupees a month, freeing their writers from hand copying these paybills over and over by the thousands.[75]

By printing the regulations, Coote could set the army's code of conduct for years to come. The army's old regulations, handwritten on some hundred sheets of paper in 1769, had been annulled, amended, and reissued so many times that they had become a chaotic and byzantine mess.[76] Their inconsistency and incompleteness made it easy for corruption to flourish as officers exploited loopholes to make extra profits.

The new regulations would combine and clarify all of the army's rules. They would standardise everything from how the troops would be paid, how they would be equipped, and even which months they would be fed beef or mutton. They would create new institutions, like the office of surveyor general, a corps of engineers, convalescent hospitals, and a fund for military orphans. And they would standardise things like how to handle the effects of the dead, how grievances would be solved, and even how many guards a general would get outside his tent. In short, they would totally reform the army.

The new regulations would curb corruption in many ways, such as requiring officers to certify their expenses to prevent them from being paid for work they had not done, forbidding officers from holding two commissions to prevent them from collecting double pay, and requiring officers to certify their muster rolls to prevent them from pocketing the salaries of troops that were dead, deserted or only existed on paper.[77] These were simple reforms, but the Company was just instituting them.

Hicky told Coote he wanted to settle on a price first. He had had difficulty getting the Company to pay him for printing their paybills. When had he sent his invoice to the Company's Commissary General, he was told it could not be authorised. Only when he had petitioned the Governor-General directly had he been paid.[78]

Coote thought for a second.

'Very well Mr Hicky, charge the Hon'ble Company for the printing of the regulations in proportion to what they have paid you for these bills,' he said.[79]

Coote's aides handed Hicky nine of the first proof sheets and told him to begin work right away.[80] It was a huge printing job, and was to total at least 38,814 pages, if not much more.[81] The regulations were extremely complex, made up of almost 1,000 separate articles, spanning 384 pages. Each page was printed double-sided and required four pulls of the press to print. Many pages had tables and grids, requiring braces and complex metal ruler work.[82]

Hicky's troubles immediately began.

First, Coote left Calcutta after giving him the project. Second, the contract, the precise details of which no longer remain, was likely made without Governor-General Warren Hastings' knowledge or permission. Third, the Governor-General's friends, Charles Wilkins and Nathaniel Halhed, had just set up another printing press outside Calcutta, and the Governor-General had ordered all Company departments to print with them.[83]

Fourth, some of the army's most powerful officers opposed the new regulations. These officers had much to lose. If the regulations were printed they would lose the perks they had grown accustomed to.

But it was not just their pockets that led many officers to oppose printing the regulations. Many opposed the regulations out of spite and wounded pride. These officers watched as Coote received incredible gifts from Governor-General Hastings, including a mansion and an allowance for any boats or elephants he needed— these perks totalled about £18,000 a year—while their perks were reduced. Coote even received anonymous death threats.[84]

Hicky borrowed Rs 4,000 for the project, hired assistants for the printing line, carpenters, blacksmiths, and brassmen to make equipment.[85] It was full-time work and he needed every man he could get. He sent a call far and wide for skilled printers.

Yet the officers stymied him at every turn. They often made him wait five or six days when he sent in proof sheets, forcing his staff to stand idle for days at a time. When he asked for assistants, they ignored him or sent frivolous excuses.

When a private in the Company army named Keely answered his call, Hicky wrote to Keely's commanding officers to have Keely transferred. He did not receive a reply for over a month. When he finally received a response, the officers told him that Keely 'did not understand much about Printing, and that he was fond of liquor,' an answer that he was convinced was an excuse.[86]

One officer more than any other opposed Hicky: Colonel Thomas Deane Pearse. He was the commander of the Company's Indian artillery corps. The regulations would disband the artillery corps, leaving Pearse without any men to command, and making Pearse determined to stop Hicky.[87]

When a man named Thomas Jones—an artilleryman with printing experience who had just arrived in India—came to Hicky's printing office to help, Hicky thought he had found a new assistant. But Pearse recalled Jones to the army.

Hicky went to Pearse and asked why Jones was recalled.

'The good of the service only, was the cause of recalling Jones,' Pearse said.

'The man was sickly,' Hicky said, promising to give Pearse two healthier men in Jones' stead.

But Pearse was adamant. 'He should never more print for any man,' he said

Hicky mentioned he needed Jones for the regulations, but Pearse again refused.

'I will not spare a man unless it is to assist in making General Coote's regulations into sky rockets,' Pearse said.[88]

Exasperated, Hicky decided to pause printing until Coote returned to Calcutta. By this time, he had completed more than 21,734 pages and had delivered these to Coote's house.[89] He asked for the rest of the regulations, telling Coote's adjunct he would finish them in due course. But Coote's adjunct refused, telling him it would be a breach of contract if he did not finish his printing on schedule.[90]

This was the last straw for Hicky. His project was at a standstill and it was unlikely he would ever complete it with so many officers opposing him. He paused his work and began to think of other ways to make money. He began to think that he could be much more than a job-printer, but someone who could provide society with a useful service.

If he could not be part of reforming society by printing regulations, he could by printing a newspaper.

Droz's Offer

Q. *What is the best way to creep into favours.*
A. *Ask Mr Droze.*
Q. *What is the best way to ruin an honest Man and his family.*
A. *Ask Mr D–e.*

      – James Augustus Hicky, *Hicky's Bengal Gazette*,
18 November 1780.

January 1780. Hicky's home, Calcutta.[91]

Three men set off through the morning's dense, dry fog, the air of winter thick with gray smoke from brick kilns. They rode east from Governor-General Hastings' luxurious palace, through White Town, skirting the brown grassy Maidan and the splendid mansions of Chowringhee Road, and into the warren of winding alleys behind them, into Black Town.

They entered Colinga, the gray of morning giving way to the haze of mid-day. The silver sun shining off the neighbourhood's many green palm trees. The cool air tinged with the heat of the sun's first rays.

This was a part of the city they rarely entered. A Calcutta without stately manors and horse riding trails, without the space for evening carriage rides and without the green walks and promenades they so enjoyed. There were no thoroughbred dogs, no lavish dinners with crystal, and no balls or dances here.

Instead, there were cracked and broken roads, wild and feral dogs, and homes made of brick and thatch and straw. It was crowded, congested, and loud. But life here was lived by all sorts of people. Here was a diverse, mostly Muslim neighbourhood, known for its prostitution and the Arabian traders who settled in it.[92] Here there were also subaltern Europeans. The neighbourhood was alive.

They dismounted near a small by-lane and approached the gate of a modest two-storey red brick house. Inside was a garden with colourful fruit trees, bamboo groves, and water tanks.

They approached the front door with an offer the man inside could not refuse.

Hicky stepped out to greet them.

He recognised them. They were important men. Their leader, Simeon Droz, the chief of the Board of Trade—the committee responsible for overseeing all trade between India and Europe—was one of the most important Company servants of all.[93] Under Droz's direction, the Board of Trade became notorious for their corruption and rigged contracts, granted to themselves under fictitious names. In his sixteen years in Bengal, Droz had moved up the ranks by staying loyal to Hastings, occupying many positions, including as a member of the Patna Council, where he managed the Company's opium exports, before being appointed to the Board of Trade.[94]

Hicky had spent the past days posting notices all over the city. He was about to launch a newspaper. The first in India. In fact, the first in Asia.

He promised to revolutionise news reporting in India. His newspaper would give Calcutta a place where everyone could read information. While Indians traditionally got their news from friends and contacts, Europeans were, and had been, reliant on newspapers for centuries. But their news came from Europe and America, arriving on ships many months after it had been published. For news from Asia, word of mouth and letters from friends were their only sources. For the first time, they would have news from around the world in one place.

With his printing press, Hicky could print news quickly and cheaply, on a scale unimaginable for newsletters that had to be copied by hand hundreds of times over. He would do away with the need for hircarrahs, the messengers who ran these newsletters from place to place. He would do away with the need for people to describe events themselves in letters. Now people could enclose snippets of his newspaper in their mail without having to describe events by hand.

He also promised his newspaper would act as a community bulletin board, where everyone could post and reply to advertisements. People would no longer have to use the city's many advertising boards. Instead, he would print their ads for the whole city to see.

His proposal came at a perfect time. News was never more in demand in Calcutta. The British were fighting four wars on three continents: against the Americans, the French, the Spanish and the Marathas. The wars were disrupting trade and making it extremely dangerous to send goods. Shipping had gotten so dangerous that insurers charged up to 30 per cent to insure goods between India and Europe, and respondentia—a type of insurance for ship captains—was 45 or 50 per cent.[95] Merchants needed to know which shipping routes were open and travellers needed to know when it was safe to sail. He could provide this information.

As the first journalist in India, he would have a monopoly over news, and he could expect many subscribers. His richest market would be the Company army. There were hundreds of European officers and thousands of British foot soldiers. His paper would let them keep track of their friends, family and comrades. In it, they could share their experiences and, through it, they could form camaraderie. Their thoughts and ideas could spread and magnify, giving them power and awareness they never had before.

Hicky was aware of the dangers of printing a newspaper. He had spent his early life in London's print industry. He had seen journalists punished and jailed for what they published, like Henry Sampson Woodfall, the printer of the famous Junius letters, who had been sued by the government for libelling the king. Woodfall walked free, but others were not so lucky. John Wilkes, who printed a pornographic poem and wrote an essay criticising the King's peace agreement with the French after the Seven Years' War, suffered for years. He was imprisoned for twenty-two months. His supporters were shot and killed in what became known as the

Massacre of St George's Fields, and he was exiled to France before finally being exonerated.[96]

The strongest reminder of all was that of William Bolts. Bolts, a Company servant from Holland, had tried to start a newspaper in Calcutta only twelve years before Hicky. Bolts announced his intention by nailing a notice to the Council House doors, promising, ominously, that he had 'many things to communicate, which most intimately concern every individual'.[97] Bolts indeed had many things to communicate that would concern his fellow Company servants. His wife had left him for another Company servant, his private trade had just been shut down, and he had been censured for amassing a personal fortune of £90,000. Instead of letting these things come to light, the Company immediately deported him.[98] It was not until Hicky came along that another person tried to launch a newspaper.

Unlike Bolts, Hicky was an unknown. He had neither connections, wealth, nor political motives to make him a threat.[99] Moreover, he promised to avoid the party politics and scandal that had doomed so many other journalists. In his proposal for his newspaper, he promised a 'rigid adherence to Truth and Facts' and a commitment to not print anything that could 'Possibly convey the smallest offence to any single Individual'.[100]

Like a ship, Hicky declared he would pilot his newspaper between the dangerous rocks of party politics. By giving politics a wide berth, he hoped to maintain his independence.

> When I first got under way in the Gazette Packett, I form'd a resolution to jog on under an easy sail, and by a well conducted Helm to shape my course right between the Rocks of contention, always observing to give these Rocks a good berth, by which means I should never have occasion to alter my course, or stand on a contrary Tack.
>
> What man with an honest good heart, and an industrious inclination, bless'd with a common share of understanding, would be a slave to any party?[101]

But his promise to stay away from politics would be harder to keep than it was to write.

The men said they had just had breakfast with Marian Hastings, wife of Governor-General Warren Hastings. They told him she wished to meet him in person.

It was well known in Calcutta how much sway she had over her husband. Many Company servants found that the fastest way to get a contract was to go through her.

The men implied that Marian could use her influence to let his newspaper be mailed for free through the post office. They mentioned no fee for their services. But in Hicky's mind no such help could come for free.

Hicky was concerned about asking a favour of Marian Hastings through these men.

'I cannot think of doing such a thing as that. I have not the pleasure of being known to her. She undoubtedly would think me very impertinent to ask her to do such a thing for me,' he said.

But they were insistent. They told him they had already fixed a meeting for tomorrow. They came close to him, their breath dropping to a whisper.

'We've come speedily from her house. Mrs Hastings has expressed her good wishes toward the success of your paper,' they said.[102]

Their insistence caused Hicky to change his mind.

The next day, he went with Droz to Hastings' Belvedere Estate. Together, they walked by its manicured gardens, retinues of servants, and tanks of drinking water, fruit trees, and rare plants. They passed two stables large enough to fit twenty-six Arab stallions, four garages capable of housing six elegant carriages, and a personal zoo that held a lion, zebra, and other exotic animals.

They approached Hastings' magnificent white-as-milk mansion. Its verandah, many windows, and grand columns made it look like the palace of a European prince.

It was truly another world from Black Town.

Hicky began to feel uneasy, like a thief in the night. Like a selfish traitor who did not have the courage to stand up for his beliefs.

Abruptly, at the last minute, he turned around and left. He turned his back on Marian and Droz and walked away.

'I thought that there was something so unmanly, so sneaking, and so treacherous in going in a clandestine manner to fawn and cringe,' he later said.

He felt relieved that he had left.

Yet he felt that he had insulted Marian Hastings and Simeon Droz by leaving. But in his heart he felt he had done the right thing.

Days later, on 29 January 1780, he printed his first *Hicky's Bengal Gazette*, the first newspaper in Asia.

Refugee Missionary

*Pray, Dear Sir, Consider, whether you or any other clergyman
of the English Nation, sent to the East Indies, would have
continued for 47 years upon the Salary of £50 per annum
and undergone the hardships, and still persevered in your
Duty, and done what I have done.*

– Johann Zacharias Kiernander to David Brown,
21 April 1788.

Eight o'clock Sunday morning, 18 January 1741, English colony of Cuddalore

Reverend Johann Zacharias Kiernander was just about to begin
his sermon when he heard the beat of the town's alarm drum.[103]

Two thousand Maratha horsemen appeared from the south,
charging the settlement.

Suddenly, the town's great guns roared like thunder and the
cannon balls whistled through the air. Up along the wall, the British
fired methodically. Their shots cascaded like hot iron from the fire.

The Marathas turned to the side, regrouping, and charged
again. Again they were repulsed. They then raided the villages
outside of town, killing and capturing anyone hiding inside their
homes before riding away.

The British maintained discipline inside the town, but rumour
upon rumour spread. Were there more horsemen? Would they
come again? When would they attack?

They came back five days later. Again, the British repulsed the
attacks. Some of the captured villagers broke free and ran to the

town for safety, selling whatever they had for food. The town became a refuge for all those escaping the war.

That night Kiernander watched from a distance as the raiders camped two miles away and built a great fire to burn their dead. Uneasiness within the town spread as the fire grew higher every hour. Everyone thought they would come again.

But the next morning they rode away. Kiernander celebrated and thanked God.

Although Cuddalore was spared, the good days never lasted long for him. He saw war every year from 1740 to 1757. First, it was the Maratha horsemen in their quest to establish an empire spanning all India. Then it was the French, in their endless wars against the English. The wars disrupted the ships bringing his salary, forcing him to live for months with no money and dwindling supplies.[104] Food became scarce. 'Twice the Marattas carried away my Milk Cows'—he lived on a mostly milk diet—'that may seem a trifle, but it was of Great consequence to me, as a poor man,' he later wrote.[105]

The world he entered was chaos. The world of a missionary.

Born in Sweden in 1711, he came from a respected family. His ancestors were priests. Two of his uncles were colonels in the Swedish army. Yet he faced personal adversities despite his status. He was bullied at his university. The senior students there once made him run through Uppsala's streets like a dog.[106]

Later, financial problems led him to counterfeit bank notes to fund his education. He was caught, but his friends bailed him out of jail and he fled to Germany. He was robbed along the way and finally ended up in the town of Halle where he met the professors of the Franckesche Stiftungen, a Lutheran Christian educational foundation. There he learned German and found himself, pledging to devote himself to Christianity. In 1739, he accepted an offer to be a missionary in India.[107]

With his parents' tear-filled letters in hand, he sailed to England to meet the Society for the Promotion of Christian Knowledge, the organisation that would pay his salary and send him to India.[108] He arrived in Cuddalore the next year.[109]

He entered his first years with boundless enthusiasm. He, more than any other missionary around him, believed the only way to win souls was to understand the people around him. With the help of tutors and books, he learned the local language, Tamil, and embraced technology, like the printing press, which he used to distribute Christian literature in towns and villages.[110]

Together, he and his senior missionary walked door-to-door, explaining in Tamil that Christianity was the one true religion.[111] At one point, he intercepted a group of men carrying timber for a Hindu ceremony. He stopped them and told them that their God was impotent because it had to be carried, whereas his Christian God never needed to be carried, but was all-powerful.[112]

He was most proud of one convert, whom he baptised and named Isaac and who lived in his Mission. One evening in 1745, Isaac's father, Rangan, and around 300 people from Isaac's village came to get Isaac.

'Give us Rangan's child! And annul his baptism!' they shouted.

'Isaac will live and die a Christian. You should also become Christians,' Kiernander calmly told them in Tamil, happy to have the opportunity to preach to such a large crowd.

The angry crowd went to the Governor but were told that Isaac had converted on his own free will. Only Isaac could decide to return to Hinduism.

The crowd returned to Kiernander's house the next week.[113] They threatened to boycott Cuddalore if he did not free Isaac.

'Give Isaac back or our whole caste will leave this town.'

Kiernander was glad to see them again.

'He is free to come if he will. Have you considered what I told you about God?'

'We do not want to hear your preaching. We have our own priests,' they said.

He took the opportunity to lecture them.

'You are coming here in vain if you do not want to hear about the true God. Your priests know nothing about him.'

Most left, but some stayed to hear him preach. He left that conversation convinced in the strength of Christianity and his ability to make converts.[114] He believed he was the one to bring India out of darkness. But his beliefs began to be challenged.

Like other missionaries, he had some success with outcastes and low castes, but not with Brahmins, the highest caste, who would lose their caste and social status if they converted.[115] His fellow Christians only made his struggle harder. Not only was he competing with the Catholic Church, but Indians often told him that, while they liked Christian tenets, they did not like the Christians they saw. 'We see so many of your European Christians who live not according to your good rules,' they said.[116]

Over the years, their words led him to question his own faith. He began to think that it was not religion that made someone good, but one's internal morals. 'I knew I had morally good people before me, who actually lived better lives than many old Name-Christians,' he wrote.[117] Perhaps, he thought, it did not matter if someone was a Christian, as long as he or she was a good person. His questioning led him into dangerous territory.

He began to drop some of the Lutheran tenets he had learned from his professors at Halle. As he spent more time in English society in Cuddalore, he improved his English and began preaching the Anglican catechism, not the Lutheran.[118] His fellow missionaries believed he was compromising their faith. He even married an Anglican woman, explaining that marrying outside his religion was not a problem. Because his wife was so young, he could indoctrinate her. 'I married her when she was just 14 years and 10 months. Therefore she has been more tractable than would perhaps have been the case with an older person,' he wrote.[119]

His successes were tempered by increasing conflicts with his fellow missionaries. Relations soured with his more established colleagues. While they criticised him for preaching Anglicanism, he criticised their translations of Christian texts, saying they were out of touch.

'One should throw the old books in the fire,' he supposedly said of them.[120]

Amid these disagreements, he found himself alone in Cuddalore. His senior missionary, Johann Geister, increasingly plagued by depression and psychiatric issues, left in 1747.[121] Personal tragedy also struck repeatedly over the next few years. His three daughters died in 1749, and his wife died after the birth of his son. He remarried in 1751, but his son died two years later, leaving him childless.[122]

But it was not religious disagreements that shook him most. His yearly £50 salary, even when it did arrive, was not enough for him to carry out his missionary duties, let alone survive on. His poverty convinced him that he needed to make his own money to be a more effective missionary. Words alone would not make converts. He needed to impress people with grandeur. He needed to prove that Christianity was a high-class, high-caste religion.

He began buying and selling goods to locals, and helping the Company buy great quantities of Swedish iron.[123] His country trade soon became more about profit than survival. He remodelled his church, and it was soon known for its splendour.[124] His business became notorious in missionary circles. Other missionaries complained he should confine himself to converting souls, not trading rupees. Two missionaries even came up to convince him to stop his business.[125]

But this conflict would come to little.

War was again brewing.

The Seven Years' War came spilling over from Europe, devastating the subcontinent as the French and British fought for dominance of trade routes to India. As the French army approached, British and Indians alike abandoned the town. Kiernander was left alone like a ghost among ruins.[126] He recorded in his journal:

> September 1757: On the 18th of this Month news came of the French army at Pondicherry in full motion and every body thought they would come and take this place. All was here in an uproar. The Malabar people ran to and fro pete-mete like madmen, and the English Gentlemen sent their Families to Tranquebar and within 2 Hours the place almost was empty, most of the inhabitants having left it.

Yet the French postponed their attack and life began to return to normal.[127]

His relief was not to last. The French came for Cuddalore the next year. Despite his pleas, the French commander, a Catholic, told him he had to leave. As a Protestant missionary he was not welcome. They took everything. 'The officers divided amongst themselves [my] shirts and stockings,'[128] leaving him with only 'one shirt on my back.'[129] He and his second wife, now pregnant, fled to the nearby settlement of Tranquebar, where they lived in abject poverty for six months, until they met a man who promised to give them free passage to Bengal.[130]

In Bengal he would have hope again. In Bengal he would start again and build the greatest, most splendid church a man had ever built. Bengal, he thought, would be the future of Christianity in India. He just needed the money to make it so. This desire to expand his church at all costs would later put him in the crosshairs of James Augustus Hicky.

Dealings with the World

This is my Resolution through God's gracious Aid, to stand to my Post and not desert it as long as a warm Drop of Blood runs through my Veins.

— Johann Zacharias Kiernander to Friedrich Wilhelm Pasche, 10 December 1784.[131]

Friday, 29 September 1758, Calcutta[132]

Kiernander arrived in Bengal with nothing but a few hundred rupees and the clothes on his back.[133]

But luck and favour were with him. He recreated in Calcutta what he had lost in Cuddalore. With the support of the Company he found a place to preach. The Governor, Robert Clive, had invited him to Calcutta and evicted the Portuguese Catholics from their small chapel, giving it to him. He formed a school, teaching children out of his home, and hiring a catechist, four teachers, and a headmaster.[134]

He was so busy he had no time for anything else. 'For the first 12 years I sat in the school myself from 7 in the morning to 11, and from 2 in the afternoon to 5,' he wrote years later. 'I was alone in everything. I had no time left me for learning the Bengal Language even if age had permitted it.'[135] His school became as successful as it was diverse. By 1759, he had 174 Armenian, English, French, and Bengali children. The next year he had 231.[136]

He worked hard to foster a flock from the ashes. His assistants grew sick or died, but he persevered and stepped in when they no longer could. He converted Catholics, Hindus of high and low castes, even a Jew. One of his greatest successes was when he convinced two Jesuit friars to publicly renounce Catholicism and join his Mission. His congregation grew because of his hard work.[137]

He struggled against a European population more concerned with the religion of riches than the riches of religion. Company servants were little interested in hearing the gospel and even less in attending church. Calcutta's first church, St Anne's, had been destroyed during a previous war, and the Company still had not bothered to build a new one. The only British places of prayer were Kiernander's small chapel and a small dark hall in the fort.[138] Faithful worshippers were few and far between.

Kiernander was beginning to feel the effects of his long years of labour. He was growing old and could not run his Mission forever. Tragedy, always close in his life, made him weary. His second wife died in 1761 in a terrible cholera epidemic. He nearly died as well. He still did not have his own schoolhouse or church. 'The conditions in which I live here, are troublesome in more respects than one,' he wrote. 'We still have no mission house, no school, no church. Who am I that I should be able to do all of this!'[139] He knew his situation could not last. He did not want to live the rest of his life in poverty. Something had to give.

That something came in the form of a new marriage. He got remarried, to a wealthy English widow. Around the same time, he received money from his brother's will in Sweden. This new money allowed him to send his son, Robert, to Europe for education. It also enabled him to think about his dreams again.[140] He was about to become one of the richest men in Bengal. For wealth begets wealth, and wealth he finally had. He could now think about building the Mission he longed for.

His dream was almost within reach.

British victories had opened North India's interior to European trade. Calcutta, the Company's gateway to Bengal, was becoming the largest and most prosperous British city in Asia. An incredible housing boom was occurring as the British came to find their fortunes. Riches were out there for those who had the means to exploit them. And means were exactly what he now had.

It was in this great demand for houses that he found his opening. He began designing, constructing and renting buildings to the many new arrivals. He saw opportunity to make money; every rupee he earned would be another rupee for his church. With enough money, he hoped to build the greatest, most glorious church in India.

But he had one last hurdle to overcome before he began. He knew it would be a problem for him, as a missionary, to succumb to greed. He had made a vow when he had first become a missionary to abstain from dealings with the world, and had been chastised once for his private trade. His first duty was to convert souls, not chase rupees.

He had tried to avoid temptation for years. But at last he could no longer resist. He knew he needed to support himself beyond his salary. 'Experience fully convinced me of the impossibility of Supporting myself and the Mission from £50 per annum,' he wrote.[141] 'Was it in these circumstances not lawful for me to exert my own labour and Industry?' he asked.[142] His long years in South India had taught him he could only rely on himself. Only he had the power to make his Mission successful.

A solution came to him after much thought and prayer. He realised that the founders of Christianity—the apostles and patriarchs in the Bible—had both worked for God and for money. If it was okay for them to profit, then it was okay for him. The patriarch Abraham was a landowner and farmer. The apostle Paul did manual labour. He saw no difference between these men and himself. He, too, was a founder of the faith. He had brought Christianity to Bengal. So long as the money he earned went back into his mission, he saw no problem.

> Temptations of various kinds broke in upon me, yet I continued still for several years in conflict with all ... I had a Tryal and Conflict with myself. I endured it under address to the Lord, petitioning Him to shew me, what was His will. At last it occurred to me, that Abraham planted groves and preached the Name of the Lord. I saw that both could stand together. That the apostle Paul worked with his own hands, that he might have for the support of himself.[143]

If the apostles and patriarchs in the Bible could make profits as well as work for God then so could he. And thus he had solved his temptation problem. Money was no longer a sin to be shunned but something to pursue, as long as it was all for the good of the Mission.

Within a decade, he became one of the leading construction contractors in the city. One of his largest projects was to build the military hospital for the Company. It was to be Calcutta's first hospital, and it was to be a massive building, with multiple floors and multiple wings.[144] To oversee the construction, he moved into a room at the construction site. To him, the ends justified the means. It did not matter that he would have to leave his Mission for months at a time to oversee construction. Even if he was away from his congregation, all the money he earned would go back to his Mission eventually.

His work was plagued with difficulties. First his architect died. Then a great famine came. It was so bad that Hindus did not have energy to burn their dead, nor Muslims to bury theirs. They dumped their dead directly into the Ganges, or left them to rot where they lay. People came in from the countryside looking like skeletons, in a desperate search for food and work. He stood like a spectator to the mounting calamity, powerless to help the displaced. '[It was] a year which will be remembered in Bengal, as long as any of the present Generation remember ... Persons who had good Information have computed the Number of those who perished at above 14,000,000 tho' others make the Loss much greater. The streets and Roads in Calcutta were daily spread with dead Bodies,' he wrote.[145]

At the same time as the famine, skilled labour for construction was in short supply, compounding his problems. The Company was rushing to complete its new fort and Company agents were scouring the country to bring workers, willing or coerced, to Calcutta.[146] When they could not find enough labour, they pressed his workers into service, paralysing his work.

Even worse, although the Company had agreed to supply him with bricks for the hospital, it had used nearly Calcutta's entire supply building the fort, leaving him unable to continue construction. 'I must either keep my bricklayers in pay, without employing them, or if I dismiss them, and they engage in other service, how difficult will it be for me to get them back when I want them,' he complained.[147]

To meet his deadline, he had to sacrifice work on his church. He took over 11,000 kilograms of bricks from his church and moved it to the hospital.[148] The delay meant that he missed his deadline, and the Company, which needed the hospital immediately for sick soldiers, ordered him to finish overseeing the project from his nearby bungalow.[149]

He had prioritised profits over preaching. But he saw no problem as long as the money went back to his Mission eventually. Once he finished the hospital, he used the money from that, and his other projects, to begin building the Mission of his dreams. At first he planned to spend Rs 30,000 on his church. But he changed his plans to make it bigger, grander, and more impressive. By the time he finished in 1771, he had spent Rs 60,000 on it.[150] He built it with mostly his own money so only he could have a claim on it. The church was his and no one else's.

One hundred and fifty feet long and forty feet wide, its red brick walls, ionic pillars, and exquisite stonework made it an imposing structure. It was only one of a few buildings known to have glass windows in Calcutta. Its grand staircase, garden, and ironwork gate made a beautiful entrance. He hoped it would be the centre of society, just like it was the centre of the city.[151]

But his church had enemies even before he completed it. His fellow missionaries outside Calcutta believed that the only reason he had been able to build such a magnificent church was because he was meddling in worldly affairs again. His professors in Halle were shocked at its splendour and cost.[152]

He faced even more hostility inside Calcutta. 'The first northwest wind will blow down the steeple … and crush it to pieces,' one told him, noting that its flat roof made it look architecturally unsound. 'The pulpit has no foundation to support it, the first time you mount it to preach, it will tumble down, and that will be the end of you,' another laughing scornfully said, a joke that Kiernander, overweight, would cause the podium to collapse.[153] To add to these insults, Calcuttans said it was a poor replacement for St Anne's, the

Company's church the Nawab's army had destroyed.[154] A church built by one man could never match the magnificence of a church built by a company, with all its financial backing behind it.

Over the next decade, he spent upwards of Rs 100,000 on his Mission.[155] When his third wife died in 1772, likely of breast cancer, he used her wealth to further his Mission. He sold her jewels to build a school that could fit up to 200 children. He then built a new Mission-House where he, his teachers, and the boarders could stay. He also built a house for himself in a quiet quarter of the city about half-an-hour away, and a bungalow on the city's southern outskirts.[156] He may have lost his wife, but he had arrived in society. He had a grand church, a school, houses, and a comfortable life. He even had two slaves.[157] He had achieved the Mission of his dreams.

He even ventured into printing. When he learned that a man in jail named James Augustus Hicky had begun a printing business, he approached Hicky to print almanacs, annual calendars with important dates and astronomical data. He gave Hicky a draft sample in November 1777 and asked Hicky how much they would cost to print. When Hicky said he would print them for Re 1 each—the same amount Kiernander had already been paying the missionaries at Tranquebar to print them—he thought it was too much.

Soon after, his son Robert purchased a printing press and began printing almanacs at the Mission. But when Kiernander saw that Hicky had copied his almanac and was selling it in the markets, he was enraged. He began giving away his almanacs for free to spite Hicky.[158]

The greed Kiernander thought he had vanquished would come back to haunt him.

He could not run his Mission forever. He was growing old and asked for a missionary to replace him. 'To whom I may deliver over the charge of my little Flock; for it affords me but Melancholy Thoughts, when I consider the uncertainty of my life,' he wrote to the Society.[159] So determined was he to find a replacement that he offered to cover the costs of any who came to join him.[160]

He was about to receive a new missionary. Never could he have imagined what would happen next.

A Nail in My Coffin

You have in particular a Colleague [Kiernander], well skilled in that Christian Warfare, almost worn out with his continual Labours, yet still of a cheerful and courageous Mind ... See therefore that you love him as a Father, listen to him as a Teacher, look up to him as an Example.

– Gottlieb Anastasius Freylinghausen, director of the Franckesche Stiftungen, to Johann Christian Diemer, 27 November 1773[161]

November 1779, The Mission, Calcutta.[162]

Johann Christian Diemer sat and smoked his long tobacco pipe. Never in his wildest nightmares had he imagined a place like Calcutta. The heat in the city was unbearable compared to the cool climes of his home on the French-German border. It was huge and festering whereas his home district was small and quaint. Like Kiernander, he had been educated at Halle. He, too, had gone to London to meet the Society before heading to India. He, too, came to India to win souls and convert heathens. He, too, had great dreams.

Yet he had come expecting a Mission ready for him. What he found was nothing like that at all. The work was hard and the servants few.[163]

Almost nothing went to plan from the beginning. He had expected to live for free in Kiernander's Mission-House. Instead he found it was under repair and it would be years before he could live in it. He had little money. Almost every last bit of his £50

salary, as well as an extra £100 Kiernander gave him, went to pay
his rent. He tried to learn Bengali with a tutor, but gave up after
learning the alphabet, finding the language too difficult. He did,
however, learn English, at least enough to write and speak in it.

He did no work for months at a time, often leaving Calcutta
to travel to the nearby Dutch colony of Chinsurah. When he was
in Calcutta, he spent many days playing the church's organ alone.
He was depressed, despairing, and despondent.[164]

He quickly grew sick, contracting tuberculosis, hacking up red
spittle, and was close to death for months. He spent much of his
time outside Calcutta trying to recover, but he continued to get
worse. By October 1776, he thought he was going to die.[165]

By December, he decided to return home. It was the ultimate
decision. He was abandoning the Mission to save himself, leaving
his whole purpose and all his dreams behind. 'I humbly beg leave
to return to Europe,' he wrote in English to the Society, 'I must
leave Calcutta and go to the Coast, as he [my doctor] much fears,
that otherwise I would soon relapse into my indisposition and
consumption.'[166]

In January, he booked a passage with a Danish ship and sailed
down the Hooghly to leave Bengal forever. His boat reached the
mouth of the river and was about to leave its pilot boat.

But he changed his mind at the last moment. He jumped on
the pilot and came back to Calcutta to give it another go.[167] As
punishment, Kiernander took away his £100 a year salary because
he had decided to leave.[168]

He slowly got better. His tuberculosis went away. Although
Kiernander had taken away his salary, he promised to do his duty
again in the Mission and to take more responsibility. Kiernander
began handing functions over to him, first giving him control of
the Mission's account books because his sight was too weak.[169]

But what should have been a promising restart soured as
discouragement turned to disappointment and disappointment
turned to disillusionment. Diemer was surprised by what he saw
in the account books. He had heard that many people donated
their wealth to the Mission as 'legacies' when they died. He had
heard talk around town that the Mission had once received a large

legacy from Captain John Griffin, a renowned captain of an East-Indiaman, who had made huge profits on private trade, smuggling between Europe and India. Griffin had bequeathed the entirety of his estate to the Mission when he died in 1770.[170] But Diemer saw it nowhere in the account books.

Instead, he saw only two small legacies, so small that they were barely worth mentioning. He wondered where all the legacies went. Where was Griffin's legacy?

He became suspicious that Kiernander had secretly pocketed Griffin's legacy. It would be one thing if a missionary gained wealth by private trade or construction, but it would be another matter entirely if Kiernander had embezzled his way to wealth.

He approached Kiernander one day.

'Are there no more legacies bequeathed to the Church than the two small insignificant legacies of Mrs Mary Handel and Mr Edward Sutton?' he asked in a thick German accent.

'No more,' Kiernander answered.

'What is become of that great legacy by Captain Griffin?'

'The estate was insufficient, and the church nothing to expect,' Kiernander said.

Diemer laughed scornfully.

'That is hard to believe. What yearly remittances from Europe, besides the bare salaries?' he asked.

'We have no occasion for any as you will find by the monthly receipts. All the charges of the Mission are answered in full,' Kiernander said.

Diemer laughed again. He quietly put the account book aside. Something was suspicious. He knew it.[171]

In March 1777, Kiernander tried to patch over his differences with Diemer by giving him charge of the Mission school. The school was one of the most successful parts of the Mission. Revenues were sometimes so great that they often subsidised the costs of other parts of the Mission. The school usually taught around 150 boarders and day students per year. Some paid for their education. Some were paid for by charities and rich individuals.[172]

The town charity—run by the Company's priests—was the school's most notable sponsor. It paid for twenty poor children to be clothed, fed, housed and educated at the Mission. They were known as the 'charity children,' and the fund that paid their expenses as the 'orphan fund'. The orphan fund also paid the salary of the man responsible for taking care of the children, known as the 'superintendent'. In this case, that was now Diemer.[173]

Although successful, the Mission school did have difficulties. Kiernander kept his teachers' salaries low, paying them Rs 60 a month. Teachers often quit because they could get higher wages elsewhere, such as Rs 100 to 300 a month as Company writers, a job that was seen as easier than being a teacher.[174]

Kiernander committed tax fraud to save money, expecting that no one would question his position as a respected holy man. He told the Supreme Council that he had transferred ownership of his Mission to the Society, and thus as a public religious institution it would be exempt from taxes. 'Having given to the Hon'ble Society for Promoting Christian Knowledge ... the Church, School & Mission house lately erected by me in Calcutta together with the Burying Ground,' he wrote, 'I humbly request that these Public Buildings & Ground may henceforth be exempted from paying any Tax or Rent whatsoever.'[175] The Council took him at his word. They never audited whether he had actually transferred ownership of his Mission to the Society. In reality, he never transferred ownership; he still owned his mission privately. His fraud was never caught.[176]

After Kiernander gave him charge of the school, Diemer went to the Company's priests and told them to transfer the orphan fund's salary to him because he had become the school's superintendent. In January 1778, the Company's priests formally recognised Diemer as the superintendent and transferred the Rs 100 a month salary to him.[177]

But when Kiernander learned that the salary had been transferred, he demanded that Diemer put it, along with all income from the school, in the communal Mission account. Kiernander also demanded that Diemer pay the salary of a new missionary out of this account.

Diemer was furious. The cost was so great that he had to let one of the teachers go.

'You make me desperate,' he said.[178] 'I thought I had found a door opened to get some rupees, but you have now shut that door, and you have thereby drove a nail in my coffin.'[179]

He stood up in anger. 'In three or four months I will remove and take the School along [with] the House,' he threatened.

But, in the end, he came to an agreement. He would pay Kiernander a monthly fee of Rs 136 and the salary for another missionary. But he would get to keep the rest of the school's income for himself.

Diemer was not happy with the agreement, and only accepted it to keep the peace. 'I, for peace's sake, consented,' he wrote to the Society.[180]

Diemer became ill again over the next few months. His tuberculosis returned and he began spitting up blood.[181] For the second time he made the ultimate choice to leave Calcutta. In November 1779, he left for Cape Town to recover. Without telling Kiernander, he left the school in the hands of one of the Company's priests. He also left his wife and son behind in the Mission-House.[182]

He expected to come back just as he had left. Nothing different. Nothing changed.

A Company Man

You are already well acquainted with the general system which I wish ... to establish in India, namely to extend the influence of the British nation to every part of India.

– Warren Hastings to Alexander Elliot,
12 January 1777.[183]

Thursday, 8 October 1750, Calcutta

The Company was everything to Warren Hastings. He was seventeen when he set sail for Calcutta. His mother had died in childbirth. His father abandoned him when he was young. His grandfather sent him to a charity school where he often went hungry. Even his one chance at climbing the social ladder was fleeting. His brief education at the famous Westminster School— among England's future poets, philosophers and prime ministers— was cut short when his uncle died and the funds for his education dried up. He was placed under the care of a distant relative who put him into an accounts school to prepare him for a life of service to the Company.[184]

The Company would be his future and his family. It would be his chance to raise himself up from his childhood. And it would be the stability that his life lacked.

He arrived in Calcutta as a writer, the Company's lowest rank. He managed account books and learned Urdu and Persian. Shy and reserved, he mixed his wine with water and left parties early rather than staying up for Calcutta's all-night debauches. After two years he was promoted and moved to a provincial factory where he oversaw the Company's silk spinning business. After two more years he was promoted to the factory's council.[185] He seemed destined to move up the Company's ranks. But his promotion was short-lived.

In 1756, the Nawab of Bengal invaded, besieging and sacking nearly all the Company factories, including Calcutta. The Nawab made the remaining British in Calcutta his prisoners, putting them in a small dungeon in Fort William. Overnight, the story went, 123 of the 146 prisoners died of heat, exhaustion and suffocation in a situation so cramped that it seared itself in British minds for centuries as 'The Black Hole'.

Up north, Hastings escaped this horror. 'I was made a prisoner,' he wrote, 'but permitted to go at large.' The Nawab treated him kindly. Under loose confinement, he escaped to an island where European refugees were gathering.[186] There, he met and married his future wife, the widow of a Black Hole victim. They had two children. But his domestic life was short-lived. His wife and daughter later died, leaving him to pin his hopes on his son whom he sent to boarding school in England.[187]

Hastings joined the British counter-attack the next year. Led by Robert Clive, later Governor of Bengal, the British recaptured Calcutta, and moved on the Nawab's capital. Clive bribed the Nawab's top commander, Mir Jafar, promising to install him as Nawab if the British won. When the Bengali middleman, Amir Chand, told Clive he wanted Rs 30 lakh and 5 per cent of the war booty for facilitating the betrayal, Clive, dreading the loss of profit from such a deal, drew up two contracts, one official, and one fraudulent to fool Amir Chand. Clive even forged the signature of a fellow commander to deceive Chand, swindling Chand out of his expected fortune.[188]

To his supporters, Clive's deception was a crowning achievement of Machiavellian politics. To his detractors, it sealed his reputation as a double-faced schemer. Clive became an example of the hypocrisy of Company rule, where forgery was acceptable for the British, but not for those they ruled. Many pointed out that British rule was not based on right, but on might alone.

The treachery cemented, the Company decimated the Nawab's forces in battle. True to his word, Clive deposed the Nawab and installed Mir Jafar on the throne. Clive and his fellow commanders used the war to personally enrich themselves, taking an estimated £1.2 million in loot and presents. Clive himself took Rs 16 lakh in loot and a jagir, a vast personal estate giving him an annual income of £27,000.[189] These presents allowed Clive to return to England revered as a war hero and wealthy enough to buy a seat in Parliament.

The Company's intrigues had not yet ended. The next Governor deposed Mir Jafar after he was suspected of plotting to overthrow the British. The Company leaders again made off with a heavy bounty, taking nearly Rs 93 lakh in presents.[190]

Like his predecessors, the new Nawab, Mir Qasim, was suspicious of the British. He drafted an army and moved his capital to a safer location. When Mir Qasim complained that Company servants were refusing to pay taxes on their trade, the Company merchants declared that he had no authority over them and refused his orders to pay.[191]

Hastings supported Mir Qasim. But Hastings was at odds with many of his fellow Company servants. He believed that Company servants did not have the right to evade taxes, taking the initiative to offer solutions to make trade fair between Indians and Europeans.[192] In December 1762, he and the Governor met with Mir Qasim and created a nine-point plan to stop trade abuses. He lobbied for the plan in Council, telling his fellow Council Members that if they followed the rule of law, their trade and their profits would increase, and they would be respected by all. But if they continued to abuse the system, they would be hated, distrusted, and their reputation would sink in the eyes of Indians.

> If our people, instead of erecting themselves into lords and oppressors of the country, confine themselves to an honest and fair trade, they will be everywhere courted and respected, and the English Name, instead of becoming a Reproach, will be universally revered; the Country will reap a Benefit from our Commerce; and the Power of the English, instead of being made a Bugbear to frighten the poor Inhabitants into a Submission to Injury and Oppression, will be regarded by them as the greatest Blessing and Protection.[193]

But the Council, many of whom benefited from their trade advantage, overruled the plan.[194]

Open hostilities broke out three months later when Qasim allied with two of the most powerful nations in North India: the Mughal Empire and the Kingdom of Awadh.[195] But Mir Qasim's war was short-lived. The Mughal Empire was a shadow of its former self. Led by weak rulers and beset by foreign invasions, it had fractured into many princedoms. The Company quickly defeated the combined armies.

The resulting treaty—which Clive also negotiated—was even more humiliating than the last. The Company took over the Kingdom of Bengal and vassalised the Kingdom of Awadh. The Company itself took £675,000 as an indemnity, while individual Company servants reportedly took up to £530,000 in plunder. In one stroke, the Company had vanquished its rivals and become one of the most powerful states in India.[196]

These campaigns marked a turning point in India's history. The Company, which had always focused more on trade than territory, became a major power. European dominance followed. The Company solidified its monopoly, taking entire control of the important salt trade, after which the price of salt jumped 200 per cent.[197] Individual Europeans used the Company's position to enrich their own. One Archibald Keir was said to have 13,000 workers extracting 12,000 tons of salt annually.[198] William Bolts had 150 Indian agents to manage his trade.[199] With profit margins two to three times of what they were in Britain, the trade in salt, tobacco, indigo, betel nut, and opium made these men rich beyond belief.

Disheartened with war and death, Hastings submitted his resignation and sailed for England. He left his £25,000 fortune behind with a friend, hoping, with interest, that it would accrue enough to let him buy his family's estate.[200]

But the reality of life in England did not match his expectations. He arrived to find his son had died.

His life lost its rudder. He began living beyond his means, giving much of his money away to relatives and drawing from his savings to buy elegant paintings and a costly horse carriage. His world came crumbling down in 1767, when he learned that his fortune had been lost through mismanagement.[201] With no money, he decided his only option was to return to India.[202] He believed it was the only way to recoup the fortune he had lost.

On Clive's recommendation, the Company's directors appointed him second-in-command of the Madras Council, the governing body of British South India. After four years of disappointment and negligence, he had to borrow money for his trip.[203] Yet he was not a man to mix with commoners. He still chose the roundhouse, the ship's most luxurious space, for his accommodation.

This time he vowed not to make the same mistakes. He vowed to repair his fame and fortune, and, if necessary, join the practices he had once condemned. He dreamed of returning to the status his family had lost generations ago. If all went to plan, he hoped to earn enough money to buy the family estate his great-grandfather had sold years ago. It was his dream and he would do whatever it took to achieve it. But his pursuit of this dream—which would launch him to the very top of the Company's government—would make him many enemies, including James Augustus Hicky.

Back to Bengal

There are cases in government in which it may be necessary to adopt expedients which are not justified on such principles as the public can be judges of.

– Warren Hastings to George Colebrooke, 1 February 1772.[204]

Saturday, 22 February 1772, Calcutta

Hastings' life had come a long way since the dark days of England. He had remarried and had quickly been promoted, showing a talent for reform. In two years, as second-in-command of the Madras Council, he had spearheaded a drive to cut out middlemen and reorganise the Company's export warehouse. His successes were so great that the Company's directors offered him their highest job: Governorship of Bengal. Bengal was their largest, most populous and most profitable territory, and it was in desperate need of reform.[205]

Hastings was just the man.

Bengal was in chaos, recovering from the worst famine in its history. Violent rains and floods, followed by nine months of drought, had caused two years of crop failures. Then huge fires wiped out many of the region's rice granaries and food stockpiles. Yet the Company had done little to stop the impending calamity. The Calcutta Council had refused to offer tax leniency, nor had it prevented Company agents from hoarding grain. Instead, it had secured enough rice for the army and had exhorted the peasants to grow more crops.[206] Their efforts, if anything, had made the crisis worse. Rice increased tenfold in cost and food became impossible to buy for all but the rich.[207]

Horrific, devastating famine came next. With no crops, no food, and no hope, the ryots, peasants, sold their cattle and then their children to meet tax collections. By the summer of 1770, people turned to cannibalism for food. Reports spread of children eating their parents, and parents eating their children. 'Certain it is that in several parts, the living have fed on the dead,' one official wrote.[208]

Provincial officials pleaded for aid, to little avail. One Bengali bureaucrat wrote to the Council that people were so hungry in his district they were wandering into the jungle to eat the leaves off trees. Others had run away to join roving gangs of bandits.

> What can I write of Dearness and Scarcity? Mankind are employed in bringing the Leaves of Trees from the Jungles for Food, and they offer their Sons and Daughters to Sale—Many of the Ryotts are daily running away and vain are all my endeavours to restrain them.[209]

When the Company sent one of its servants, Gerard Ducarel, to investigate the district of Purnea, he had the horror to find half the ryots already dead and disease spreading.

> The Situation of Misery in which I have found Purnea is not less striking than that of the Pergunnahs—The first Object I have had to attend to was to guard against the Horrors of Pestilence being added to those of Famine; by providing for the removal of the Number of Dead Bodies, which were laying in different Parts of the Town, and with which the Air was infected to a very great Degree—the Report of the Number that has been buried for these three days past exceeds one Thousand ... I do not believe I should exaggerate in saying that half the Ryotts were dead.[210]

By the time the famine ended, more than ten million people, or over a third of Bengal's population, had died.[211] Whole tracts of land returned to jungle.

The famine exacerbated Bengal's instability as Company servants used their powers to enforce taxation. With the threat of the army, Company supervisors combined the powers of regional trade monopoly, judge, and tax collector to enforce payments. They and their agents confined, flogged, or tortured ryots to extract payments.[212] The Company's provincial councils, far away from Calcutta, ran their factory towns like fiefdoms.

The rule of law broke down as ryots began leaving their farms. Those who did not become bandits were attracted to armed groups of Muslim and Hindu religious ascetics. These bands openly fought the Company's tax collectors. For the next decade, the Company would fight gruelling guerilla wars against these bands.[213]

Tax collection kept pace despite the famine. Although so many ryots had died, the Company actually collected more at the height of the famine than before, helped in part by a levy requiring the living to make up for the taxes of the dead.[214] Company servants worked with near impunity and no oversight. Their only direction was to maximise revenues, and this they did with frightful efficiency. This was the situation Hastings entered.

Hastings put his new political ideas into practice to confine the chaos shortly after arriving in Bengal, ideas that ten years ago he would have shuddered to think about. He tackled the increased crime and brigandry with harsh measures, executing bandits in front of the villagers as public examples, and enslaving their families. He hoped that selling families into slavery would prevent crime as well as raise money. Slavery, he believed, would both reduce the cost of maintaining prisons and would get rid of troublesome members of society. 'The community will suffer no loss by the want of such troublesome members,' he told his Council.[215]

Hastings dismantled whatever power Indians still held at the highest levels in Bengal. He stripped the Nawab of Bengal of his remaining power and he appointed a woman, Munni Begum, to be the Nawab's guardian, a move calculated to insult the Nawab's importance in an era of male-dominated rule. He reorganised the justice system and put himself and his council at the head of the Company's top courts.[216] He also put himself at the head of a committee to oversee tax collection. He used these moves to personally enrich himself, accepting a Rs 150,000 present from Munni Begum in return for her appointment, adding to the vast personal fortune he was collecting.[217]

Hastings reformed the Company's bureaucracy next, hoping that many of his actions would prevent the abuses he saw in his earlier service. He stabilised the Company's trade by founding a central bank. He created regular post stops to ensure delivery of mail, limited private trade, and enforced a tariff on Company and European merchants. He set price floors to protect artisans from selling their goods below the cost of production. Lastly, he encouraged Company servants to record observations on Indian languages and cultures, hoping their knowledge would help them better understand and rule India.[218]

But Hastings' most precious goal was not reform. It was power. He set the Company on a course to spread British rule throughout India. The fracturing of the Mughal Empire granted him unexpected opportunities. His first target was the state of Cooch Behar, a former vassal of the Mughal Empire.

Hastings launched an invasion. After a bloody, poorly documented, and largely forgotten war, Hastings negotiated a peace that sealed Cooch Behar's fate as a Company vassal.[219] He justified this annexation by saying that Cooch Behar's strategic position on the Company's northern flank meant it was too important not to conquer.[220] By annexing Cooch Behar and making Cooch Behar's Maharaja pay for it, he added to the Company's territory, all at no expense to its shareholders.

Hastings' next move was his greatest diplomatic coup. In 1773 he formed a plan with the Nawab of Awadh to invade Rohilkhand, another former Mughal vassal. The Nawab of Awadh asked Hastings to help him punish the Rohillas for not paying an earlier debt. 'The English Gentlemen will thoroughly exterminate them, and settle me in their country,' the Nawab suggested.[221]

Seeing an opportunity to expand the Company's influence, Hastings proposed a meeting to coordinate their plan. 'I have long thought that the union of the Rohilla country with yours ... would be an advisable point for you to attain,' he wrote.[222] After three weeks of private talks, they agreed that Hastings would lend the Nawab the Company army. In return, the Nawab would pay the Company Rs 40 lakh.[223] Since Awadh was already within the

Company's sphere of influence, territory it conquered was really territory that the Company conquered.

On 17 April 1774, the Nawab and the Company army launched their invasion. The Rohillas were defeated only six days later in a battle that quickly turned into a rout.[224] Afterwards, as the Company brigades remained in standing order, the Nawab's troops plundered the Rohilla camp and marched into Rohilla cities, looting an estimated Rs 50 lakh.

The Company's soldiers grew jealous as they watched the plundering. The British commander twice asked Hastings if the British troops could share in the plunder, warning Hastings that the troops might not obey another war of aggression without any extra payment for their service. 'It may be dangerous ever to try an experiment of this kind again, or to put the temper and patience of any part of your troops so much to the proof,' the Commander, Colonel Alexander Champion wrote.[225]

Reports of army discontent were followed by reports of widespread atrocities. An estimated 100,000 Rohilla refugees fled from the advancing armies, while many Hindu zamindars, landholders, shut their forts to Rohillas seeking shelter.[226] Wild rumours spread in the British camp that the Nawab had raped the daughter of a Rohilla chief and had murdered every man, woman, and child in a village after a British officer offhandedly mentioned that children had thrown stones at his hunting dogs.[227] After the battle, the Nawab's army dragged hundreds of captive women on carts into camp. 'We arrived at Bissoulee, where the whole army were witnesses of scenes that cannot be described,' Champion wrote.[228]

Champion reinforced his claims of the Nawab's cruelty by sending Hastings a letter from the widow of the Rohilla regent, Hafiz Rahmat Khan. She and her husband used to rule a hundred thousand people, now she had nothing. Once the most powerful woman of her nation, she was imprisoned and she and her children were starving.

Hafez Rhamet Khan for forty years governed this country, and the very beasts of the forests trembled at his bravery. The will of God is restless: he is slain, and to his children not an atom remains, but they are cast from their habitations, naked, exposed to the winds, the heats, and the burning sand, and perishing for want of even rice and water. How shall I either write or speak my condition? My sighs dry my ink and scorch my paper ... Yesterday I was mistress of a hundred thousand people; to-day I am in want even of a cup of water ... I am taken like a beast in a snare, without resting place by night or shade by day. From you, Sir, I hope justice and compassion, for I am as a bird confined in a cage; 'tis better to give up life by the dagger than famish thus by hunger and thirst. You, I hope, Sir, will reflect on my state, or my misfortunes will be doubled. I have nothing left. Pardon this paper.[229]

Many Company soldiers were ashamed that they had taken part in a war full of atrocities. But most of all, they were angry that they had not been paid their *prize money*, loot. Money would have made their complaints go away, and they blamed Hastings for not giving it.[230] The soldiers would be mad at Hastings for years to come. And they would turn to Hicky and his press to express their anger.

Instead of allowing the troops to take part in the plunder, Hastings dismissed their complaints, denied their reports of atrocities, and rejected their claims to prize money. 'It is to be avoided like poison,' he wrote of plunder.[231] Hastings justified the war by saying that the Rohillas were foreigners who did not belong in India. 'They are a tribe of Afgans or Patans; freebooters,' he wrote.[232] The war had achieved two of Hastings' goals. It would bring money to the Company, and it would expand its sphere of influence. It was a win-win.

In retreat to the Himalayan foothills, the Rohillas became desperate. By the first week of October, they had eaten all their horses and camels and disease had broken out. The Nawab's peace terms were brutal. Around forty-five to seventy thousand people—most of what remained of the Rohillas—were forced off their land and expelled across the river Ganges. What became of many of them is lost to history.[233]

News of the treaty reached Calcutta on October 19. The war had been won, but at a great cost to the loyalty of the army. This war had been won, but a new one was about to begin.

Four Guns Short

I see this glorious empire, which I was sent to save and govern, tottering upon the verge of ruin.

— Philip Francis to John Bourke,
30 November 1774.[234]

Noon, Wednesday, 19 October 1774, Chand Paul Ghat, Calcutta

The new members of the Supreme Council counted the fiery crackle of each of Fort William's great guns as their ship neared the city. They anticipated a full twenty-one-gun salute. Instead, the guns went silent at seventeen.

Sir Philip Francis was not disturbed, but his fellow Council members, General John Clavering and Colonel George Monson, sticklers for military rules, grimaced as they noticed the error. They were Parliament's new government in India, sent from England to take over the Company. They had been expecting full honours. Instead, they felt slighted.

The whole party and their families landed. They had expected Hastings to send out an honour guard. There was none. They had expected an official to greet them at the docks. There was no one.

They walked, hot and confused, to Hastings' house. There they found him waiting in a plain shirt, surrounded by his Council. As they sat down for lunch that first day, not even wine served in ale glasses could quell their suspicions.[235] They believed there had to be a reason for the chilly reception.

The reason was that they had come to take away Hastings' power—and he suspected it.

The Company's slide into insolvency had taken place over several years. The growth of British power in Bengal created a bubble as many bought Company stock expecting great returns. Yet, revenues had not kept pace despite the Company's victories. The great famine had sapped Company profits. Exports declined. Large stockpiles of goods began to accrue in London. Tea, the Company's largest export, was undercut by smugglers and an American boycott. The Company's directors, afraid any change would signal weakness, further drained the Company's finances by keeping the Company's dividend high. Finally, a great credit crisis struck London and financial collapse seemed imminent. By the summer of 1773, Parliament passed a law to overhaul the Company: the Regulating Act.[236]

The Company had been bailed out, but it came at a heavy cost. For the first time in history, it would be accountable not just to profit, but to Parliament. Francis, Clavering, and Monson saw themselves as that accountability.

The Regulating Act was designed to stabilise the Company by reducing corruption and curbing personal profits. The Act made it illegal for these new Supreme Council members to take presents, accept second positions, or engage in private trade. It gave them extraordinarily high salaries, £25,000 for Hastings and £10,000 for each councillor. The idea was to make these men loyal to British interests as a whole.

Yet the Regulating Act was still a compromise. The newcomers on the Supreme Council would be balanced by old Company hands: Hastings and another long-serving Company servant, Richard Barwell. Every decision on the Council would be decided by vote, and although Hastings had a tie-breaking vote, three votes was the majority. Three votes would rule.

Francis, Clavering, and Monson came out to investigate Hastings' administration and undo his actions. Their first target was the Rohilla War. They had made up their minds that Hastings had illegally used the Company army as mercenaries in a war of aggression. And, although they did not say so in their official

correspondence, they privately suspected he had been bribed to
go to war.[237]

With their three votes to Hastings and Barwell's two, Francis,
Clavering, and Monson immediately took control of the Company
and reversed many of Hastings' policies. They withdrew the
Company army from Awadh and declared that they would live
in peace with their neighbours.[238] They wrote a massive seventy-
four point letter announcing they were formally investigating
if Hastings had abetted atrocities during the Rohilla War. They
wrote that as long as they were in charge, the Company's army
would never again be used for conquest.

> Long before this Letter can reach England, you will have
> been informed of the engagements entered into by the late
> Administration with Shuja Dowla [The Nawab of Awadh], and
> the assistance given him to invade and subdue the Rohillas. The
> first accounts we heard of these transactions filled us with anxiety
> and surprise. We thought it our duty to enquire minutely into
> them, not only for your information, but for our own direction ...
>
> The general principle on which we have acted, and which we
> mean to make the rule of our future policy and conduct, is ...
> to maintain PEACE in INDIA. ... Adhering to this system, we
> never can engage your arms in any offensive operations for the
> aggrandizement of one Indian State at the expence of another;
> much less could we have suffered the little States ... to be
> swallowed up by the great ones. Had we arrived in this Country
> ten months sooner, we should have saved a nation.[239]

The new councillors represented a change in what was
permissible in war. They believed that burning and looting,
encouraged ten years earlier, was no longer acceptable.

They believed Hastings' wars were unjust and impractical and
that the best way for the Company to regain its prosperity would
be to abandon conquest. Francis was the most adamant of them all.
'Look to the facts, gentlemen,' he wrote to the Company's directors,
'it is your civil servants who involved the Company in offensive
wars, and in schemes of conquest by which no public interest could
be promoted.'[240] 'Under a European government Bengal cannot

flourish,' he added.[241] Unless the Company restricted itself only to trade, he believed it would eventually 'invade the laws, religion, manners and prejudices of the people.'[242] He believed that profit and governance together could only lead to abuse.

Francis, Clavering, and Monson next set their sights on Hastings' personal corruption. On 11 March 1775, with preparations complete, Francis presented a letter in the Supreme Council from an old enemy of Hastings, a Bengali administrator named Nanda Kumar, claiming that Hastings had accepted two bribes, one for Rs 104,105 to have Nanda Kumar's son appointed the Nawab of Bengal's administrator, and one for Rs 250,000 to appoint Munni Begum the Nawab's guardian. Over the next few days, Francis, Clavering, and Monson listened to evidence that Hastings had accepted further bribes, including an allegation that Hastings, Barwell and, others had illegally shared in profits a tax collector made in his collections. With all this mounting evidence, Hastings' position looked tenuous at best.[243]

Instead of defending himself, Hastings went on the offensive. In a complex series of intrigues, one of the witnesses against Hastings retracted his testimony, claiming that he had been coerced. Hastings and Barwell then publicly announced that they were suing Nanda Kumar and others for conspiring to bring false charges. Hastings' associates also dredged up a case that had been held in legal limbo in the Company's courts for years. They claimed that Nanda Kumar had defrauded the Company by forging a bond which he used to collect Rs 48,021. Forgery carried the death penalty according to English law. Nanda Kumar was found guilty and executed three months after his arrest.[244] As suddenly as it had begun, Francis, Clavering, and Monson's investigation into Hastings' corruption ceased.

More than ending the investigation into Hastings' corruption, Nanda Kumar's execution sent a chilling warning to Indian accusers of British officials. The prosecution of Nanda Kumar became an example of the hypocrisy of Company rule, where forgery was acceptable for the British but not for those they governed. Nanda Kumar's execution may have ended investigations into Hastings' corruption, but it would have echoes that would ring for decades.

Over the next few years, Hastings clawed his way back to power. First Monson and then Clavering died, leaving only Francis against him. By January 1778, Hastings got his first opportunity in years to conquer new territory. When news arrived from Bombay that a faction of Maratha chiefs was plotting a coup, he immediately decided to support the coup's leaders, ordering an army to march to Bombay to support the pretender.[245] If the coup succeeded, he could install the pretender as his puppet and bring one more Indian state under his orbit. In theory, it was a brilliant plan.

But before he could see his plan through, news arrived that France and Britain were at war, and that the Marathas had joined the war, defeating the Company's Bombay Council in a humiliating battle. The Marathas surrounded Bombay's army, killing over a thousand Company troops and forcing the rest to surrender. The Company had lost the war in only a month.

Yet Hastings refused to accept the treaty. He claimed that the Bombay Council had no authority to sue for peace.[246] Instead, he ordered the war to continue.

A brutal, bloody, and protracted war began. Many thousands would die. Over the next few years more nations would jump into the fray. The war would soon engulf almost the entirety of India and would earn Hastings the ire of James Augustus Hicky.

PART II

THE NEWSPAPER

Open to all Parties, but Influenced by None

Calcutta has grown populous enough to support a Newspaper, of which I send you a specimen. In a little Time I conclude it will be as full of Scandal as the Morning Post.

– Philip Francis to Andrew Ross,
12 February 1780.[247]

Saturday, 29 January 1780.
Hicky's Printing Office. No.67, Radha Bazar.

It had been ninety years since Calcutta was founded and his was the first.

Hicky's Bengal Gazette was a sensation.

'As a novelty every person read it, and was delighted,' Hicky's old lawyer, William Hickey, wrote.

People were happy to finally have a newspaper. Printed on Saturdays, each issue was four pages and cost Re 1, similar in price to newspapers in England at the time. Hicky dedicated the first two or three pages to news and opinion letters, with the remainder being for advertisements. He tried to cover everything that might be important to Calcutta, devoting many sections to politics, world news, and events in India. He encouraged people to write him letters and poems.

He tried to be witty and satirical. He gave nicknames to the city's most colourful characters. One that stuck was 'Nosey Jargon'—an overly inquisitive jabberer—for the city's surveyor and head of public works, Edward Tiretta. Tiretta, a talkative man who came from Italy and spoke an odd amalgam of English, French, Portuguese, and Hindustani, had a reputation for being flamboyant, minueting his handsome physique in crimson suits of rich velvet, even in the heat of summer. Hicky jabbed at Tiretta's reputation, writing that Tiretta had a 'happy Turn for EXCAVATIONS and *Diving into the Bottom of things'*, a joke that Tiretta's job as director of public works might also be a euphemism for his sexual orientation.[248] These nicknames, and his light-hearted reporting, made his paper an entertaining read for many.

People were also glad that Hicky made their lives easier. They could enclose his newspaper in letters to their friends and relatives instead of writing all the details of events. 'As I propose sending you a regular supply of Calcutta Gazettes there can be no necessity to fill my letters with political information,' one woman wrote to her sister in England.[249]

Hicky saw his newspaper as a forum where people of many backgrounds could voice ideas for the betterment of society. As he promised, he avoided politics. And he refused to print any partisan letters. He once rejected one letter because it, 'breathes strongly of faction'.[250] He maintained neutrality, careful not to discuss anything controversial.

He wanted his paper to serve society, so the first topic he ventured into was city improvement. He published articles calling on the Company to invest more on infrastructure, road construction, and general sanitation, things the city lacked compared to its European peers. One of his correspondents, who lived near the Portuguese cemetery, urged the Company to regulate burials. The cemetery was overflowing, with over 400 bodies buried every year in shallow graves without coffins. The monsoon rains often exposed the corpses. Their decaying matter mixed with drinking tanks, poisoning the water and causing disease. 'I [hope] thro' the channel of your paper ... to remove it,' his correspondent wrote.[251]

Another topic was road maintenance. One of his correspondents pressed the Company to repair and rebuild the city's roads.[252] Another wrote that the Company needed to clean up the 'dead carcasses of animals putrefying in the streets'. While this correspondent was dismayed that animals were left to rot in the open, he was more shocked that the Company had not buried human corpses lying in the street. How 'trivial is the shock' of dead animals, the correspondent wrote, when 'the miserable corpse[s] of our Fellow Creatures' were lying naked on the streets.[253]

As Hicky ventured into more topics, he touched upon the role that women should fill in society. Typical for his time, he and his writers supported the belief that men were superior to women.

His male writers opined that women should be chaste, faithful, and submissive. Their role was to satisfy and please their husbands. Their value was in how many children they could produce, and their responsibility was to preserve society's moral values.[254] One of his correspondents wrote:

> A Good Wife I think Mr Hicky is one who ever mindfull of the Solemn Contract which she has entered into, is strictly and conscientiously virtuous, constant, and faithfull to her Husband; also chaste, pure and unblemished in every thought Word and Deed—She ought to be humble and modest from reason and conviction, submissive from choice, and obedient from inclination ... [She must make] it her constant study to appear truly amiable in the Eyes of her *Husband*, being conscious that every thing which promotes his happiness, must in the End contribute to her own.[255]

Hicky devoted many columns to the idea that women should be subservient, quoting sections from a book, *Thoughts on the times but chiefly on the profligacy of our women,* which argued that women should remain 'modest', 'virtuous' and be educated only for the pleasure of men. They should be taught only subjects like dancing, music and French. By reprinting many sections from this book, he spread the idea that education made women less sexually attractive, that it stripped them of their femininity, and that women's biology made them intellectually inferior and unable to participate in serious male-only conversation.

While Hicky and his writers argued women should fill a restricted sexual role, they also sometimes applied restrictions to themselves. When he had extra space, Hicky reprinted sections from a 1772 book, *The Fatal Consequences of Adultery*, which argued it should be illegal for someone to marry the person they committed adultery with. 'Our modern fine gentlemen look upon this crime as mere gallantry ... But what honour can there be in that man, who violates the laws of friendship, the laws of his country, the laws of reason and the laws of God,' he quoted.[256] The book's hope was to reduce adultery by reducing the incentive to commit it. Still, the burden fell hardest on women, who unlike men, would have to live with society's judgment of their actions.

Hicky adapted his patriarchal stance to India. In particular, he focused on the profession of male-midwifery, a profession that had been newly introduced to Calcutta. In Europe, men had become midwives, displacing women from this traditional role. While in Europe there was some resistance to male midwives because they were believed to violate decency between men and women and could lead to improper lust, in India the resistance to male midwives was more complex. Not only were they thought to violate decency, they were seen as foreign invaders of Indian customs.

Hicky, who opposed male midwives because of patriarchy, joined Anglo-Indian women who opposed them because they were foreign. Into the debate, he printed a letter from his first female writer, a lower class Anglo-Indian woman known as Old Nell.

Despite his beliefs, Hicky published her article, allowing a woman into a male sphere at a time when women, most of all women of colour, were marginalised.[257] For although his own views on women's role in society may have differed from hers, he acted on his paper's slogan to be open to all parties. He let her write despite her status, perhaps because she did not challenge his belief that a woman's value was her womb.

Old Nell recalled passing the office of one European male midwife who set up shop in Black Town. She could not imagine the male midwife getting any business as the only people who walked by were Anglo-Indians, Muslims, or Hindus. Few could read English anyway, so they would have little idea what 'man-midwife' meant. 'Therefore I say Mr Hicky, the man must be mistaken and might as well have wrote up *Man-Monster* to the Ignorant crowd that pass,' she wrote.

Old Nell was the daughter of an Irish man and an Indian woman. Unlike many other poor Anglo-Indian women, she was literate. Her father had taught her how to read and write. Yet she was unable or unwilling to take advantage of her education. She lived as a farmer, growing root vegetables. She was proud of her work. Every morning she picked vegetables and every day she sold them at the market. Her daily routine and diet of nutritious foods like congee and curries kept her healthy.

She revealed that her lifestyle kept her in better health than European women. She claimed that if they exercised as she did they would have no need for a male midwife, or any midwife at all. They could give birth without assistance. 'Nature will always act her part, if not prevented by luxury and Indolence,' she wrote. She said her diet, lifestyle, and education would allow her to rear healthier children than any European woman; she could produce six healthy sons even if her skin was not as white as a European's. And in that, she said, she was equal to any woman, white or otherwise.

> You must know Mr Hicky, my Husband is a Gardner, I am therefore up at Day break plucking my Roots, and washing them for Market, from whence I return generally by Nine, but some times sooner, Eat a hearty breakfast (not of Ship Slop Tea) but good Congee, after which I attend to the domestic affairs of our little Cottage, whilst my Husband is Ploughing, and working in the Grounds. Our Dinner is generally made of wholesome Curries, or the Poultry of our Yard, and Congee again serves us for supper. Thus we enjoy sound and perfect health, and I will venture to affirm, that I can turn out, six as fine Choping Boys and Girls, as any in the Parish, and without the assistance of a Man-Mid-wife.
>
> And tho' my Skin is not so white as your fine Ladies, it is as plump, and as sleek as the best of them.
>
> Old Nell[258]

Another contradiction of Hicky's reporting was that while he printed articles arguing that women should be chaste, he also printed articles supporting women's right to control their own sexuality. Perhaps shocking his more prudish readers, he printed

one topic more taboo than others: female· masturbation. Hicky
cared little about norms which considered female masturbation
a selfish pleasure that degraded a woman's purity and lowered
society's honour.

Hicky reported a conversation between two women, one of
whom was engaged to a man nicknamed Jack Hydrocele, because
of rumours that he had a hydrocele, a testicular deformity that
could inhibit sex. When the woman was asked if the rumours about
her future husband were true, she said yes, her future husband
did have a hydrocele. Her friend said she was sorry for her, for
without a man she would not be able to get sexual pleasure.

'For, to tell you the truth, you might as well be Married to your
maid as to [him],' she said.

To her friend's shock, the woman said she could very well cater
for herself.

> I shall take the liberty to follow the example of the *sensible* and
> *fashionable* part of my Sex particularly in *catering* for myself, and
> in laughing at those *Squeamish* and *vulgar* creatures who may
> have the *impertinence* to blame me for doing myself *Natural
> justice.*[259]

She did not care what other people said about her. She could do
herself justice, so to speak.

Instead of shaming her, Hicky mocked those who criticised her.
He noted that her other suitors had retired to a brothel to 'procure
a sort of half oblivion of that imaginary happiness which they
think Jack Hydrocele is in possession of'.

Hicky was also unusual for reporting on the poor and lower
classes. He expressed a level of class consciousness well before his
time, shaped and developed by his background as a subaltern and
his experience in debtors' prison.

He printed an article from a Company officer at the Gwalior
fort in Central India. The army was reorganising the fort to make
it more defensible, hiring labourers to do the work. The officer
wrote to Hicky that he had spotted a girl, about age ten, and
could not stop staring at her. There was something about her
appearance, her 'sweetness of countenance', that made him want

to learn more about her. He told his *hircarrah*, messenger, to find out where the girl lived and who her parents were.

The next morning the girl's mother came to his house. She told him that she had always been poor, that her husband had died and that she had earned a living making wool but was now too old to work and had to rely on her daughter. He was shocked that they could survive on three paisa, or 3/64 of a rupee, a day. He asked if he could see her daughter, taking out a bag of 100 rupees and giving some to her. '*Wah wah; Burrah Sahib hai!*' Wow wow, you are a great man! the woman cried. She had never seen so much money in her life. He suggested they come and live with him. They could have all the money they wanted, he promised. But the mother grew suspicious. She asked why a foreigner like him would want two Indian women to live with him.

He was embarrassed by his offer and said that he had a wife and children down the river and they could live with them instead. He thought his offer was an act of charity that would free them from a life of hard labour.

But Hicky reported that his charity was not wanted. Moreover, he was viewed with suspicion. The mother came back an hour later and threw the money back at him, saying the only reason that white men gave money to little girls was for bad intentions. She said she would rather kill her daughter with her own hands than let her become a slave to any man, and that his story of having a wife was all a 'dirty lie'.[260]

Her reply shocked him. After they left, he fell deep into thought. He found himself surprised that such a poor woman, least of all a heathen, could have such honour and courage to refuse him. She did not have the education, refinement, nor enlightened ideals of his fellow Europeans. He had a revelation; it was not enlightenment ideals or Christianity that made people good or bad. A person's religion did not matter, nor their education or social class. Anyone from any background, man or woman, could be good and righteous.

Why said I should we value ourselves for our Education, or Religion when we find such sentiments in these poor ignorant

Heathens? Where will you find such instances of virtue with us, under such temptations for vice? Blush Oh ye people of a more enlighten'd age, Nation and manners, blush for your depravity. Come here and see ... what innate Natural Honour is, let the stoics and Philosophers tell me to eternity that there is no such thing as innate principles, that they are all the effects of Education. I tell them, I'll prove to them that it is false, here was native honour unsullied by Indolence and luxury, unadorn'd by Education, and unsupported or protected by any thing.

He never saw the mother and child again. He wanted to say that he was not ashamed nor meant them dishonour or harm, a thought he shared with the whole world via Hicky's newspaper.

I would give 1000 Rupees this moment that they were with [me], but that's now impossible, for I have made every enquiry in my power, and can hear Nothing of them, they are removed I suppose to some other place. I'm sorry for it, for I wish'd them both well, and still do, nor have I a thought concerning either, that I would be asham'd to expose to the whole World.[261]

The conclusion Hicky let people draw was that goodness did not come from class, education, or modernity. Goodness was innate. Indian women were not inferior to their European counterparts.

But his article still treated Indians as noble savages. Their goodness came from the fact that they were pure and untouched by the corruption of the modern era. He implied that Indians lived simple lives with simple thoughts in simple times. Hicky may have seen Indians as having the potential to be equal, but throughout his writing, he often did not describe them as actually his equals.

Despite this disconnect, Hicky did not write solely about Europeans. By reporting the tragedies and happiness of Europeans as well as the Bengali poor, he covered news others might have passed over. For example, he reported a miraculous story of how one woman survived giving birth amid a great fire. He covered the demise of a palm sap picker who fell to his death from a coconut tree. He reported boats that overturned in the Hooghly river and the commoners who drowned. He reported the violence of British sailors who seized men in punch houses to force them into the navy.[262] In bringing stories like these to light, he saw himself as a servant to society, covering topics of which many would have been ignorant.

At some points, he went a step further. His support of the poor could turn into criticism of the rich. When one Bengali chief drove his chariot over a poor man and killed him on the spot, Hicky exposed how the chief covered up the murder. Instead of murder charges going to the Supreme Court, the chief paid off the deceased's wife and children; they needed money to survive. 'The matter we hear has been hushed up for twenty Rupees,' Hicky reported.[263]

Hicky covered one issue that affected the poor more than any other: Calcutta's terrifying fires. Because many poor Bengalis used grass from the Hooghly to thatch their roofs, fires broke out frequently and spread rapidly, often burning down thousands of houses at a time. Months of extreme heat during the dry season and Calcutta's narrow roads and unpaved streets made it tough to control these fires.[264]

Calcutta was hit by one of the greatest of these fires ever in March. Every house, from Bow Bazar in the city's north to Colinga in the east, went up in flames. 'The dreadful havoc the late fire has made amongst the poor Bengalis is almost incredible,' Hicky wrote.[265] Above fifteen thousand straw houses stood gutted. One hundred and ninety died, 'burned and suffocated by the smoak and flames', he reported. In one house, sixteen people were burnt alive.[266] In another, five men went in at different times to save two women and a child, but all were suffocated. Women ran to place their babies in Lal Dighi, the city's main source of drinking water. Looters took advantage of the chaos, burglarising homes. The destruction was so bad that old residents said it was the worst fire in a lifetime.[267]

Thousands were left homeless, with no food, water, or clothing. Even Hicky was affected. His bungalow and little out houses in his garden had been consumed. He called for action in his newspaper, asking the rich and powerful to give food, and more importantly, shelter and clothing. He insisted the Company do something to help.

To the Benevolent and Powerful.

Be it known that fifteen thousand Inhabitants of Calcutta are since the late Fires in extreme Distress, their small possessions having been consumed ... but a more dreadful foe awaits them, lingering Diseases, exposed to the extremes of heat and cold, destitute of clothes and dwellings, to feed them may only prolong their misery: many of the Aged have laid down content to die and the Infants wailing in their Mothers bosoms increase the calamity beyond the power of language to describe ... Ye Patrons of the Unfortunate, Exert your influence, clothe [them] and give them habitations.[268]

Hicky soon discovered that he had influence. Many people, including Company servants, read his newspaper. After his articles on the putrefying carcasses in the streets, the police superintendent posted a notice in his paper asking where the dead were so they could be picked up.[269] He got an even greater response to the fire. On June 26, after he published his call to action, the Supreme Council issued a proposal to forbid thatch houses within Calcutta, and to enact a 14.7 per cent property tax to repair the city's roads. This proposal, called the *Bye-Law*, would later become a lightning rod for dissent because many saw it as illegal taxation without representation.[270]

Slowly, Hicky began to change. He became more political as he saw the power his newspaper wielded. His friendships with other subalterns and his time trading in India likely convinced him to turn to politics. By allowing subalterns to advocate for their rights in his paper, he saw himself providing a public service. But by doing so, he began to drift away from the neutrality he had earlier espoused. He changed his masthead to proclaim that his newspaper was 'Open to all Parties, *but influenced by* None'—borrowing this slogan from Revolutionary American newspapers—to emphasise his independence, and to indicate he would be accepting more controversial topics.[271]

The first of these topics was war. At first Hicky supported British wars, in particular the fight against American Revolutionaries. He hewed to the party line that American colonists should submit to British authority and that their rebellion was sedition.[272] In one poem—a common way of expressing political beliefs—he accused the Americans of rebelling because they were too selfish to pay taxes. He compared the Americans to frogs and predicted that their joy would turn to sorrow when they learned their ally, the French king, was no friend of democracy, but planned to conquer America after the revolution was over. In the end, he predicted the Americans would be eaten like frogs by the French stork-king.

Rejoice, Americans, rejoice!
Praise ye the Lord with heart and voice;
The treaty's sign'd with faithful France,
And now like Frenchmen, sing and dance!
But when your Joy gives way to reason
And friendly hints are not deemed treason
Let me as well as I am able,
Present your Congress with a fable.

Tired out with happiness, the frogs
Sedition croak'd thro' all their bogs
And then to Jove the restless race,
Made out their melancholy case …

None but ourselves are fit to rule us:
We are too large, too free a nation,
To be incumber'd with taxation.
We pray for peace but wish confusion
Then right or wrong a revolution! …

The Stork grew hungry, long'd for fish!
The monarch could not have his wish
In rage he to the marshes flies;
And made a meal of his allies;
Then grew so fond of well-fed frogs
He made a larder of the bogs!

Say, Yankies, don't you feel compunction,
At your unnatural, rash conjunction?
Can love for you in him take root,
Who's Catholic and absolute?
I'll tell these croakers how he'll treat 'em!
Frenchmen, like Storks, love frog, to eat 'em.[273]

There were pressing issues Hicky felt he could not avoid. He slowly began to criticise corruption in the Company. But he was careful to criticise only those who were far away from Calcutta. He limited his attacks to a person and a place both mentally and physically distant from Calcutta: the Governor of Madras, Sir Thomas Rumbold, who had been recalled to England to answer charges in front of Parliament. Hicky sarcastically wrote that Rumbold was a 'great man' for 'only' amassing a fortune of about £600,000 while in India, much of it from bribes and extortion.[274] For now, this was Hicky's only mention of corruption.

Hicky began to air long-standing grievances about pay and promotion. The subalterns who had fought in the Rohilla War seven years ago felt betrayed and deceived that they had never received prize money. Many were convinced the Company's directors and Parliament wanted to wash their hands of Hastings' war. No politician in England wished to be seen condoning an immoral war.

Hicky printed the subalterns' letters, hoping that publicity would resolve their grievances. He published a letter from an officer who had served in the war and who had seen one of his veterans at Calcutta's Old Fort. The officer asked the veteran if the young girl by his side was his daughter. The veteran replied she was not. She was the daughter of his comrade who had been killed in the war. He was taking care of her now, he explained:

> Your Honour knows I have been too long in India to have a Child so young as her. But [she] is the Orphan of my old Comrade Thomas Beck, Corporal in the file that was hacked down just on our left. He never rightly recovered but died a little after you left us. As your Honour knew him to be a good Man and got him made a Serjant, had he lived he would have saved something for his Poor Child. When on his death Bed Grasping my Hand [he] said 'George you loved me: Love my Child as well, and she will not miss her father.'

The veteran continued speaking, with tears in his eyes, that if he had prize money he could provide better for his comrade's daughter. Other troops in more recent conflicts had gotten prize money, but he had not.[275] He said he was deceived. He was now certain he had fought for a bad cause and that was why he was being punished.

> May you Sir never know the loss of a Friend—Poor Tom! All he had he gave, in his Knap Sack was found a few Shafts of Linen and this Breast Buckle, tho' I have no occasion for that to remind me of him, while this little one is exactly like him lives. I am fonder of her then I could be of my own. I have got his Will by which he left me his Prize Money.—Ah! Your Honour, we have been cruelly deceived. I am sure you was too, as you believed those fine promises true or, you would not have caused them to be read at the Head of the Company. I begin now to think true what a number of people then used to say. That we were fighting in a bad Cause, or else why should those who took the ships; and Chandernagore, get prize Money and we not? ... It is our duty to obey and we were told they were our Enemies. Such a sum as mine and Tom's would be of great service to me.[276]

Hicky also used his newspaper to criticise the army's promotion system. Promotion was tediously slow. It could often take a decade for a cadet to be promoted. Moreover, the Company army had fewer officers per solider than the British army, especially at the higher ranks, meaning there were fewer promotion opportunities for cadets. Furthermore, while in theory the Company army promoted by seniority, in reality, the well-connected and rich could subvert the system by returning to England to wait their turn for promotion.[277] Poor subalterns learned with dismay that the system was corrupted by connections and money.

In July, Hicky published a letter from a cadet who grumbled that he stood little more chance of being promoted now than he had when he had enlisted a decade earlier. He did not know what to do, other than to write to Hicky and hope that the publicity might cause change.

> It is a disagreeable reflexion, Sir, for a young Man like me ... to think, that I am likely to remain in this Schorching, unhealthy Climate for 12 or 14 Years and unless I have interest at the fountain head ... have the most valuable part of my life spent,

and my health destroy'd in the service ... and at the same time
see many inferior Officers, return to their native Countries in
affluence... Oh ye in power think of this, and let some kind of
equal distribution take place.
      Yours,
      A poor Cadet.[278]

Hicky covered not just European soldiers, but also Indian
sepoys who fought at the bottom of the Company's ranks. When
lightning struck the military base at Kanpur in June, it set off a
fire that destroyed much of the camp. The sepoys suffered the
most. Their pay was already months behind, forcing them to
borrow money to buy supplies. Now much of what they owned
was destroyed. 'The poor black Troops have suffered much by it
and their situation is now truelly miserable ... they are always
kept three Months in Arrears, so that being obliged to borrow
from mercenary usurers at an exorbitant Interest for their daily
subsistence, it reduces their pay to a very small Pittance indeed,'
wrote one of his correspondents.[279]

Hicky turned against the war as death tolls mounted.
The biggest turning point was the horrific Battle of Pollilur in
September, when the king of Mysore, Hyder Ali, and his 90,000-
man army ambushed one of the Company armies in South India.
The Company commander formed his force in a hollow square
and frantically wrote for help. But it all was for naught. A rocket
hit one of his ammunition wagons and ripped a hole in his line.
The Mysorean cavalry charged in and the square collapsed.

The battle became butchery as the Company army was
decimated. Over 3,000 out of the 5,700 soldiers were killed. It was
the single biggest British military defeat in India in a generation.
After the battle, the British commander was strapped to a cannon
and forced to watch as the severed heads of his fellow officers were
paraded before him. The youngest soldiers were dressed as women
for their captors' entertainment. Three hundred were forcibly
circumcised. The survivors were marched naked or semi-naked
into dungeons and fed a diet of toxic rice until they slowly died.[280]

The battle shocked Hicky's belief that the British were superior
to any enemy in India. As reports filtered in over the next few

months, he learned just how disastrous the battle was, and how incompetent the Company generals had been. The chief of the Company forces in South India, Hector Munro, stood only four miles away and ignored repeated requests for help. Instead of coming to their aid, he dumped all his artillery into local lakes and fled.[281] To make matters worse, after the battle, Hyder Ali besieged most of South India and cut Madras from any supplies.[282]

The battle made Hicky question why the British were fighting in India. The casualties made the war seem pointless, and he accused the Company of squandering its soldiers' lives. 'More Europeans have been *ignominiously Sacrificed* in the late ill concerted and disgraceful Campaigns,' he wrote, 'than were lost ... in ... the whole of the last War.'[283]

He began to question whether his fellow British were good and Indians bad.[284] When Hyder Ali's army captured Arcot, it was thought they massacred anyone they found. Hicky reported a much different reality. He reported that Hyder had actually escorted the captured Company troops to friendly territory, let them write letters home, and even had his own hircarrahs deliver their letters. 'How noble and General like was this act,' Hicky wrote. 'How much we wrong the Infidels of those remote and savage Nations, when we suppose them capable of acting a more base part than we do ourselves.'[285] Where Hicky once saw only a rapacious warlord, he now saw a complex leader, capable of the same humanity as his fellow British.

With ever-increasing scepticism, he used his paper to report on the war's humanitarian tragedy. As Hyder laid waste to the countryside with fire and sword, thousands of people came flooding into Madras.[286] Mothers walked with infants at their breasts. Fathers led their families on foot.[287] The city was full to the brink. 'The houses and streets of that place are now so full that they can scarcely find rooms to lay themselves down,' he wrote.[288]

He reported the terrible effects of war. The price of rice shot up thirty times. [289] Famine came next. 'The poor Natives near that place are all starving,' he wrote.[290] People were 'DYING EVEN AT THE WAREHOUSE DOORS—Everyday numbers perish in this manner, 5 women with infants in their arms waiting for their turn dropt down dead with hunger'.[291] The human horrors were almost too much to bear, and he saw it as his duty to point them out.

His war coverage gained him an international audience. Many British newspapers such as the *London Courant, London Chronicle, Public Advertiser, British Evening Post,* and the *Lady's Magazine* reprinted his news, often verbatim. So did many monthly and yearly journals. His news even reached America, where newspapers such as the *New Jersey Gazette* and *Providence Gazette* were quick to reprint British defeats.[292] His paper also reached non-English speaking audiences. French journals like the *Journal Politique* and the *Mercure de France* translated his articles about British battles in India.[293] Even the German *Politisches Journal* summarised his reporting.[294] Many other journals, whose records no longer exist, likely reprinted his news. As the only newspaper in Asia, his gazette became an important source of information.

During these months Hicky had made his newspaper an independent voice for reform. But his increasing scepticism also made him more willing to question those in power and to break cultural norms. He saw his mission to tell the truth: open to all parties, but influenced by none. He spotlighted the subalterns that occupied the lower rungs of society, shut out from patronage and prestige. And he gave them the means to express their complaints. All he could hope for was that those in power would respond.

But his success meant that others saw a good business opportunity. An event was about to come that would make it easier for any competitor with the right connections to challenge him.

These Evils Must Come

For a House divided against itself, cannot stand.
– Johann Christian Diemer to Michael Hallings,
Secretary of the Society, 1780.[295]

Monday, 31 July 1780, The Mission Church

Diemer had been gone for nine long months to Cape Town and back. His health was perfect. His tuberculosis was gone. He felt rested and ready for new challenges.

But he was astonished when he returned. Kiernander had evicted his wife and family from the Mission house and had dismissed his schoolteacher and schoolchildren from the schoolhouse. A new school was founded with new teachers in its place.[296] And a new missionary now lived in the house where his wife and son once were.

His status as a missionary taken away, he felt humiliated.

He was convinced Kiernander wanted the school back to turn a profit.

'[Since] he never expected my Recovery and Return to Calcutta, he flattered himself with the Hope of receiving so many Boarders and Scholars as would have yielded his Mission a greater benefit, than that he chose to suffer the loss of, by turning the Charity Children and my Boarders out of his school,' Diemer wrote to the Society.[297]

His relationship with Kiernander, already fraught, turned outright hostile. He wanted to confront Kiernander, and he began preparing just what to say when they would meet. He would not stand for what happened, and was determined to keep his Rs 100 salary from the town charity.

He came head to head with Kiernander one morning when they met in the house of a member of their congregation. He took Kiernander aside to the garden and recited his prepared speech.

'All people wonder, that you, such an old man, whose eve of life is fast emerging to the shadows of the grave, and whom the sepulcher is already yawning to close upon, that you should be so avaricious and take to yourself the hundred rupees house rent for the school, and not allow it to me, who has the charge of the school,' he said, speaking slowly and eloquently.

'I have never taken those hundred rupees for myself, but have made use of them to defray the charges of the Mission, as you know I have also desired you to do,' Kiernander said, taken aback by Diemer's eloquence.

'No. You have received those hundred rupees and why cannot I now have them?' Diemer pressed on.

'It is true, I have monthly received them from the [town charity], but I have also disbursed them for the Mission,' Kiernander said.

Kiernander turned his back and began to walk away.

But Diemer was not finished.

'It is your Mission, and you are to support that, but those hundred rupees belong to me who takes care of the school, as well as the money for what the [day students] pay. That is what all people say is just.'

As Kiernander walked away, six years of spoiled hopes boiled up inside Diemer.

'These evils must come, but woe be to the man, through whom they come,' he called out.[298]

Diemer decided he would leave the Mission forever. He felt sick just to be there.

He wrote to Kiernander the next week that he was officially leaving. He said he was willing to preach and officiate marriages but would have nothing to do with the day-to-day work of the Mission. Separation, he believed, was the only way to preserve the peace between them.

When I take a Retrospective view of the Efforts I have made, the Struggles I have had ... to maintain that Peace and Harmony, that ought to subsist between us particularly as Clergymen, yet without Effect; I must conclude there is such an unhappy Difference of Sentiments between us, as cannot harmonize. Therefore to avoid that Scandal in future which may by our Differences fall as well upon ourselves as our holy Profession, I am come to the Resolution to decline all farther Meetings or Conferences.[299]

He thought Kiernander would agree that they should part ways in peace.

He was wrong.

The next week he received a furious letter from Kiernander. Six years flashed before him as he read it. Six years of futility, suffering, and sickness. It was clear nothing would change. The Mission was and would always be Kiernander's private property, run like a personal fiefdom.

'You have struggled hard to maintain your own obstinate self will,' the letter read.

'You have done things of your own accord to the Detriment of the Mission,' it read.

'You will not yield to Reason and Equity,' it read.

'You have deserted from your own charge ... and run where God has not sent you,' it read.

'Lord ... have mercy upon you, and make you sensible of your perverse doings!' it read.[300]

These were vicious words. Words that required answers.

He put the letter down.

After all those years of depression and worry, he found himself accused of laziness, abandoning the Mission, and forgetting his oath to serve God. He would not let this stand. Rage boiled inside him. He would get revenge.

He began plotting.

The Duel

In a word, I have power, and I will employ it.
—Warren Hastings, November 1780.[301]

12.30 p.m. Monday, 14 August 1780. On the Hooghly River.[302]

The wind swept by Governor-General Hastings' head as his servants sailed him down to Calcutta. The southern sky looked gray and ominous. The monsoon was on its way.

Hastings' mood matched the weather, melancholy and sad, drawn and tired, stiff and cramped. He had been fighting his enemy Philip Francis for six years for control of the Council.

It was time for it to come to an end.

He only wanted to have the power he long desired.

It was nightfall by the time he reached Calcutta. He stepped off the boat and went directly to his mansion and found a letter he had written over a month ago, but hadn't sent, addressed to the Company's directors, about Francis.

I do not trust to his promise of Candour; convinced that he is incapable of it, and that his sole purpose and wish are to embarrass and defeat every measure which I may undertake … every disappointment and misfortune have been aggravated by him, and every fabricated tale of armies devoted to famine and to massacre, have found their first and most ready way to his office … I judge of his public conduct by my experience of his private, which I have found to be void of truth and honour. This is a severe charge, but temperately and deliberately made … The only redress for a fraud for which the law has made no provision, is the exposure of it.[303]

He sent a hircarrah running with the letter. There was no going back now.

He was infuriated by Francis, who had promised to support the Maratha war. Yet Francis had vetoed his orders to send reinforcements.[304] The army needed reinforcements immediately, before the monsoon made roads impassable.

He deeply believed that Francis vetoed the reinforcements only to spite him, and to frustrate him so much that he would resign, so Francis could become Governor-General himself.

But Francis' tactic had the opposite effect. Hastings could never let such a man become Governor-General.[305]

The next day, after the Council meeting, Francis asked if they could speak in private. Francis took him aside in a private room, took a paper out of his pocket, and looked down at it.[306]

'You must be sensible, Sir,' Francis read, 'that no answer I can give to the matter of that paper can be adequate to the dishonour done me ... You have left me no alternative but to demand personal satisfaction of you for the affronts you have offered me.'[307]

They agreed to meet in two days' time outside Belvedere, Hastings' estate. This area was favoured ground for duellists. Shaded, secluded, leafy, and green, it had even earned a moniker for the two trees under which so many duels had been fought: the 'Two Trees of Destruction'. [308]

17 August. Hastings' Esplanade Mansion. 4.15 a.m.

Hastings woke to a knock on his door by Colonel Pearse.

It was early, too early, he thought. Calcutta was quiet. Only the shrill yells of jackals pierced the night.

He laid down on the couch to close his eyes for a few more moments of rest. A half hour later they popped open again.

He would have to kill a man this morning.

He got dressed and stepped into Colonel Pearse's carriage.

He saluted soldiers as he rode south past the New Fort. But his mind was on other things. What would happen if he were shot and killed? He knew his wife Marian would grieve for him. But what about his plans to expand the British Empire? All would come to naught.

On the other hand, even if he were to kill Francis, his plans might still be ruined. He would have to stand trial for murder.[309]

His mind drifted to a happier time, to his vacation last month. He and Marian had enjoyed a packed breakfast on his private boat, sailing up to the Dutch settlement of Chinsurah. Amid balls and minuets, he had distracted himself from the war on the Company's frontiers, and his war with Francis.[310]

His mind snapped back to the present. Dawn's first rays were rising when he reached his Belvedere estate. Outside, he saw Francis and Francis' aide, Colonel Watson, on the road. They had been waiting for nearly half-an-hour.

He and Pearse dismounted.

They found a small brown dirt path just outside the western gate of his estate. The air was still and the ground was dry and parched. Scarcely a breath moved. The monsoon had still not come.[311]

Pearse handed him a pistol. Watson measured fourteen paces and drew a line in the dirt.

Hastings lifted his foot. Pearse counted his steps. One, two, three…

He took a breath. 'Fourteen,' Pearse counted.

He stopped.

He had only fired a gun a couple of times in his life. He did not know what to do.

'Do you stand before the line or behind it?' he asked Francis.

Francis looked down. Francis had never shot a gun either.

'Behind it,' Francis said.

Hastings stepped forward.

'It is a rule that neither of you are to quit the ground till you have discharged your pistols,' Pearse interrupted.

'You both should fire together without taking any advantage,' Watson added.

Hastings was still confused.

'Does that mean we ought to fire by word, or your command?' he asked.

'You should fire together as nearly as can be,' Watson said.

Hastings turned to face Francis, looking at Francis' sideways body, right arm raised high, slowly coming level to his chest.

Francis aimed his pistol once.

Hastings' heart raced.

Twice.

He winced.

Three times.

Click.

He exhaled. Silence. Francis' powder was wet and his gun did not fire.

Out of the corner of his eye, Hastings saw an old Bengali lady beckon for others to watch. A small crowd began to form. He and Francis made a strange and entertaining sight: two white men in breeches duelling to the death.

Pearse refilled Francis' powder.

Again he watched Francis prepare. But this time he was determined to fire first.

He cocked and aimed his pistol; Francis levelled his at the same time. They fired together.

Click.

Boom.

Francis staggered and fell. He tried to sit up but his arms gave way. A growing spot of red blood stained his shoulder.

'I am dead,' Francis cried gently.

Hastings ran to his side.

'Good God!' he said.

Hastings and Watson compressed Francis's wound. Pearse ran to Belvedere for help. Surgeons came and cut the bullet out of Francis' shoulder and bled Francis twice. They said he was lucky to be alive. A rib had deflected the ball away from his chest.[312]

News of the duel reached Calcutta within hours. Many saw it as a trial by combat where God granted the victor the right to rule.[313]

Francis told Hastings that he was going to leave India. Relief washed over Hastings, opening into a boundless future.

'I shall have no competitor to oppose my designs, to encourage disobedience to my authority ... to excite and foment popular odium against me ... In a word, I have power, and I will employ it,' he wrote.[314]

There was no one to oppose him. The absolute power he had long coveted was now his.

After seven long years he could rule as he pleased. He immediately moved to assert control. His first target was the Supreme Court. The Court had been founded by Parliament to bring equal and blind justice to India and had been a thorn in his side since its foundation. It had obstructed the Company's tax collection, and had issued many habeas corpus orders to review the arrests of those his tax collectors had jailed.

Two cases angered him more than any others. In the first, the Court had found one of his provincial Councils—the Patna Council—guilty of forcing a woman off her lands, surrounding her at an Islamic shrine, and trying to starve her out and force her to live with her nephew-in-law.[315] In the second, the Court had sent the sheriff to arrest one of his tax collectors. The Court had declared him in contempt for ordering the army to seize the sheriff, and jailed his lawyer for telling him the sheriff's route.[316]

He struck upon a brilliant plan to sideline the Court and solidify his control over the Company. In the months following the duel, he targeted the Chief Justice, Sir Elijah Impey. Impey had once been his childhood friend; they had attended the Westminster School together. Impey was also politically ambitious, and had asked to be given a seat on the Supreme Council six times. Hastings leveraged Impey's ambition and suggested the next best thing. If Impey would agree not to obstruct the Company's tax collectors, he would give Impey, and Impey alone, entire control of every court in Bengal. To sweeten the deal, he offered Impey a Rs 5,000 a month salary and Rs 600 a month for office fees, amounting to almost an extra two-thirds of Impey's salary as Chief Justice.[317]

On October 10, he formally offered Impey the new court system, which he called the Sadr Diwani Adalat, the Central Indian Court.[318] Cases that would have once gone to the Supreme Court would now go to Impey. The Supreme Court would be obsolete for all cases outside Calcutta. The Sadr Diwani Adalat would be Bengal's highest court.

Hastings began to bestow patronage to every office under his control over the next few months. He appointed Impey's friends and relatives to plum Company positions. He appointed one the Remembrancer of Criminal Courts, with a large Rs 1,000 a month salary. He made another the Company's senior advocate with a similarly large salary.[319] And he appointed a third friend, John Rider, to Simeon Droz's Board of Trade, giving Rider a Rs 1,100 a month salary, even backdating Rider's salary to the moment Rider arrived in Calcutta. Moreover, because the Board of Trade was full, he allowed Rider to receive a salary while waiting for the next vacancy.[320]

Hastings believed his means were for good ends. 'I am conscious of the rectitude of my intentions,' he wrote.[321] He believed Impey's appointment would bring harmony to the Company. His provincial councils and tax collectors would be able to collect tax without having to fear the justice system.[322] By giving Impey control of the judiciary, he controlled Impey. Their fates and fortunes were now bound together.

After Impey, he courted Sir Robert Chambers, the Supreme Court's second judge. He took advantage of Chambers' well-known struggles with money. Chambers' investments in real estate, including the purchase of a £6,000 mansion, as well as one of Kiernander's luxurious garden houses, had put him in financial straits.[323] Also, like Impey, Chambers had asked many times to be placed on the Supreme Council.

He gave Chambers' brother a plum position on Impey's new Adalat, making him its Persian interpreter.[324] He later appointed Chambers to be the judge of an entirely new court, the Court of Chinsurah, giving Chambers a Rs 3,000 a month salary for this ceremonial position. With these bribes, Hastings moved not just one, but two judges deeper into his embrace. Only the Supreme Court's last justice, John Hyde, stubbornly remained outside his patronage, rejecting his overtures.[325]

Hastings had bound the judges to his will and had compromised the Supreme Court's independence. No part of government, no person, was out of his reach. Power was his. And he employed it.

A Rival

We hear that the Editors of the INDIA GAZETTE ... have come to a resolution to render their Gazette of as much real utility as possible, by Printing it on a fine soft Paper and of such a size that it may be sufficient for a whole weeks offerings in the TEMPLE of CLOACINA; so that their friends will in future have something for their Money.

– James Augustus Hicky, *Hicky's Bengal Gazette*,
5 May 1781.

Saturday, 4 October 1780, The India Gazette Office.

Bernard Messink and Peter Reed had kept their plan to launch a newspaper secret for months. At first, they started by telling Hicky's subscribers one by one to drop their subscriptions.[326]

Then they turned to Kiernander to get a printing press and types. On their behalf, Kiernander sent a letter to his fellow missionaries in Tranquebar, in South India, asking for a set of used types and 'an old press, but still in good condition.'[327]

On October 4, Messink and Reed asked the Supreme Council to let them mail their newspaper for free through the post office, and to be made the Company's official printers. They must have known their request would be granted, for although they were told that Hastings had already made another Company servant the Company's official printer, they were granted free postage.[328] Hastings' order gave them an advantage over Hicky who had to pay for his own postage.

Neither Reed nor Messink appear to have any printing

experience. Messink came to printing from theatre and spent his youth in London before moving to Calcutta. A talented actor, singer, and director, he made Calcutta's theatre an instant success. The most well-to-do and powerful—including army officers like General Gilbert Ironside, Supreme Council members like Hastings and Barwell, and Supreme Court Justices Impey, Chambers, and Hyde—became his subscribers, and he grew wealthy and well-connected.[329]

Reed came from Bengal's salt trade, where he worked for over a decade. He also served on the Calcutta Committee of Revenue.[330] Reed saw a newspaper as a profitable business venture, and his experience taught him how to avoid the pitfalls of others. He had acted as William Bolts' lawyer and representative after the Company had deported Bolts.[331] That lesson had taught him that the best way to succeed was to avoid politics, or, better yet, support those in power.

With patronage secured, Messink and Reed posted notices in all Calcutta's public places, announcing they were launching a newspaper.[332] On November 18, they printed their first *India Gazette*.

They became Hicky's one and only competitor.

They differed from Hicky in almost every way. Like the liberal Whig and conservative Tory newspapers in England, they and Hicky represented two different sides of the political spectrum. Where Hicky covered the poor, they focused on the rich. Where Hicky was lewd, they were dull and dry. Where Hicky emphasised independence, they made no secret they had Hastings' support.

From the beginning, they spread the belief of British superiority. In one of their more telling features, they devoted many pages to the diary of a deceased Company servant named Henry Wildmore. With a busy social life, Wildmore did very little work indeed. Between smoking hookah, playing cards, racing horses, and watching performances of dancing girls, Wildmore returned home to beat his servants, which he recorded in his diary. On a Monday, he kicked one of his servants down the stairs for having the 'impudence' to disturb him as he was waking up post a hangover. The next day he recorded: 'after breakfast, sit down to Persian, beat my Moonshee several times for not being able to explain himself in English.' Later that day he 'abused' his bania for forgetting to pay an IOU. He also flogged his Indian barber for being late. He almost cut short the flogging because he received a letter to report to work. But he deflected the letter by writing he had the flu, and instead took the night off to dance at the Harmonic Tavern.[333]

Messink and Reed did not print Wildmore's journal sarcastically or jokingly. In a preface to Wildmore's journal, their correspondent dismissed Wildmore's violence against Indians as only 'trifling incidents' that would not detract from the 'pleasure' of reading his journal. While their intent was to lampoon Company servants for wiling away their time instead of being industrious, the real effect was to show how acceptable violence was against the Indian lower class.

Wildmore's journal was not a unique example of how Messink and Reed abetted violence and impunity. They spread the belief of British superiority in many other articles. One of their correspondents thought Indians were inferior because they did not understand British wit. After learning a joke at a party, their correspondent said he went home and retold it to his munshi. 'I found however it was to no purpose; the Brute answered he could not understand either its excellence or use,' he wrote. His munshi replied that while the joke might be witty in English, it was rude in Persian. Their correspondent wrote that he was 'much nettled' that his munshi did not understand him and asked Messink to support him. 'Pray Mr [Messink] write a Paper in defence of this sort of wit,' he pleaded.[334]

Messink and Reed accused Indians of corrupting British values. In one scathing article, Messink blamed the sloth of Company servants on the fact that they were 'obliged' to socialise 'with the Natives'. Messink believed that Indians were lazy because indolence was built into their culture. Their 'morning and evening prayer, might with great reason be supposed to be "Teach me O guardian genius how to procrastinate",' he wrote.[335] In Messink's world, British and Indians should keep separate, because Indians would sap the purity of essence that made British superior.

Where Hicky wrote for and about subalterns, they published articles for the upper-class, writing about cotillion dances, or the proper behaviour of young men in front of ladies.[336] One article they printed was a call to stop spitting bread pellets at one another at the dinner table—a common practice at large, raucous, drunken parties—calling it, without irony, a 'barbarous' practice.[337] A second article argued that people should drive their carriages on the left to avoid accidents. In another issue, they devoted their full front page to an actor's complaints that other actors' servants had absconded with prop knives to open oysters for their employers' suppers, and had let dogs run wild on stage.[338]

Where Hicky treated Indians as noble savages, Messink and Reed believed Europeans would always be superior. While on the face of it, they adopted Hastings' idea that it was important to understand Indians to rule them, their claims did not match their actions. One of their articles purported to explain the origins of Shia Islam. Instead, it devolved into a two-column denunciation of Islam, explaining how the Shia were 'bigotted', driven by 'blind zeal', corrupted by Hindu 'superstitious rituals', and best avoided during Ramadan when they could be 'worked up into Madness'. Their author concluded that Muslims should be watched carefully during religious festivals. Their susceptibility to violence 'ought to be a lesson to government', to keep a watchful eye on them.[339]

Messink and Reed made good on their promise to avoid politics. They told their contributors that they would reject anything that did not 'come within our plan', refusing any letters about politics.[340] Ultimately, they printed only seventeen opinion articles for their entire first year. Many of these focused on trade policy. They did not print a single article against the Company or Hastings. Nor did they print a single article that supported freedom of the Press or freedom of speech. At a time of great upheaval, their focus signalled their self-censorship and their close relation with Hastings.[341] Their lack of opinion columns was itself an acknowledgement of Hastings' authority.

They had an obvious reason to muffle themselves: financial rewards. They became the Company's de facto mouthpiece, as the Company's departments used their paper for advertisements and

public notices.[342] Merchants recognised that they had wealthier
subscribers so they printed more advertisements for luxury goods
in their gazette than Hicky's, making their gazette the preferred
place for products like private boat rental companies, hunting
dogs, garden houses, and dinner clubs.[343] Some of their common
advertisements were services like buying and shipping diamonds
home to England, a form of wealth that could be easily hidden.[344]
Company servants, like Hastings, who often sent their wealth
home as diamonds, would have found these offers enticing.[345]
Even Kiernander advertised in their gazette, offering to print legal
forms for the Supreme Court.

Perhaps their close connections to Hastings and other powerful
Company servants were why they supported Hastings. The
opinions they did print attacked freedom of the Press.[346] They
found Hicky dangerous, disloyal, and insolent. They argued that
Hicky was himself oppressive for attacking people in his paper.
'Freedom of the Press' wrote one of their contributors, 'is often
converted into a destructive engine of Public Oppression and
Private wrong'.[347] 'I am shocked to observe the constant endeavors
of malcontents to effect a total subversion of peace and harmony
amongst us,' wrote another.[348] To them, Hicky was dangerous
because he disturbed Calcutta's peace and harmony, and acted
against the interests of his country.

They believed Hicky should be censored because he spread
dissent, threatened social superiors, and subverted British
interests. 'That there are in Bengal, some who are ill-affected to
the true interests of their country, is, I think, evident from the
many inflammatory letters and Paragraphs that have appeared
in the Bengal Gazette, which seem to breathe a strong spirit of
discontent,' one of their correspondents wrote.[349] The abuse of
liberty of the Press, 'calls for the pruning hand of authority. These
chronicles are carried to distant countries; and the mischief is
completed, by their becoming the general opinion of mankind,'
wrote another.[350] True patriots, their writers wrote, supported
their rulers. To them, Hicky was no patriot.

Like Hicky, Messink and Reed came from abroad. But in
truth Messink and Reed came from a very different culture. They

affiliated with people that made great fortunes, lived in mansions, and returned home with enough money to buy seats in Parliament. Hicky affiliated with subalterns on the fringes; men who came seeking fortune but frustrated by an unfair system.

It was to this frustration that Hicky turned next.

Suppression

Without paying any compliment to rank, every one of the parties concerned shall be arraigned on Saturday next, and referred to the Public either to acquit or condemn them.

– James Augustus Hicky, *Hicky's Bengal Gazette*,
4 November 1780.[351]

Saturday, 11 November 1780, Hicky's Printing Office

Hicky was more than upset when he learned that Messink and Reed had been given free postage.[352]

Their free postage meant only one thing to him: there was a grand conspiracy to ruin him.[353] Of this he was certain. Certain that a powerful force was against him. And that powerful force must have been Simeon Droz, the chief of the Board of Trade, who had led him to Marian Hastings. And there could only be one reason why: his refusal to pay a bribe.

He saw injustice and began plotting revenge.

He decided he would tell the public his story, from the time his shipping business had failed and he was thrown in jail for debt. Instead of 'melancholy reflections and indolence', he turned to printing to free himself from jail. He worked long hours for two years, often from six in the morning to one or two at night and earned enough money to finally pay back his debts, 'denying himself any necessaries of life'.

He wrote in his newspaper why he became a journalist.

I have no particular passion for publishing of News Papers. I have no propensity [for them].

I was not bred to a slavish Life, of hard work, yet I take a pleasure in enslaving my body, in order to purchase freedom for my mind and soul.

I wanted no girded chariot, or seat in Parliament, I wanted no pomp or asiatic pageantry. I wanted to pay my debts like an honest Man, secure three things which I once thought I should be able to accomplish in six years, by jogging on simply and inoffensively with my little paper ... I hoped to pay off all my debts, and secure six thousand Pounds in England in order to support me in my old days in a land of freedom and Liberty. To purchase a little House in the middle of a Garden, rise with the lark, sew my own Peas or Beans, Graft or inoculate my own Trees, according to the seasons of the year and live in peace with all mankind. And when it pleased GOD to summon me to another world, to enjoy the pleasure, of laying my hand on my breast, and with a comforted old heart to have it in my power to say I thank you my GOD I have paid all my debts and that by the sweat of my Brow. That I never did in all my life, wrong Man, Woman, or child, of six pence, or the value of it.

He did not want wealth. Nor did he want fame. He only wanted to earn enough money to retire to England and to live a simple life.

Yet after all his hard labour, he felt threatened and intimidated.

These, ye horrid schemers, are the comforts which I was in hopes to enjoy, and would without doubt had not the Devil the Master you daily serve, prompted you to raise schemes to ruin me and my little Family, but that GOD who has brought me thro' all my misfortunes will I hope bring me thro' this.

He believed that the corruption had gotten so extreme that God was going to punish Company servants for their greed and pride, something that he already believed was happening with the recent military defeats.

Acts like these has call'd the Vengeance of GOD down on these once peaceable settlements. But GOD being merciful has suspended them for some years in hopes, of your amendment, but finding that ye still grow more, and more hardened, daily in the practice of oppression and secret Villainy. He has withdrew his all merciful and suspending hand. The long suspended Vengeance now seems to fall on all of the Country's territorial possessions, the wanton unbounded pride and insatiable avarice of some bad people has brought all this upon us.

Having built the suspense, he exposed Droz. He explained how Droz had gotten him to go to Marian Hastings and ask for protection for his paper.

Mr Droze in company with two other gentlemen came to my house ... they had breakfasted that morning with Mrs Hastings ... they had heard her express her best wishes toward the success of my paper, and ... they had come speedily from her House, and the next day was fixed for the meeting.

He had travelled all the way to Belvedere, but he had refused at the last minute. 'Not being able to reconcile myself to the act, I returned without waiting on Mrs Hastings,' he wrote.

He was careful not to assign any blame on Marian, but cast all on Droz.

I thought that there was something so unmanly, so sneaking, and so treacherous in going in a clandestine manner to fawn and cringe, and take an advantage of a good natured Woman. To draw her into a promise of getting that done for me which I knew would be highly improper to ask her Husband.

He believed Droz had intimidated Messink and Reed into starting a newspaper. One of his correspondents reported overhearing Messink in conversation.

'I was led on by a leading Man, one of the [Board of Trade],' Messink supposedly said, 'he insists on my doing of it. Should I refuse, it might prove my ruin.'[354]

He exposed Droz as a man who pretended to be good in public, but in private was a self-serving character assassin. He stood no chance against Droz. 'The Man who is conscientious, and would willingly do as he would wish to be done by stands no chance,' he wrote. Droz was not to be trusted in politics or in battle, and his advice would endanger all those who listened.

> He who gave me this advice is what you call a leading Man, a header of plots, a Tragedy King, who is passionately fond of aping the actions of Great and good Men (what he never will be). This is the Public character he frequently assumes. It's all a counterfeit, unnatural and forced. – But in private he acts his natural part: the premeditated dark and deep assassin, the slave and tool of a party. The King of the mummers. – A fellow not to be trusted in the Senate or the field, for he would no longer be faithful than it suited his own interest, or answered his own caprice.
>
> And he who would take his advice (providing he could do it with impunity) would cut a throat, bury a state, or blow up a Magazine.
>
> What man can be safe where such artful schemes are practiced?
>
> If the secret springs and Wheels of Court in this part of the World are moved thus, then there is no protection for a British *subject* since the *British Flag* is deprived and despoiled of its influences and occasionally becomes a clout to wipe the shoes of every petty Tyrant in this distant part of the Globe.
>
> J. A. Hicky.[355]

13 November, Council House, Calcutta

The whole city had seen Droz's name dragged through the mud. Hastings was determined to do something. No man should be able to get away with calling the head of the Board of Trade a slave and tool of a party, someone who would cut a throat, bury a state, or blow up a magazine. This was insolence of the highest order. He had to do something to recover Droz's honour from the mud Hicky had dragged it through.

Droz defended himself in a letter to the Council, assuring them that Hicky's claims were all lies; he had never solicited a bribe, nor had helped Messink and Reed.

> To the Hon'ble Warren Hastings, Esq., Governor General And Council of Fort William.
>
> Honourable Sir and Sirs, – Forgive me if I trespass on your time by this address.

The unmerited and insolent abuse bestow'd on me in a Weekly publication of Mr Hicky's paper obliges me to solicit you for redress. I am convinced it is your wish to protect every individual residing under your Government who conducts himself with propriety, and as Mr Hicky must undoubtedly as a British Subject be under your Orders, I flatter myself you will not permit such daring and wanton Insolence to pass unnoticed.

Give me leave to assure you Gentlemen that Mr Hicky is without a Cause for this attack, for even the reason he assigns for making it is not true. I have not been at all instrumental in encouraging a paper in Opposition to his, if I had I could not be wrong, but I mention the circumstance to show how prone this Man is to do mischief.

I flatter myself you will excuse the liberty I take in intruding on your more weighty concerns. I would not have attempted it, but that I think I owe it to my Character, and Station in the service, and to the Community in general, who are all equally liable to be insulted, to seek for redress by every proper and Legal method.

I am with respect, Hon'ble Sir and Sirs, Your most obedient and Most humble servant.

Calcutta, 12ᵗʰ November 1780
Simeon Droz

Hastings was decisive and calculated. He proposed that Hicky be forbid from mailing any newspapers through the post office and forbid anyone else from mailing them on Hicky's behalf. He gave the postmaster general the right to inspect any mail suspected of containing Hicky's newspaper. He then announced the decree to the public.

FORT WILLIAM, 14 Nov. 1780

Public notice is hereby given that as a weekly newspaper called the Bengal Gazette or Calcutta General Advertiser, printed by J. A. HICKY, has lately been found to contain several improper Paragraphs tending to vilify private characters and to disturb the peace of the settlement, it is no longer permitted to be circulated thro' the channel of the General Post-Office.

By Order of the Hon'ble Governor General and Council,
E. Hay, Acting Secretary.[356]

Hicky was now convinced he was a victim of arbitrary tyranny. No longer did he believe he was fighting a single Company servant, but the whole Company system. He believed the decree was illegal under British law and was passed only by the will of a despot.

In his next issue he ran a front-page feature on arbitrary revenge. 'The weakest, the meanest, the most cowardly souls are ever the most cruel and revengeful,' he wrote. 'Cruelty is the vice of cowards only.'[357] He mentioned no names, but it was obvious he blamed Droz for sending a letter to Hastings.

The Council's decree hurt his business; he estimated he would lose Rs 400 a month in subscriptions, or about a fifth of his monthly profit.[358] Yet the order was most damaging not because of money, but because it would limit his influence. It would be much more difficult for him to circulate his newspapers to other cities, or to troops on the front lines. His paper would no longer have the power it once had.

To mitigate their decree, he hired twenty hircarrahs to deliver his newspapers in Calcutta.[359] Outside Calcutta, he asked friends and subscribers to carry his newspapers for him. He knew many would never see his newspaper again, but he saw no alternative.

Despite the Council's crackdown, his paper remained as popular as ever, and his subscriptions actually increased.[360] 'The Harcarrahs that I see running thro' the town on Saturday Morning with the Bengal Gazette clearly proves that, indeed till dinner time there is very little else talked of,' one of his contributors wrote. Moreover, subscribers signed a public letter saying they would continue to support him, in defiance of the Council's decree.[361] Individuals also wrote in. 'Should it come to a hearing the Court will be crowded,' one promised.[362]

Another called him the 'Papa of the Bengal Press', encouraged him to 'stand forth for the liberty of the press,' and to be the 'scourge of all bad ministers and evil Councellors.'[363] Even someone from Cossimbazar—a stronghold of Company servants employed to interact with the Nawab of Bengal—wrote that his fellow servants still preferred *Hicky's Gazette*. 'Your Competitors seem to me to have very great occasion for the Hand of POWER to support them, while you, on the other side, are entirely substantive; standing by yourself,' he wrote.[364] Hicky was still popular in Bengal, perhaps more now than ever.

Hicky continued the fight. The next week, he wrote an article with the bombast that would characterise the rest of his paper. He claimed that as a British subject he had a right to print a newspaper that no Company, nor any king, could wrest from his hands. He told his readers that the Council's order did not intimidate him. Even if he had to compose ballads and sell his paper through the streets, even if he was thrown in jail, he would keep on printing. He said he would sacrifice his liberty and his life for his paper. He meant every word.

> To the PUBLIC.
>
> MR HICKY, begs leave to inform his friends and the Public in general, that the most cowardly, unmanly, and illegal methods has been made use of, to prevent the sale of his News-paper, by procuring an Order from the Council, to prevent their going by the Post ...
>
> He is not to be intimidated by such trifles, for before he will bow, cringe, or fawn, to any of his oppressors was the whole sale of his Paper to be stopped, He wou'd compose Ballads, and sell thro' the streets of Calcutta, as Homer did.
>
> He has now but three things to lose: his Honour in the support of his Paper, his Liberty, and his Life. The two latter he will hazard in defence of the former. For he is determined to make it the scourge of all despotic and arbitrary tyrants, should they illegally deprive him of his Liberty, and confine him in a jail. He is determined to Print there with every becoming spirit, suited, to his case, and the deserts of his Oppressors.
>
> And let them see that he is a Freeman of the first City in the British Empire ... and that he has a power to print a Newspaper that no East India Company nor the King their Master can wrest out of his hands. It is beyond the prerogative of the British Crown to invest the Company or their servants with such a power.[365]

Hicky saw the decree as a form of slavery. He felt he had been robbed of his freedom of speech and of his rights. He saw it as obvious proof that the laws of England meant little in India, and that despotism ruled. In England, he told his readers, he could be

sued in Court, the dispute settled in front of a jury of his peers.
But in Calcutta, he had no such rights. Hastings was the source
of all power.

With Hastings' dictatorial powers, Hicky's challenge now was
to prove that he should have the same rights in India that he
would have in England. He felt this like the warm blood coursing
through his veins.

To the PUBLIC.

The very hard treatment I met with last Saturday night in
being denied a Passport for my Newspapers at the Post Office, is
the strongest proof of arbitrary power and influence that can be
given ...

If a Printer in England is guilty of offences against the Crown
he is taken into custody and tried by the laws of his Country
under the tender protection of a Jury of his own Countrymen.
This is the Glorious birth right and priviledge of an Englishman,
and whilst I pen these words I feel my heart glow with honest
indignation and my blood run comfortly warm thro my veins.
What then am I to think of the usage I received last Saturday
in denying my Letters a passport? They not only enslaved me,
but they also enslave my subscribers, by denying them of the
pleasure of receiving the Papers they had subscribed to. The
Laws of my country are here and [so are] the Hon'ble the Lords
the Kings Judges.

If I have offended against the Laws of my country, let me be
tried by them, and a Jury of my country men, and if my crime
comes within the Letter of the Law, then the Jury will give such
damages, as the Nature of my crime and my circumstances will
point out.

In England if a Man is accused of Robbery, Treason, or Murder,
his person is secured, but his Family is not ruined by Stopping of
his letters at the Post-Office. It cannot be done. It is beyond the
prerogative of the British Crown to put such an act in Execution.

J. A. HICKY.[366]

After this article, Hicky announced that he was beginning a
movement against tyranny. He would have to rely on popular
support for his survival, and would need to convince people they

lived under tyranny. And he would need to convince them to do something about it.

He expected he would suffer for his new political positions, but he believed he would at least have vindication and satisfaction for exposing those who harmed him. 'I will produce Letters calculated to injure the reputation of my Paper, and also to ruin the Reputation of two very great Men, and drag the Authors to public Justice, the World will then see how far I have been injured,' he wrote.[367] Who these two men were, he left unnamed, but his message was clear: he had already lost his fortune once. He was willing to lose it again, even if it meant sacrificing everything.

In this contest, his ability to carry public opinion was his biggest strength. But it was also his most dangerous weakness. The one man who could oppose Hastings had been vanquished, the one Court that could check Hastings had been corrupted, and now he, the one journalist who could expose Hastings, had been suppressed.

The fight may have seemed already over. In truth, it had just begun.

His Platform

Englishmen, in all Countries, seem to expect to be governed exactly as they are in England. 'Ubi Imperator, Ibi Roma.' [Where the Emperor is, there is Rome] They carry an Atmosphere of Liberty about them wherever they go. They are such enthusiasts for Liberty they will not by compulsion be saved from being burnt or drowned, but call it Tyranny to attempt to do so.

– Justice John Hyde, 23 November 1780.[368]

Saturday, 25 November 1780, Hicky's Printing Office

Hicky meant every word of his threat. With the help of anonymous correspondents, he started an anti-tyranny, anti-corruption, and pro-free speech campaign using his newspaper as his platform. Where he once only believed he needed to emphasise things like city improvement, he now saw his mission to drag those in power to public justice.[369]

His new focus was remarkable. Like no one in India before, he began to believe his duty was to spotlight malfeasance, fraud, and abuse of power. He embraced notions of rights to life, liberty, and the pursuit of happiness that were coursing through Western Europe and America, adopting them in India. He began to believe that these rights were inalienable, that no one, not even a king, had the right to take them away. And, if he believed it was wrong to take away his rights as an individual, then he believed it was doubly wrong to take away the rights of the public.

Through his writing, he made it clear that if Company servants used their positions to enrich themselves at the public's expense, he would use his newspaper to shame and expose them.

He also believed that if such a thing as the public existed, then it was worth fighting for. He believed that if he did not fight, then the public would become like slaves, their rights, their freedoms, and even their reason to live stripped from them. He was determined to fight for an ideal of liberty, where every man— or at least European men—would have the same rights in Bengal as they did in Britain.[370]

This was the heart of his struggle. He mobilised his correspondents to join, and began publishing articles that he would have once rejected for being too political. With their help, he began criticising Hastings' regime on almost every issue.

His correspondents focused on three main means of corruption: contracts, nepotism, and taxation without representation. They first attacked Hastings' many no-bid contracts.

With only two to three hundred Company servants ruling a population of millions, the Company relied on contractors for almost all basic services. From opium, salt, silk, and rice contracts that sourced goods for its international trade, to elephant, boat, and tent contracts that supplied its army, contracts were the building blocks that kept the Company going. Contracts were also a shadowy way to dispense patronage. They were often given to men who took no part in the actual work done, or were used like shells and divided into many shares, where each man involved took a cut. Embezzlement was so common with contracts that sometimes two-thirds or more were skimmed off the top.[371]

While Hastings gave contracts to win influence, Hicky's correspondents believed contracts should be fairly given to the lowest bidder, as the law required. They pointed out that while the Company's directors had mandated competitive bidding on all contracts, and Parliament's Regulating Act made this mandate law, Hastings still handed contracts to favourites or to those with powerful friends back in England.[372] 'These lucrative contracts, instead of being disposed of as Justice points out, and Equity demands ... by public notice to the lowest Bidder, are invariably bestowed either upon some obsequious follower, or to some Man who has Interest at home,' one wrote.[373]

Hicky's writers focused on a few of the most notorious contracts. The most notorious of them all was the 'army contract'—arguably the Company's most important contract—to feed the soldiers and source the bullocks that transported the army's supplies and artillery. In 1779, Hastings pushed through a measure to rewrite the contract and give it, without any bid process, to Charles Croftes, a Company servant with powerful friends in England.

Hastings made this already profitable contract much more profitable. He tripled the value of the contract from about Rs 390,704 to Rs 996,174 per year.[374] And he made it even more lucrative in practice. Compared to the old contract, the Company would pay the contractor more than twice as much for each bullock supplied, and over 30 per cent more for each soldier's food. He also authorised the contractor to source bullocks as needed in times of war. Since the Company was nearly always at war, this meant the contract was effectively limitless.

Hicky turned to satire to describe it. He began nicknaming Croftes, 'Charley Bullock', and ironically, 'Idle Charley the Bankrupt Merchant'. Hicky's writers were outraged because they believed the army contract, out of all contracts, should be free from corruption because both the artillery that formed the core of British military superiority, and the stomachs of thousands of troops, relied on it. In the words of one correspondent, the army contract was, 'the most extraordinary in its nature which was perhaps ever granted'.[375]

Hicky's correspondents alleged that the contract was so incredibly lucrative because Hastings was using it like a shell to reward his friends. They believed its real spoils were meant not just for Croftes, but for others. 'Charley sold it,' one alleged.[376]

They were also alarmed at the contract's sheer scale, which would have made those who held it rich on an almost unimaginable level. According to one correspondent, once all the contract's extra perks were added up, it was worth about Rs 1,077,500 per year for bullocks alone. Another estimated the whole contract cost about Rs 40 lakh per year.[377]

The second contract Hicky focused on was the Poolbundy Contract, the contract to repair the poolbundy, river embankments. In 1778, Hastings and Barwell gave a man named Archibald Fraser the Poolbundy Contract for Burdwan district. Like Croftes, Fraser's profits must have been incredible. The old contractor was paid Rs 25,000 a year, while Fraser would be paid nearly Rs 90,000 a year for the same work. Fraser was also allowed to submit bills on honour for any extra work, making the contract nearly limitless.

There was something worse than profits that scared Hicky. Fraser was the cousin of Chief Justice Elijah Impey. Fraser also lived in Impey's house, and was the Supreme Court's Sealer and Examiner, where he already earned a large salary of Rs 8,000 a year for those offices.

This was a potential conflict of interest of the highest order.[378] Hicky believed the reason for the contract was obvious: Hastings wanted to influence Impey.

In April 1781, Hicky's fears came true when he learned that Impey had indeed taken a cut of the profits. One of his correspondents alleged that Fraser had given Impey's children Rs 100,000, implying that Impey was too smart to take money directly, which would be illegal. 'I am sure [this] must give infinite Pleasure to the people of Bengal,' his correspondent wrote sarcastically, 'for [Impey's] unbiased, spirited, steady, and independent conduct in dealing out impartial Justice and opposing an arbitrary and Tyrannical [Administration].'[379] Because of this contract, Hicky nicknamed Impey 'Lord Poolbundy', both to criticise Impey's corruption and his elitism.

The Poolbundy Contract shook Hicky's faith in the independence of the Supreme Court. But, if he saw the Poolbundy Contract as the first step in the Court's corruption, then he saw Hastings' appointment of Impey to the Sadr Diwani Adalat as the fatal wound to the Court's integrity. In a poem, one of his correspondents described how Impey took Fraser—nicknamed Archibald Sealer in the poem—under his wing like a student and told him to abandon his principles if he wanted to get rich. The Company might lose a little money, but that money would be little missed in a hundred years hence. India's wealth was for the taking. All Fraser needed to do was let his conscience rest.[380]

> Poolbundy once in a high fit of crowing
> Exclaimed thus to Archibald Sealer the Knowing!
> Mr Hastings the feeling, Just, and the wise
> Has appointed Ad–l–ts, whose payment at large
> My dear little Archy! are under my charge ...
> By which should the Company lose a few pence,
> They ne'er will perceive it in a hundred years hence
> And as long as we jointly can manage the Rudder
> No doubt, but I'm snug in my post at the Sudder [Sadr
>   Diwani Adalat]
> When I talk to Sir Robert or dear brother Hyde
> And bid them throw qualms all, and scruples aside
> They preach up old conscience, till I lose all patience,
> And leave them poor d–ls to their own meditations
> As for you, my friend Sealer, I trust you're grown wise
> From my bright example and candid advice
> Do never let consciousness mollest or offend you
> For conscience should sleep all the time we're in India ...[381]

Hicky believed the Sadr Diwani Adalat appointment was plain bribery. And he was convinced Impey's corruption would lead to a broader corruption of justice where the Supreme Court would put money before constitutional values, and the people would no longer be protected.[382]

Hicky soon experienced the corruption he so feared. On 9 January 1781, the Supreme Court unanimously voted to approve the Bye-Law, the Supreme Council's ordinance—which had been proposed back in June—that would forbid straw houses and enact a 14.7 per cent property tax to repair the city's roads.[383]

Hicky was silent when the Bye-Law was first announced. He could actually claim it was his reporting on fires that had led to its proposal in the first place. But so much had changed. He was now using his newspaper for advocacy. His perspective had also shifted, and, rather than focusing on the fact that the Bye-Law would reduce fires and improve roads, he focused on the fact that it was made without the public's consent.[384]

Hicky believed that corruption was why the Supreme Court judges had approved the Bye-Law. Impey he charged with being bought by Hastings. Chambers he charged with conflict of interest. Besides being a judge, Chambers was the head police commissioner and would not only oversee collecting the Bye-Law tax, but would have the right to pay himself for his labour, giving him a personal stake in passing it.[385]

Hicky began to mock Chambers as 'Sir Viner Pliant' in his newspaper, an allusion that even an upright man could be plied with temptation. Chambers had once been the prestigious Vinerian professor of law at Oxford University. Of all the judges, Hicky believed only Justice John Hyde had voted in clear conscience, bestowing on him the moniker, 'Justice Balance'.

Hicky made Impey and Chambers notorious for their involvement with the Bye-Law. His correspondents were convinced the Bye-Law was a massive fraud to enrich the judges and their acolytes. One correspondent, pseudonymed *Anti Poolbundy*, claimed that Hastings had conceived the Bye-Law to placate Impey and others who were clamoring for bribes. It would quiet the 'mouths of troublesome Harpies, and throw Fortunes into the Pockets of Favorites and Dependents,' his correspondent wrote.[386]

Some of his other correspondents were even more explicit in their condemnation. A pseudonymed correspondent, *An Enemy to Bribery*, revealed that the Council had once rejected a cheaper proposal that would have used the Company's treasury to repair the city's roads. *An Enemy to Bribery* alleged that a tax was passed instead because Impey, Chambers, and Chambers' brother wanted to share the profits of this 'shameful business' between them. *An Enemy to Bribery* further estimated that three-fourths of the Bye-Law's 'unconstitutional and stupendous' tax would be given as bribes, divided into shares of Rs 100,000 each: Impey would receive three shares, or Rs 300,000, Chambers Rs 200,000, and the rest would go to Chambers' brother and others.[387]

Hicky's correspondents blamed the system as much as they blamed corruption for the Bye-Law. The Bye-Law was passed by two undemocratic bodies, the Supreme Court and the Supreme Council. They believed this system effectively shut out the poor. 'Great inequalities' one of his contributors wrote, 'have perverted the principles of representation.'[388] Without representation, only those close to Hastings' could have their concerns heard. The well connected secured their wealth, while the poor languished.

Despite his correspondents' condemnation, Hicky was conflicted by the Bye-Law. He agreed that something had to be done to curb the devastation from the fires. Yet he believed the evils of taxation without representation overpowered the good the law was intended for. He saw the Bye-Law as an act of tyranny that robbed people of their participation in government and made them like slaves subject to the will of a despot. The people would have no representation, no way to have their voices heard and no way to protect their rights. While Hastings' friends would benefit, he believed everyone else would suffer, most of all the poor, who could least afford to pay.

Hicky took special care to report the Bye-Law's effects on the lower classes. He reported that it was so incomprehensible to the poor that the only way they could understand it was to view it in almost apocalyptical terms, working themselves into a religious fervour and believing it was divine retribution 'inflicted by the *Chastising Angel*' for their sins.[389]

Like the poor he reported on, Hicky also began working himself into a fever pitch over the Bye-Law. He publicly printed that Hastings and the judges should be smitten for their sins, and prepare themselves for the afterlife, where all would equal before God. 'The rich Tyrants, oppressors (of the Poor and Friendless in this part of the World) ought now to look back into their past actions, and ... make some small atonement for their past Sins, and prepare their Souls for another World, where there is no distinction of Rank,' he wrote.[390] If they could not be punished in this life, then Hicky hoped they would be punished in the next.

Hicky must have known that these were dangerous words to print. For, much of the world, especially his social superiors, would see them as insolence. At a time when even the widest ideals of representation only included landholding white men, he was unusual in that he believed government should not just be for the rich, but for the poor as well.

He warned that taxation without representation would have consequences. It had caused a revolution in America and so it might also in Calcutta. The Americans had revolted instead of paying taxes to a government that did not represent them, and were now, in the word of one of his correspondents, 'making a glorious Effort ... through streams of Blood' to fight for their independence.[391] The same thing could happen in Calcutta.

How different Hicky was from only months ago. Rather than mocking the Americans, he now lionised them. Where he had once publicly supported the British war in America, he now called it an 'absurd farce'.[392] He hoped his readers would see that what was happening in America could happen in Calcutta. That a corrupt, undemocratic and tyrannical government could impose a tax without the people's consent, and that the people should stand up for their rights.

He had made a full transition from viewing his newspaper as a public service to one in which he saw himself as the defender of the people's rights. In the contracts and the Bye-Law, he saw a violation of notions of life and liberty that he now believed was his mission to protect. He hoped to awake his fellow Calcuttans so they could see the tyranny they lived under.

It would not be long before he began to publish articles that more than simply warned of revolution, but called for it. It was to this dangerous territory that he turned next.

Colonel Pearse

Q. *What is the greatest vice?*
A. *Poverty.*
Q. *What is the most cardinal virtue?*
A. *Riches.*

– James Augustus Hicky, Hicky's Bengal Gazette,
11 November 1780.

Saturday, 10 February 1781. The border of Bengal, south bank of the Subarnarekha River.

The eyes of five thousand men were on Colonel Pearse as he tied a deserter to the barrel of a cannon and raised his hand in the air.

He wavered for a second, his hand motionless, his thoughts raced. Hastings had ordered him to form an army and march into the war. He needed to maintain discipline. He needed his army together. If one man had to die to set an example, then so be it.

His mind cleared, he gave the signal.

The cannon roared like a red firecracker. Whizzing pieces of flesh and bone flew into the air and hung for one long sickening moment before landing on the muddy ground piece by piece with dull thuds. The barrel's gray smoke simmered like a whisper. Shards of rope that once held the deserter dangled on the ground.

Five thousand men stood silent, eyes on him.

The silence tore through the rain and fog, through the months of marching, and through the many more to come.

The closer he had gotten to the border, the more men that

deserted. At first it was only a few. But then, fifty-six fled in a single night.

He knew his men were silently shaping soliloquies in their minds, thinking this was not their fight, this was not their war, this was not their time to march a thousand miles to fight an enemy they had never seen.

He thought blowing the deserter from the cannon would quiet them.[393]

'I hope it will put a total stop to the desertions ... my feelings very nearly made me say pardon instead of give the signal, but this is not a time to give way,' he wrote to Hastings.

Slowly, he relaxed. He took a deep breath and ordered his men to form up. He could not fail Hastings now, not while all hopes were pinned on him.

He had Hastings' letter in his hand.

'March on,' it read.

Between him and Madras stood the 30,000 to 40,000-man army of Berar, commanded by prince Chimnaji Bhonsle. He did not know whether they would be friends or enemies. On one hand, they looked poised to invade. On the other, they had moved slowly. They could have attacked months ago if they had wanted to.[394]

'Force your way,' it read.

The next few weeks would determine if he would be greeted with open arms or unsheathed swords. He knew Hastings had sent an envoy with terms of peace and gold to Chimnaji. But he would likely arrive before any treaty could be signed. He would be the stick to Hastings' carrot, the intimidation that would persuade Chimnaji to the negotiating table.

'Give them due warning, & avoid being the aggressor; but do not stop to negociate,' it read.[395]

He was nervous. Over 1,500 kilometres of mud, uncharted roads and unknown land separated him from Madras. No British army had ever attempted such a march along the east coast of India before. His men were unprepared, demoralised, and riddled by corruption. Their equipment was already failing and he could not find enough for them to eat, so he sent foraging parties to take by force what he could not get by consent.

'You will hear of what the people may call ravages, but when the orders I have given are laid before you, you will see the necessity I was driven to,' he wrote to Hastings.

And yet, he felt there was little he could do. The Company's contractors, not he, were responsible for supplies, and they should be responsible for fixing them. They had obviously cut corners. His bullocks were weak and many had already died.[396] His sepoys had no tents, so they would sleep in the open. His officers' tents were so poorly made he did not think they would last the march.

'The first northwester will send half to Pieces,' he wrote.[397]

He felt there was little he could do for morale either. The sepoys in one battalion had been six months without pay and marched thirty to forty miles a day to reach their meeting point. They had sold everything they owned, including their wives' jewellery, for food. When they reached Calcutta they threatened to riot. Only when he discovered that their commanding officer had embezzled their pay did he fix the problem, court-martialling the officer and sending the remaining sepoys into other units.[398]

He wished he could do more. When he mustered his troops and counted their ranks, he was shocked to learn that part of his army existed only on paper. His subordinates had been collecting the pay of troops who were no more real than ghosts. Although the shortage of soldiers concerned him, what really worried him was that he could not trust his junior officers, men he would need to trust in battle.

'I plainly tell you, you must not trust any man's honour who has a possibility of playing tricks with your troops,' he wrote to Hastings.[399]

He gathered himself and wondered if blowing the deserter from the cannon was the right decision. Would it convince his men to stay obedient? Would they march all the way to Madras? Or would they vent their frustration? Would they blame him?

He hoped that his march would be quick. But hope was all he had.

The next few months would be very long indeed.

Colonel Snail

ADVERTISEMENT EXTRAORDINARY, WANTED
A Resolution not to bribe, or a determination not to be bribed.
LOST. – *The dignity of high Life, in an attention to trifles.*
STOLEN. – *into the Country – the inhabitants of the Esplanade,*
STRAY'D. – *sincerity, and common honesty,*
FOUND. – *that the Idea of liberty, is fast verging to slavery …*
ON SALE. – *For ready money – whatever ought to be*
purchased by merit only.
SCAVENGERS. CONTRACTS – *Any person willing to oppress*
the poor, may hear of full employment.
— Hicky's Bengal Gazette, 5 May 1781.

Saturday, 13 January 1781. Hicky's Printing Office, No. 67 Radha Bazar.

Vent frustration is exactly what Pearse's men did, and they went straight to Hicky.

Hicky encouraged them. The march brought Pearse back into the public eye and Hicky saw his chance for revenge. He wanted to wreck Pearse's reputation like Pearse had wrecked his contract with Coote.

He criticised Pearse from the moment the march began, attacking Pearse for corruption and for conduct unbecoming a British military officer.[400] He claimed Pearse kept a harem and was dishonouring the army by adopting the lifestyle of a Mughal ruler. He also mocked Pearse for having a full upright portrait painted before leaving Calcutta, for his harem to remember him.

Pearse's posture was not the only thing full length and erect, Hicky implied.

'The C—l is painted out at *full length* and ERECT, surrounded by his whole *Seraglio* of Oriental Virgins,' he wrote.[401]

The troops sent Hicky information, which he then printed in his newspaper. Based upon what they sent him, he further attacked Pearse's reputation, blaming Pearse for thinking more about his harem—especially his favourite paramour, Sall—than his troops.[402] He wrote that Pearse thought so much of Sall that he sometimes accidentally said her name while giving orders. 'The truth of the above is well known by all his Officers, in fact, so much so, that he generally gives the word Sall as a Parole in Orders,' he wrote. He also reported that Pearse had given Sall great gifts, including a large Rs 1,200 monthly allowance, a chariot to race around Calcutta's horse track and even a private garden house.[403]

In another article, he satirically claimed that Pearse had volunteered to be circumcised to become more pleasing to Sall, a Muslim, before leaving and also reported that Pearse had enthusiastically agreed to the operation: anything to prove his devotion to the women of India.

> Such is the refined Gallantry of the serious Col. P– and such his Mahometan Devotion to the Native Beauties of Hindostan, that we hear he consented to be C–r–m–ed, to facilitate his approaches, and render his Devoirs to Sall, the more pleasing, the Lady being absolutely obdurate, unless the Col. wou'd adopt her Cast. To his everlasting Fame the Amorous! Detachment commander, spiritedly submitted to the operation.[404]

The farther Pearse marched away from Calcutta, the more bitter Hicky's reporting became. Fuelled by leaks from Pearse's subordinate officers, Hicky reported that Pearse was treating the march more like a personal shopping trip than a military expedition. While stopping at the city of Cuttack, Hicky alleged that Pearse had collected many Indian curios and had sent them under armed guard to his harem, along with a letter to Sall promising everlasting love and chastity until he could see her again.

'She is his dream by night, and thoughts by Day,' Hicky wrote bitingly, adding, 'It would be better for the Service if he devoted his time a little more to the care of his Detachment.'[405]

Hicky blamed Pearse for the desertions, believing that had Pearse taken more care of the men, they would have been proud to serve and their morale would have improved. Instead, he claimed Pearse's cringing manner, marching like cowards through the night, was the reason so many had run.

> It is really a disgrace to the English Arms that Col. P– should have ... Marched in so Cringing a manner ... [this] has been the Cause of Discontent amongst the Troops for no soldier of spirit could tamely submit to such insults ... The Detachment were well disposed for real service and it is a pity they had not been indulged with having one Field day with Chumnagee's Army, it would have prevented that desertion which have happened in the Detachment.[406]

Hicky's writing was like a signal to the army's subalterns that it was open season on Pearse in his gazette.[407] They jumped on Hicky's invitation and made their unhappiness known, writing many letters to Hicky that he published.

At first, they vented their frustration that an artillery officer had been chosen to command an infantry detachment, claiming that Hastings picked Pearse because of loyalty, not competence. 'Surely there can not have been so great a mortality among your Field Officers of Infantry, to have rendered such an innovation absolutely necessary,' one wrote.[408] They also grumbled that Pearse focused on needless paperwork and complicated orders. 'Col. P– gives us damn'd long Orders, and a deal of useless trouble,' another wrote.[409]

Some soldiers went so far as to emphasise they were more loyal to Hicky than to Pearse. One, pseudonymed *No Oppressor*, wrote that all Pearse's officers wished to continue receiving Hicky's paper despite no longer being in Calcutta. No Oppressor said they had even gotten together and agreed to purchase large orders of his gazettes per week to make it worthwhile for him to hire hircarrahs to deliver them. 'You are supported from *every* Quarter,' No Oppressor wrote, adding that Hastings' suppression was '*A most arbitrary* act.'[410] Because of this special connection, these soldiers continued to receive *Hicky's Gazette*, and they continued to write to him.

Their frustration mounted as they marched south along India's coast. They reported that Pearse had stopped the detachment for ten days to accept expensive presents from a local raja in Odisha, including an elephant, two camels, a palanquin, clothing, and horses.[411] They were envious, and pointed out that while they lived in tattered tents, Pearse lived in luxury, and had taken to riding the elephant to command them. They came up with a nickname for Pearse, which Hicky printed: Colonel Snail. Like a snail, they said Pearse was short, squat, 'slimy, and filthy', and moved slowly. 'Any thing sticks to him that comes into Contact with him', one soldier wrote. With Hicky's newspaper, they hoped the nickname would 'stick to him like the slime upon the Snails back.'[412]

But what really concerned them was what would happen if they were attacked. They worried that they were marching like sitting ducks, two by two in a line so long it stretched into the horizon, a formation that would have been impossible to defend. They also marched with unfixed bayonets. 'Risum teneatis Amici?' *Can you help but laugh, friends?* one wrote to Hicky with fatalistic humour.[413]

Hicky worried that Chimnaji would consider Pearse's march an act of war and attack Bengal. One of his correspondents sent him a secret letter that had been intercepted from Mudhaji Bhonsle— the king of Berar and Chimnaji's father—to Mirza Najaf Khan, the Mughal Emperor's top general, in which Mudhaji suggested they ally together to attack the British.[414]

Mudhaji wrote that all India, Hindu and Muslim, needed to unite and fight the Company. Otherwise, they would be picked off one by one. The Company had insulted his majesty, the Mughal Emperor, vassalised the Nawabs of Awadh and Bengal, Shuja-ud-Daula and Mir Jafar, and even deceived its own allies by promising to give them land, but keeping it to itself.[415] The Company had no friends left in India. It was now or never to drive it out of India.

Hicky printed the letter because he felt it was urgent for the public to know the dangers Pearse's march was causing. Not only did it appear that Berar was planning to attack, but Mudhaji was enlisting others like the Mughal Empire to join the war. The Mughal Empire may have been a shadow of its former self, but the Emperor was still the nominal ruler of much of India. The symbolism of him joining the war would be huge. Overstretched, outnumbered, and already fighting many wars, Hicky knew the Company could ill-afford another enemy, and he wanted the public to know the possible consequences of Hastings' decisions.

The letter also compared the English to vultures preying on Indian nations. By printing this letter Hicky was now willing to print an opinion describing his fellow English as no better, and possibly worse, than the Indians they ruled. Most of all, he was not afraid to show it in his newspaper.

> Extract of a Letter intercepted on the Road to Nigif Cawn's Camp, near Agra, translated at Cawnpore.
>
> You may be sure that I am very serious in this Business—is it not as clear as the Sun that these restless and insatiable foreigners, aim at universal conquest? We must all unite, great and small; in one chain of friendship, and confederacy—The whole world can witness their infidelity, and ingratitude to his August Majesty, to yourself also, who art the right hand of his Majesty. Have they not been deceitful? What is the condition of Sujah ud Dowlah's Son and of Meer Jaffier's family? Have not the very Crannies of those English Soudagirs [Merchants] fed upon their vitals like Vultures?—The inconsiderable Zemindar of Gohad was their only Ally in this War. They took, by Surprise, Gwalior as his Auxiliaries—but they keep it to themselves, and his eyes are opened, in short they have not one friend in Hindostan, and the Carnatic is out of their grasp, I hope you will consider these things and give ear for the sake of the general good ... it will not be longer necessary to wear a double face, or to make use of two tongues. My Son Chumnagee, with a potent Army shall soon speak the language of my heart ... Let me always hear of your health. May your happiness be as lasting as time. What can I say more.
>
> The only legible part of the impression on the seal was: MUDAGEE.[416]

Over the next weeks, Hicky's prediction that Pearse would be attacked appeared to come true when confused rumours reached Calcutta that Chimnaji had attacked Bengal and was plundering villages, while overwhelmed Company border guards holed up in their forts and villagers fled into the jungle, leaving the country desolated.[417]

Hicky's reports caused fear and anguish in Calcutta. Some believed the raiders were the vanguard of an invasion. Their number was wildly estimated at 7,000, and it was thought nothing would stop them till they got to the gates of Calcutta. 'They destroy every thing as they advance. They are not contented with plunder only, but have been Guilty of the most Horrid acts of cruelties, in Killing both Men, Women, and Children,' one border guard wrote to Hicky.[418]

Hicky spread the panic in his newspaper. Alarm grew in Calcutta by the minute. His contributors feared that the city would be sacked just like in 1756. Some of his writers even publicly wondered if the Company deserved such an invasion. Perhaps it was retribution for the Company's greed and conquest. When the 'enemy rush in like a torrent', one wrote, 'then the Inhabitants of Bengal, when your golden dreams are fled, will you lament your supineness, your negligence and corruption.'[419]

His correspondents believed that Pearse's march would lead the Company to disaster. They accused Hastings of starting the war in the first place, and of gross negligence and incompetence. One correspondent, *A By Stander,* wrote that sending Pearse away was not only poor strategy, it was irresponsible and dangerous. It left Bengal defenceless and put the lives of thousands at risk. Moreover, the fact that the Company could not repulse the raiders dishonoured the British name because it showed they were unable to defend themselves. His correspondent prophesied that others would take advantage of the Company's weakness, leading to even more chaos.

Independent of the indelible disgrace this irruption is to our Arms, and even to our very name, how must it irreparably sink us in the opinion of all the native Powers; and what a particularly ill

effect it must have upon our present Military operations upon
the Coast, that it be seen either that we are unable to repel these
invaders like Men, or that we are sunk into that contemptible state,
to be obliged to purchase their absence, and their quiet with the
fortunes, and property of our Employers. – Shade of the immortal
Clive if Sublunary concerns still fall under thy observation, how
must it wrong thy heart to see these Marauders, whom thou
reduced to dependence, and taught to tremble at the name of
Englishmen ... advance their hostile flags in that Dominion which
thou, with consummate wisdom, and encountering a thousand
dangers, didst annex to the power of Britain! Shed one spark
of thy unfailing courage, one Ray of thy superior intellect upon
thy miserable successor, who disgraces the seat which filled the
reflected lustre on thy whole Nation, and reduces the name of
Briton to contumely and contempt! ...
      A By Stander.[420]

Had this article merely criticised Hastings' strategy, it may
have gone unnoticed. But it called Hastings, Clive's 'miserable
successor', and accused him of reducing the British name to
'contumely and contempt'. These words could only be taken as a
personal attack.

As much as Hicky predicted doom, he was wrong. After
protracted negotiation, Hastings signed a treaty with Chimnaji,
and the two became allies, not enemies. With the treaty signed,
Pearse could continue his march to his ultimate destination of
Madras without fear of attack along the way.

In return for peace, the Company would give Chimnaji a huge
fortune, Rs 16 lakh.[421] The Company would also lend Berar troops
to help conquer territory from a neighbour.

Hicky reported the treaty the next day. But he reported the
treaty with disgust, believing that Hastings had degraded the
Company's honour by both paying for peace and letting Berar
use Company soldiers as mercenaries. He believed Berar was just
the next state that Hastings wished to conquer, and that the treaty
was yet more proof Hastings was bent on total domination, and
would force the Company into perpetual, legally dubious wars
until all India was conquered. He saw the treaty as Hastings'

standard strategy: first lending Company troops, then using them to extract concessions, then finally using them to conquer, as with Cooch Behar, Awadh, and the Rohillas.

The real sufferers, Hicky told his readers, would be the poor 'Johns', the soldiers who would fight and die for Hastings' (the Great Mogul) dreams of conquest.

> We are well advised that a treaty is on the Carpet between the Great Mogul on the part of poor sinking John Company, and Rajah Ram Pundit on the part of the Berar Chief.
>
> We have not yet been able to learn the particulars of this intended, extraordinary Alliance but the Public may depend upon their being held out and depicted to them in their genuine colours, the moment we can obtain a true and exact knowledge of things. It is confidently whispered however, that the probable consequences of it will be the entailing of a perpetual War on the Company, infamy and dishonour on our Arms, and inevitable perdition on Poor sinking John—to whom ... if he had not locked up his Eyes and his Understanding, he might long have foreseen and prevented the dismal Catastrophe which awaits him and which has been brought upon him by the Wild, Pusilanimous, disgraceful, and wicked Policy of his all Despotic, and infatuated Agent the Great Mogul.
>
> We are told, but hope we are misinformed, that immense sums of Money have been lately smuggled out of the Settlement in the Night Time and sent by Bearers, to Chumnagees Camp. It surely cannot be that the Nation has sunk so low as to become Tributary to this Padjy Chief.—A Chief whom we ought to hold in the most Sovereign contempt and whom we ought to have taught to tremble at the very idea of our Prowess ...
>
> It is reported that the G. Mogul, is seized with a fit of Dispondency and Political despair, and that the Faculty are of opinion his Pereneal Spring is out of order.[422]

Again, Hicky's article would have gone unnoticed. But again he attacked Hastings personally, calling Hastings an 'all Despotic' 'Great Mogul', and insinuating that stress from the wars had damaged Hastings 'pereneal spring', giving Hastings erectile dysfunction.

In a time when personal honour could mean more than life, Hicky must have known this mockery was insolence of the highest order. To talk of things like someone's romantic life, let alone someone's intimate physical details, could only be taken as a personal attack. Such things were just not discussed, at least not in public. If it was not already the case, he could be sure he gained new enemies. While his personal attacks may have only been insolent, his willingness to let his newspaper be the voice of aggrieved subalterns meant he would begin to be perceived as a real threat to authority and discipline.

These words would not go unnoticed.

On the March

Good God where will that man's wickedness end?
— Colonel Thomas Deane Pearse to Warren Hastings,
25 March 1781.[423]

Eleven o'clock Sunday evening, 18 March 1781, Ganjam, Odisha

Colonel Pearse's head throbbed from his hangover from last night's St Patrick's Day celebration. He did not usually drink, but the last month had been hell, and he needed a drink. The sweeping rain, the scorching sun, the disintegrating tents and scrawny bullocks, it was as if God was against him.

It had been weeks since he had received a letter from Hastings. He was getting nervous now. They used to exchange letters nearly every day. Maybe something had happened. Maybe his hircarrahs had been waylaid on the road.

Pearse feared Hastings had been reading Hicky's newspaper. Maybe Hastings believed Hicky's lies. Maybe that was why he had not heard a line for these many long weeks. Maybe Hastings' silence was punishment for his lack of progress.

He fretted anxiously.

He was weeks behind schedule. The land had been so unforgiving that he had marched less than ten kilometres a day and still had over a thousand to go.

Long hours of marching had taken its toll on his men. His subalterns were unhappy. Their tents had mostly fallen apart. His sepoys were sleeping with no tents at all. Many of the bullocks had died. Morale was low all around. Blowing the deserter from the cannon had done little to stem the desertions; over four hundred of his five thousand men had left him.[424]

'Our men are totally unprovided for this climate,' he wrote.

Moreover, before the treaty had been signed, Chimnaji had made his march as miserable as possible. Chimnaji's cavalry had intercepted his hircarrahs, had encouraged his sepoys to desert, and had scared local merchants from selling food to him except at exorbitant prices. His sepoys complained they were hungry and could not afford rice to eat.

He grumbled. And all his negative thoughts came out with his hangover. He heard he had been ridiculed even by his best friends back in Calcutta because of Hicky. This was painful enough, but he could not bear to lose Hastings' friendship and confidence as well, something he prized more than anything on earth. He begged Hastings to write to him:

I had seen Hicky's importunacies. I compared the date of your last to me with the appearance of those lies in print & with the Letters I received from friends who told me I was ridiculed & censured [even] by my best friends in consequence of those libels—and I own I did think that you had been infected by them & had withdrawn at least part of your regard for me; & that in that critical time some envious demon had suggested to you that I meant to waste my time at Soobunreeka & caused you to write to me on the 13th of February to press me to march on. But when I proceeded further to reflect that I had not had a single line tho' you must have received Letters telling you of my march & progress, it confirmed me in the Opinion that I had fallen in your esteem. But I shall not give it harbour in my Breast as I knew I have not done anything I might to blush at. I am certain I have not lost what I prize more than anything on earth. However I still think myself highly honoured if you will attend me a quarter of an hour for a letter …

Dear Sir,
Your devoted servant
T. D. Pearse[425]

But on the plus side, he added in his letter, the local sheep were very large and delicious, or at least tasted as good as the pariah dogs he had been eating.

'To make amends, nature has given stature enough to the sheep which are larger than pariah Dogs & not much unlike them in taste,' he added.[426]

He sealed the letter and sent it off, and the next morning continued his march.

Over the next few weeks he walked through a world that looked like the odds and ends of a carpenter's shop.[427] Craggy yellow rocks jutted out from the rich red earth. Sand and pools of brackish blue-green water dotted the land. His men trudged on, marching during the day, and sleeping in the open at night.

In the mornings, white mists and gray fogs occluded his way. In the days, the sun's heat scorched his skin. In the evenings, long winds swept the shore. At night, when the rains came, he could feel the wet, sideways wind even through his great coat.

Something terrible began to happen as the marching continued. His men began to get sick by the hundreds, vomitting, feverish, and collapsing. Many dropped dead where they stood.[428]

Every day he was greeted with fresh death and dismay. Soon nearly two thousand men, almost half his army was sick. He began leaving men along the way, hoping they would get better later. His camp followers, servants, bullock drivers, and bearers began running away.

He was filled with fear. While he was drinking, his army had been dying.

'Whilst we were rejoicing … our Camp was drinking the air of death & destruction,' he wrote.

He blamed the sickness on locals who used the sap of euphorbia, a poisonous plant, to wash their clothes. His soldiers had filled their flasks from ponds along their march, and drank the poisoned water.

He worried that news of the epidemic could reach Hicky and that the Company's enemies would read of it. He could not afford a leak in such a precarious time. Anxious that his subalterns might

write news of it to Hicky, he insisted that Hastings should not
believe any exaggerated tales these newsmongers might spread.

> Dear Sir,
>
> Though I was determined not to alarm you, yet as we have
> news mongers enough ready to do mischief, I beg leave to tell you
> that my army has met with a disaster which no foresight could
> guard against. In short, the whole have drunk poison and great
> numbers are killed and many are dying.
>
> It seems the people here use Euphorbium juice for soap and
> our people, not knowing it, drank out of the ponds in which they
> washed – many dropped down dead, others dying ... It was only
> this morning, by accident, that I learnt the cause assigned for this
> dreadful attack, and have now taken every precaution against it.
>
> I am Dear Sir
> Your faithfull Servant
> March 23, 1781
> Colonel Pearse[429]

He huddled down in a small village, his army too sick to move.
He ordered the villagers out and his men to wait for the calamity
to end.

It worked. Slowly his men began to recover. By the time the
epidemic was over he had lost nearly one thousand men, a fifth of
his five-thousand-man army.[430]

'Oh my dear friend I have had such a Trial that I can hardly
relate it ... death was raging in my Camp with horrors not to be
described,' he wrote to Hastings.[431]

Things began to improve. He took steps to care for his troops.
He found tents so his sepoys would no longer have to sleep in the
open. He issued orders in both Hindi and English so his sepoys
would know their rights, he required that his sepoys be given full
pay. And, although his subordinate officers called him a fool for
missing out on easy money, he refused to take a cut of the profits
from goods that camp followers sold his troops.

Morale improved.

'This is new but good indeed for us,' the sepoys told him.

Refreshed, he began to move again. The terrain became easier.
His sick began to get better. Finally, the march went quickly.

Then, news arrived that Hastings had signed a peace treaty with Berar. Pearse was glad to learn of the treaty, but shocked to hear that Hicky had ridiculed Hastings as an 'all Despotic' 'Great Mogul' with erectile dysfunction.

He wrote to Hastings that Hicky needed to be shut down. Hicky had insulted them both professionally and personally. The whole world could see it. And what would the world think if they did nothing while Hicky's writers stabbed them like cowards in the dark? Finally, he could convince Hastings that Hicky was too dangerous to their honour, or even to their lives. The threat of mass mutiny, or even revolution was too real.

He had warned Hastings once that letting Hicky print in the first place was dangerous. Now, he warned him again: Hicky must be shut down.

> I really wonder at your patience in suffering such a scoundrel as Hicky to publish loads of abuse every Saturday. We do not get [the paper] here nor have for these six weeks, but we hear of the abuse from other quarters with the same expressions of astonishment. It is true the wretch himself is not the author but some pitiful scoundrel who dares not avow his insolence & wishes to stab in the dark. Yet still such a thing as that Gazette in such a place as this is not allowable & such good sir was my opinion when you too readily agreed to the first publication of a newspaper. I then told you the year would not pass before it became the channel of personal & public abuse & it is so.
>
> I am, Dear Sir
> Your faithful Servant,
> T. D. Pearse [432]

In a settlement where honour could mean more than life, Hicky played a dangerous game. He would pay for his words.

But he was not done yet.

For the Good of the Mission

'Tis right excellent Fun, for the Town; – how it chuckles,
That, old Grey Beard, at last, gets a rap on the Knuckles.

– Anonymous Poet, *Hicky's Bengal Gazette*,
12 May 1781.

Saturday, 31 March 1781, Hicky's Printing Office, No. 67, Radha Bazar

Hicky knew he had a golden scoop the moment he picked up a packet from Johann Christian Diemer.[433]

The packet explained everything. How Kiernander had embezzled from the orphan fund, given consecrated types to Messink and Reed, rented warehouses, and even tried to sell his Mission to the Company.

Finally, Hicky understood how Messink and Reed had gotten their types.

He saw his chance to expose the corruption of the clergyman, to reveal how a holy man had succumbed to the temptation of riches and fortune. Most of all, he saw his chance for revenge.

He gathered information. Attacking Kiernander—wealthy and well-connected Kiernander—would involve incredible risk.

But Hicky believed it was his duty to expose Kiernander. He believed he would actually be defending religion by exposing greed that corrupted it. Moreover, Hicky was angered that Kiernander had recently announced he would begin printing documents for the public, further encroaching on Hicky's printing business.[434]

On March 31, using documents Diemer likely supplied him with, Hicky surprised everyone with a front-page article that damned Kiernander for gross corruption, avarice, and dishonesty.

He accused Kiernander of forgetting the sanctity of his function as a priest, and for abandoning vows that forbade him from dealing with the world. He accused Kiernander of lusting after lucre and for acting exactly opposite of the biblical pious Samaritan, someone who helps others out of the goodness of their heart. He accused Kiernander of selling types that had been consecrated for religious purposes. And he accused Kiernander of embezzling Captain Griffin's legacy, renting warehouses to the Company, and stealing from the orphan fund.

These were incriminating charges for anyone. They were absolutely damning for a priest.[435]

For the good of the Mission.

The Reverend Padre Kiernander Missionary, having by a late Advertisement in Mess's Reed's and Messink's *Monitorial Gazette*, informed the Public that he had commenced the Business of printing in all its various branches, by which it appears that a part of the types sent out on the behalf of *the Mission* to assist the Pious design of propagating the Gospel in Foreign Parts, are now employed in Printing *Warrants* Summons, writs of Latitats, and special Capias – those *Blister Plaisters* of the Law.[436]

And furthermore, forgetful of the Reverence due to our most Holy Religion—the Sanctity of his peculiar function, and the confidence reposed in his Evangelic piety by the Gospel Society in London, Mr Kiernander has sold or disposed of part of the said consecrated Types, to Mr Messink of the Play House in order more effectually to enable him to accomplish (with the Blessing of *the Sublime*—I ask pardon for the mistake. I mean the Supreme Council) the ruin and destruction of Mr Hicky, and his innocent Family.

That Man whose Eve of Life is fast verging to the shadow of Death—whose Silver Head bows down Loaded with the Blossoms of the Grave, and whom the Sepulcher is already yawning to close

upon—that such a Man, and in so sacred a function should be
influenced by any considerations—much less those of FILTHY
Lucre and detestable avarice, to do so mean, and un-neighbourly
a deed toward Mr Hicky as to sell these types to aid the meanest,
partial, and most ungenerous of purposes. But this in fact has
been the case. And such the *obligation* Mr Hicky lays under (as an
industrious and struggling neighbor) to the Charitable good will
of this Pious-SAMARITAN, Mr Kiernander.

Hicky then listed a litany of charges against Kiernander,
including misappropriation, dishonesty, greed, and embezzling
legacies. He also attacked the Company's priests, accusing them
of seeking fortune by running the charity like an ecclesiastical
farm—treating donations like harvesting vegetables—implying
that Kiernander was not the only priest who sought illicit fortune.

He ended with quotes from the Bible, predicting that Kiernander
would be condemned by his own actions.

Mr Hicky does not enquire what is the amount of Captain
Griffin's Property, left as a Legacy to the said Society in the hands
of Mr Kiernander. Nor does Mr Hicky ask with what propriety
Mr Kiernander could Solicit Money from a Charitable Fund in
England toward Erecting what is call'd his CHURCH near this
Great Tank. Nor by *what right* or authority he could presume to
Offer the same for sale, or Hire, to the Governor and Council of
Bengal, (altho refused by them). Nor does Mr Hicky inquire what
the Annual Profits and advantages of the said Church have been to
Mr Kiernander since its Erection, or whether it has proved *more –
or equally* profitable, as the Building of *Godowns*, or Warehouses
on Holy consecrated Public Ground to be occupied without
scruple, by the Pious, and very immaculate Board of Trade.

Mr Hicky would only ask the Pious, and Learned ecclesiastics
who do so much Honour to the Pulpit, of Calcutta, whether the
Church Dues, and fees &c. arising from the said ecclesiastical
farm do not of Legal right either belong to the orphan fund, or
to the joint capital stock of the charitable society, with whose
Property the said Church was *Built* and for whose sole use the
Legacy left by Captain Griffin was intended and does entirely
belong, together with many other Legacies of a Similar kind

which *have Lapsed* to the present incumbent within these last 15 or 20 Years. Mr Hicky now Subjoins Mr Kiernander's Letter to the Gospel Society, Prefaced by the following few words from the New Testament, a MOTTO *well suited* to the occasion.

'*Out of thine mouth shall thou be condemn'd and there shall arise many wolves in Sheep's Clothing ... Whose* GOD *is their Belly – Preferring Filthy Lucre to Godliness.*'

'*These Evils must come, but woe be to the Man thro' whom they come.*'

'*And Nathan said unto David*
THOU *Art the Man.*'[437]

After the article, he appended Kiernander's *Mission Report*, which Kiernander sent annually to the Society. In it, Kiernander reported that Griffin had given his legacy to the Mission, and that the Society and the professors at Halle were to be its trustees. Griffin's legacy was to be used to pay for repairs and salaries.

Since Hicky had reported that Griffin's legacy had lapsed into Kiernander's hands in the above article, to him Kiernander's Mission Report was proof that Kiernander had embezzled Griffin's legacy. He quoted from the report:

Captain John Griffin, deceased ... *has bequeathed the Residue of his Estate to the New Church at Calcutta*; directing that the yearly interest be applied towards the Repairs of the said Church, and the Salaries of one or more Missionaries and Schoolmasters; and appointing the SOCIETY for promoting Christian Knowledge, in Conjunction with the Reverend the Director of the Orphan-House at Halle in Saxony, Trustees for the RIGHT Application of the Request.[438]

Hicky did not annotate Kiernander's Mission Report, he just let the insinuation lie: If Griffin had bequeathed his legacy to the Mission, but the legacy had disappeared, then Kiernander must have stolen it.

Hicky had not just attacked Kiernander's work, he had attacked Kiernander personally. He had attacked the reputation Kiernander had been building in Calcutta for over twenty years. He wrote things that no innocent man should suffer in silence.

His claims would reach every person in Calcutta, India and beyond. The world could read his reporting. Through his Press, he could ruin Kiernander's reputation and maybe even destroy Kiernander's Mission.

He had launched a major blow. Some men would have turned the other cheek.

But Kiernander was not that kind of man.

In Darkness

*Until I be gone into the Silent grave, and can no more
answer for myself, then that Lyar and Slanderer may ride
on in Triumph, and I be sent out of the World with Infamy.*

– Johann Zacharias Kiernander to Michael Hallings,
Secretary of the Society, 27 October 1783.[439]

Thursday, 12 April 1781, The Mission

Kiernander listened as a young man, Christopher Meyer, read
Hicky's article out loud for him. Blinded with cataracts, he could
not read the article himself. He listened as he was accused of
terrible faults. Rumours he knew were nothing but lies.[440]

'The Reverend Padre Kiernander Missionary,' Meyer read,
'has sold or disposed of part of the said consecrated Types to Mr
Messink of the Play House in order more effectually to enable him
to accomplish (with the Blessing of *the Sublime*—I ask pardon for
the mistake. I mean the Supreme Council) the ruin and destruction
of Mr Hicky, and his innocent Family.'

Meyer continued. 'That Man whose Eve of Life is fast verging
to the shadow of Death—whose Silver Head bows down Loaded
with the Blossoms of the Grave, and whom the Sepulcher is
already yawning to close upon—'

Kiernander had heard these words before. He immediately
knew what they sounded like. Diemer's words. They were not just
similar. They were exactly the same.

Meyer kept reading. 'That such a Man, and in so sacred a
function should be influenced by any considerations—much less

those of FILTHY Lucre and detestable avarice, to do so mean, and un-neighbourly a deed toward Mr Hicky as to sell these types.'

Kiernander brimmed with anger. He knew he had not sold types for lucre and avarice. It was a gross accusation for a man of God who was above dealings with the world.

The words flew by, each stung more than the last.

> 'Annual Profits and advantages of the said Church'
> 'Warehouses on Holy consecrated Public Ground.'
> 'The Church Dues, and fees'
> 'Belong to the orphan fund,'
> 'Captain Griffin's Property'
> 'Lapsed to the present incumbent.'

Meyer finished: 'These Evils must come, but woe be to the Man thro' whom they come.'

His temper flared. These were Diemer's words. He was not going to let this stand. He knew what he had to do. Sue Hicky.[441]

Rumours quickly swirled. Later, one of the Company's priests, Reverend William Johnson, came to him and asked if he meant to sue Hicky.

'If there were at Calcutta as many lying devils, as there are bricks in the walls in all the houses, I would face them all before the bar of justice in the Supreme Court,' he said.

'You should not show such a warmth of disposition,' Johnson said, trying to get him to forget about it.

'No. I cannot drop it,' he said, indignantly. He knew he had to fight back and protect his reputation from Hicky.

'Hicky has published many worse things against me, but I will take no notice of it,' Johnson said, looking at him.

A guilty conscience cannot clear itself, Kiernander thought to himself. His was clear. Johnson's was not. Johnson had actually been the one building warehouses on consecrated ground, not him.[442]

Hicky's article could not have come at a worse time. Kiernander felt weak and frail and under siege, without the strength to repel Hicky's attack.

'I had a most violent Cold in my Head, which so filled my Eyes ... that I lost the little sight I had till then recovered, so that

I am now intirely in darkness,' he wrote in one letter, adding: 'The Mission here lies under great Distress, and labours under many Hardships.'[443]

Sorrow was all around. The pox had carried off many of his schoolchildren. That, combined with Diemer taking the charity children away, left him with only forty-two students, a fraction of what he once had.[444] Most of his Mission was sick as well. His schoolmaster had fallen ill, and so for the last year it was only his son and a few assistants running the school.[445]

His fellow missionaries were desperate, too. Hyder Ali's army was pressing its advance toward Madras, plundering everything in its wake. They had pillaged the missionaries at Tranquebar, who lived outside the town's fort.[446] And while those inside the fort's walls were safe from Hyder's army, they were not safe from starvation. 'In the Streets of our Town from seven to twenty Persons are every Day carried off by Famine,' the missionaries wrote.[447] 'Men are like Wandering skeletons.'[448]

It looked as if all Christianity was under siege in India. In May, a doctor couched Kiernander's eyes and restored some of his sight. Reinvigorated, Kiernander prepared for his most important trial yet. He was determined to get the vindication he so desired.

Over the next few weeks, he asked Calcutta's lawyers if they would represent him. All seemed to be afraid of Hicky, so he went to Judge Chambers and asked if he could be his own lawyer.[449]

Chambers told him not to worry. There was already another prosecution on foot, and it was initiated by the most powerful man in the city.

Night's Assassins

Mr Hicky asks no favours of the GREAT *... he Laughs at their impotence, and promises the delinquents ample retaliation through the Channel of his Press.*

– James Augustus Hicky, *Hicky's Bengal Gazette*, 14 April 1781.

Between Two and Three o'clock Thursday morning, 5 April 1781, Calcutta

Hicky woke with a start, and stumbled over to his bedroom window. He peered into the blackness, bleary eyed and confused.

He heard yells and screams from below.

'[What is] the cause of so much noise?' he opened his window and yelled.

He saw figures running in the dark. Three men were trying to break into his house. Two were Europeans and had cut open the rope that held his back gate shut with curved knives.

He rushed downstairs. But the men had fled before he made it down.[450]

He asked his servants who these people were.

They said one was Frederick Charles, the owner of a public house in the city, and Messink's assistant at the theatre.

Hicky had bad blood with Charles. When he had practised medicine in his first years in Calcutta, Charles had once refused to pay for a surgery he performed. He had to sue Charles to get his money back.[451]

Hicky pondered for a second. Why would these people

break into his house deep in the night? Why would they wish to attack him?

Then, everything came together like pieces of a puzzle.

Behind Charles, he saw Messink. And behind Messink, he saw Hastings.

He was convinced it was an assassination attempt. Or, if not, at least a threat to silence him. He feared another attempt on his life, so he hired sepoys to guard his home and told his servants not to let anyone in without his express permission.[452]

The warning might have scared some men, but it made him bold. If it was a warning to silence him, then he would do just the opposite. He was not intimidated. He would fight till every muscle in his body failed him rather than surrender his right to print. He became convinced he needed to wake the consciousness of the people and show them the tyranny they lived under.

He saw himself as the scourge of tyrants, the defender of free speech, and the protector of the people. He saw himself as the only remaining hope against corruption and oppression. In a place where fundamental rights had been overturned and where the people lived in slavery, he believed the someone like him, someone with a free Press, might restore the people's rights and redeem their freedoms.

Reflections in Consequence of the late attempt made to Assassinate the Printer of the Original Bengal Gazette.

Mr Hicky verily believes that fate decreed that he should come out to India to be a Scourge to Tyrannical Villains, and upstart Schemers ... Mr Hicky is determined to go on and persevere ... unawed by the frowns of arbitrary Tyrants in power (Men who wou'd sell their souls as well as the Country's interest for Rupees) ...

He is resolved to defend his Person in those attacks until every Muscle and Sinew in his Body fails him, and shou'd he be doom'd to fall a Victim to satiate the Malice of unprincipled Plunderers in power ... Mr Hicky will fall contentedly, considering himself as a Martyr in Support of the property of his Countrymen, and in the support of the LIBERTY OF THE PRESS ...

Mr Hicky considers the Liberty of the Press, to be essential to the very existence of an Englishman, and a free Government.

The Subject should have full Liberty to declare his principles, and opinions, and every act which tends to coerce that Liberty is Tyrannical and injurious to the COMMUNITY. – The Press is the Medium through which opinions are disseminated amongst the People, (Vox Populi, Vox Dei) the voice of the People is the voice of GOD – It is the constitutional Censor and controller of Princes, the accuser of bad Ministers; and the most efficacious Machine to protect and shield the Subject from Tyranny and Despotism.

The Liberty of the Press is of such infinite consequence, that if the constitution was overturned, and the people involved in an abject State of Slavery, a Man of Spirit with a FREE PRESS might soon restore the one, and redeem the other, and without it the bravest People on Earth, cannot long preserve their rights and Liberties.[453]

Over the next few weeks Hicky' writing grew hotter, just like the weather. He was no longer just going to point out despotism, he was going to call people to fight it. His next articles were his most extreme.

Two editions later, he published an article from someone written under the pseudonym, *Cassius*. Cassius told the Company's troops that they should think twice before fighting for Hastings, claiming that Hastings ruled as if he were a king, and had no qualms about sacrificing their throats for his dreams of conquest. Cassius reminded the soldiers that their ultimate loyalty should be to the British people, not to this 'Great Mogul', and that if Hastings disobeyed the Company's directors, then they should have no reason to obey Hastings.

Even Cassius' pseudonym was strategic. Cassius was the Roman senator who led a plot to kill Julius Caesar and restore the Roman Republic. The name itself was a warning: beware of those who wish to become Emperors. Cassius's connection between Ancient Rome and Bengal was none too subtle. And his lesson was clear: rise up and overthrow Hastings before it was too late.

A hint at a distance to the Proprietors of India Stock.

MOST seriously is to be apprehended, that the Great Mogul's inattention to the immediate and positive orders of the Divan, will be productive of very fatal consequences to this Tottering

Empire ... As he throws off his subordination to [the Directors], it must be expected that Officers of Abilities who are placed in independent Commands, will if they find it for their purpose, hold themselves no longer answerable to a Government that he conducts as tho' it was his by inheritance ... Beware of a combination of the tendency of Lepidus, with Anthony, and Octavius, think of their proscription, and reflect that you have all of you Connections in this Country, that are more or less dear to you, whose throats are perhaps devoted to the wild Chimeras of a Madman.

   Cassius[454]

The article brought Hicky to the edge of sedition. It suggested that the army mutiny and maybe even carry out a coup. It claimed that Hastings had forfeited the right to rule because he put soldiers' lives at risk for dreams of conquest, sacrificing their throats to the 'wild Chimeras of a Madman'.

Hicky had changed his role from being an advocate to a provocateur. His call for officers to question their loyalty was dangerous. The Company army had not always been the most loyal institution. It had a history of mutiny, such as in 1764 when a European mutiny sparked a second sepoy mutiny that was only shut down by blowing the ringleaders from cannons.[455] Just months ago, the sepoys at Visakhapatnam rioted rather than get on boats to join the war at Madras.[456]

Hicky added another spark to the mix. His newspaper was a sounding board for the army's subalterns, letting them and their comrades express their opinions. Emboldened by ideals of life, liberty, and equality, subalterns could use his newspaper to sound out a coup. A coup could end Hastings' career, and possibly his life, in a single stroke. These were the risks Hastings faced if Hicky continued printing.

In article after article, Hicky's contributors took on tones reminiscent of revolution. They proposed that the people should stand up for their rights, especially the right to free speech. 'There's nothing more sacred ... than the liberty of the Press, I am persuaded that Millions would become as Martyrs at its Altars, the defence of it is a Cause of Glory,' one wrote.[457] 'The meanest

Subject of England ... is as much Protected in his Life, Liberty and property, as the greatest,' another wrote.[458] 'Priviledges are not to be invaded nor [the people's] Liberties torn from them, without a noble Struggle and patriotic Opposition,' a third wrote.[459]

Yet, these articles only talked about revolt as an abstract concept.

One of Hicky's writers was about to propose actual revolution. His writer, pseudonymed *Britannicus,* claimed that if the Company taxed the people without their consent then not only did the people have the right to fight back, they should fight back. If they had no other options, then at least they had revolt.

Britannicus claimed that the rights of British subjects, upheld by centuries of common law and documents like the Magna Carta, were being violated. In Bengal, Britannicus claimed, the people paid taxes but had no rights. They had no Parliament. They had no independent Judiciary. They had only Hastings.

And, they had only one answer: revolution.

To the Inhabitants of Bengal, Countrymen and Friends ...

I will not wrong either your Understandings or your feelings, by supposing you ignorant of, or insensible to, the oppression which now prevails; but I wish to inspire you with something more—to expose to you the weakness and inferiority of your oppressors. To lay before you your own comparative greatness, and to display to you your Power ...

This then is the original compact viz. That Government shall consult the welfare of the People; and that the People shall obey Government on that condition. When that condition is neglected or violated, the People are no longer bound to obey.

We have seen, and God forbid that it should be otherwise, that the People can and may assert and defend their liberties when directly invaded ... The Spirit of the Constitution requires a full and fair representation of the People; on that, and that alone, depends the right of Taxation; if then the People are unfairly or imperfectly represented, or not represented at all, that Right falls to the Ground ...

If the Spirit of Magna Charta is not quite Extinct [the people] will receive full Redress: but if Law and Justice are annihilated— If the British Constitution is destroyed from its Foundation—If

Liberty is irrecoverably lost—Every Englishman should join in the Sentiment of Cato, *Indifferent is my Choice to live or die*.
      Britannicus.[460]

'*Indifferent is my Choice to live or die,*'—Hicky's contributor reminded the public of the last words of Cato, the Roman senator who had fought for the Republic and fell on his sword rather than submitting to Caesar.[461] The implication was clear: they, too, should fight for freedom. For if they did not, it would not matter whether they lived or died. All was the same under tyranny.

It was no longer about revolt against the idea of oppression in some distant place, it was about revolt here, now, at this very moment, against Hastings.

Sledgehammers on Tuesday

A Governor who wishes to silence the Press may properly be compared to those Tyrants, who put out the Eyes of their slaves that they might more chearfully turn a Millstone.

– Britannicus, *Hicky's Bengal Gazette* Extraordinary, 25 June 1781.[462]

Two o'clock Tuesday afternoon, 12 June 1781, Calcutta

Hicky peeked through the gaps of his window lattice as an armed gang of European and Indian policemen surrounded his home and pounded his gate with sledgehammers. Badges on their breasts marked them as CP, Calcutta Police.[463]

Hundreds of onlookers gathered outside to watch what was happening. It was odd for so many armed men to be in this part of town.

The policemen broke Hicky's gate and rushed into his yard.

Hicky grabbed his sword and ran outside to meet them.

'I will put the two first men to death who would dare offer to advance a single step farther,' he said, adding, 'who sent you here?'

'Sir Elijah Impey, the Chief Justice of the Supreme Court,' the undersheriff announced.

'Produce a legal authority to support what you say.'

'Here it is, Sir.'

He read the warrant. They had come to arrest him for libel.

He told them to wait.

'I will not have a finger laid on me. Go back to the Court and give my respectful compliments to the Chief Justice. Inform him that I am all obedience to the laws of my King and country, and that I have declared upon my honour that I will attend him in court as soon as I can get my clothes on.'

He dressed and arrived at the Court House forty-five minutes later. But the judges had adjourned Court for the day, and would only set bail tomorrow. They threw him in jail for the night.

The next morning he was dragged into the Court House and brought before the judges. He approached them, in their red robes at a green table in the centre of the room. Lawyers, aides, and functionaries darted all around like a hive of bees.

A grand jury of twenty-three men sat on the side. Hicky recognised some of them. They were almost all Company servants or contractors, or had some connection with Hastings.

I have often heard that Christ was crucified between two thieves, and I am now going to be arraigned between fifty pence liars, he thought to himself.[464]

The Court read the charges against him.

Five counts of libel, three from Hastings. The first was for his article that accused Hastings of being Clive's 'miserable successor'. The second was for calling Hastings a 'Wild, Pusilanimous, disgraceful, and wicked', 'Despotic, and infatuated Agent the Great Mogul', and insinuating Hastings had erectile dysfunction. The third was for calling the troops to mutiny, and maybe even launch a coup, because their throats were 'perhaps devoted to the wild Chimeras of a Madman'.

Two counts of libel from Kiernander, both from his article, '*For the good of the* MISSION'. The first was for nearly the entirety of the article, for ironically calling Kiernander a 'pious Samaritan' motivated by 'filthy lucre and detestable avarice', insinuating that Kiernander built 'Warehouses on Holy Consecrated Public Ground' for private profit, claiming that Kiernander embezzled from the orphan fund and from Griffin's legacy, and for accusing Kiernander of running the Mission like an 'ecclesiastical farm'. The second count was a failsafe, only intended to be used if

Kiernander could not convince the jury that the whole article was a libel. It was only for calling Kiernander a 'pious Samaritan' motivated by 'filthy lucre and detestable avarice.'

The grand jury agreed that criminal charges should be brought on all five counts. Judge Hyde at first suggested Rs 4,000 for bail. But Impey proposed Rs 40,000, which, with Chambers' assent, became the bail amount.[465] It was an astronomical sum, about twice what Hicky made from his newspaper per year, and far above what he could pay.

Hicky sent the judges two petitions asking for bail to be lowered. He told the judges that they had violated his right to reasonable bail, citing one of England's foundational documents, the English Bill of Rights, which read that 'excessive bail ought not to be required.' He also cited the leading law books of the day: *Blackstone's Commentaries*, *Hawkins' Pleas of the Crown*, and *Edward Coke's Reports*, which indicated that excessive bail was a 'great grievance' to the accused. He even cited an obscure case, the Duke of Schomberg v. Murray, in which a man, Murray, was accused of defaming an English Lord, a great charge known as scandalum magnatum, but was still given reasonable bail.[466]

At the same time, Hicky appealed to the public. He printed one of these two petitions in his newspaper and remarked that while he was given high bail, journalists in England had been given reasonable bail, even when accused of great crimes. Henry Sampson Woodfall's bail had been only half his, and Woodfall had been charged with libeling the King.

'The measures pursued against me are so singularly harassing and oppressive, that it seems reserved for this Country, to beat down the sences which the Laws of England [have] placed to guard the subject's Liberty,' Hicky wrote.[467] His meaning was clear: rights in Bengal had been corrupted, and he wanted the world to know it.[468]

But the judges refused.

Unable to post bail, Hicky prepared for his trial as best as he could from his jail cell.

He still printed his newspaper, even though in jail. He turned to his best weapon: satire. The next week, he printed a fake playbill mocking Hastings, Impey, and Kiernander for tyranny and corruption. His title, *Tyranny in Full Bloom*, was a none too subtle observation that the Company was corrupt to the core. Hastings starred as the villain, playing four different parts: the tyrannical 'grand Turk', the despotic 'Great Mogul', the misguided 'Don Quixote' fighting invisible enemies, and the bloodthirsty warmonger, the 'Tyger of War'.

Impey starred as hanging 'Judge Jeffreys', an historical English judge notable for sentencing hundreds to the gallows, and as 'Ven Poolbundy' for the Poolbundy contract. Judge Chambers featured as 'Sir Limber' and 'Sir Viner Pliant' for sacrificing his reputation and bending himself to Hastings' will. Only Judge Hyde was spared, cast as the overweight but honest 'Cram Turkey' and 'Justice Balance'.

Hicky reserved a special place for Kiernander, singling him out as 'Mammon', the human incarnation of greed and one of the seven deadly sins.

Hicky then took aim at the rest of Hastings' crew. He cast Hastings' lawyer, Henry Davies, as the unscrupulous 'Double Fee Ferret Whore' for his past work prosecuting debtors at the infamous Marshalsea prison in London. Messink featured as a lowly 'link boy', lighting the way for his master, Hastings. The grand jury that indicted him were cast as 'Slaves, Train Bearers, Toad Eaters, and sycophants', loyal to Hastings and Impey.

While he cast his enemies as corrupt and evil fools, he cast himself as 'Cato', the famous Roman Senator who fought to save the Roman Republic. He pinned his hopes on petty jury—the jury in front of whom he would have his trial—hoping to influence them by calling them his 'honest independent disinterested Liberty Boys', and promising they would have the public's adoration if they defended him and the freedom of the speech.

Play Bill *Extraordinary*

At the New Theatre near the *Court House* is now in
Rehearsal
A Tragedy call'd Tyranny in Full Bloom, or the Devil to Pay –
With the Farce of All in the Wrong
DRAMATIS PERSONAE

Sir F's Wronghead	by the grand Turk [Hastings]
Judge Jeffreys	by Ven Poolbundy [Impey]
Sir *Limber*	by Sir Viner Pliant [Chambers]
Justice Balance	by Cram Turkey [Hyde]
Dildo whipper Snapper per Balance's foot'n	by *Raw Town Guinea Pig* [George Wroughton]
Judas Iscariot *touching* the 40 Pieces	by the Rever. Mr *Tally Ho* [Rev. William Johnson]
Don Quixote fighting with Windmills	by the Great Mogul commonly called the Tyger of War [Hastings]
Double Fee Ferret Whore	by C'r Avis from the *Marshalsea* [Henry Davies]
Idle Charley the bankrupt Merchant	by Mr Bullock [Charles Croftes]
Sawney Bull Head	by Burdwan *fammoy*
Cato, also the *True Born Englishman*	by Mr Hicky
Mammon	by a Germ. missio'y [Kiernander]
Irish Link Boy crying *(a brass Farthing your Honour)*	by Sir Barnaby Grizzle [Messink]
Slaves, Train Bearers, Toad *Eaters,* and sycophants	by the Grand Jury
Liberty Boys	by the honest independent disinterested Petty Jury

Between the Play and the Farce will be introduced a Dance of *Demons* of Revenge by the Calcutta Lawyers and their *Banyans.* – The Dance to conclude with the song of.

> 'From Mortal *sighs*, We draw the groan
> To make *their* Sorrows, like our own.'

Which Sir Barnaby promises to accompany on the *Bassoon,* assisted by his Germ. Missionary Brother-Printer [Kiernander]. Two Ghosts will be introduced for the sake of Variety.

1st Ghost by Nunducomar
2nd Ghost by Peter Nimmuck [Reed]

Councellor *Murder English* from *Gothland,* will entertain the Audience with a dolefull Ditty on the *Hurdy Gurdy* about his *card Losses* and *Pluckings* at Lady *Poolbundy's Routs.*[469]

If anything, Hicky's playbill indicated that he was not going to be cowed.

Freedom of the Press in Calcutta was about to be put on trial. In anticipation of a packed house, Hicky came to court ready to fight.

Hastings v. Hicky

*The Governor General and Council have powers; I do not
say they could have been legally exerted in the Present case.*

– Justice John Hyde, 26 June 1781.[470]

Tuesday, 26 June 1781, Supreme Court House, Calcutta

A hircarrah stood on the crumbling steps of the Court House in
the fierce morning sun, a stack of two-page special edition *Hicky's
Bengal Gazette Extraordinary* in his arms. Passers-by were glad
to escape the brown dirt plaza outside, next to the stinking great
tank, and enter the Court House's cool, dark archways.[471] Under
the mildewed, cracked-paint pillars, they read the gazette, printed
the day before.

> CALCUTTA Monday 25th June 1781
>
> Tomorrow the very important TRIAL of MR JAMES AUGUSTUS
> HICKY will come on at the Court House in Calcutta, on the Fate
> of which materially depend the inestimable Liberty of the PRESS,
> the security of the property, and the boasted Liberty of all British
> Subjects in this Part of the World ...
>
> Let such know that a libel on which a man is criminally indicted
> is in a strict sense a malicious defamation, expressed in printing
> or writing, so that if a jury does not think it answers that exact
> description they must in conscience find him not guilty.[472]

The extraordinary gazette continued, with a warning from
Hicky that his case was not just about one newspaper. Freedom

of speech was on trial. If he lost, not just his newspaper but the people's voice would be lost. Their last protector would be gone.

'We shall then be in the Condition of the sheep ... when our Dogs, our Guardians, are gone our House may be robbed whilst we sleep,' the gazette read.

Hicky included a list of the grand jury that had indicted him. Thus, he stripped them of their anonymity; he wanted to show his readers that his trials had been rigged before they began, that the jury had been packed with his enemies. The grand jury were either members of Company committees, contractors, residents at foreign courts, or those who had some connection with Hastings. Even the postmaster general had been on the grand jury, so had the Bye-Law's tax collector, and also the army contractor, Charles 'Charley Bullock' Croftes.[473]

9.08 a.m., inside the Court House

Hicky stood at the bar in front of the judges as the court sat in sweltering silence. He came ready to cause chaos, starting by objecting to Impey sitting on his trial:

'I have an objection to mention before my trial goes on. My enemies report I have treated the Lord Chief Justice with disrespect in some publications. I am not conscious of any such offense, for I have the highest respect for his Lordship's abilities and private character. Yet, as some prejudice may have been taken from those publications, I object to Sir Elijah Impey sitting on my trial.'

Impey was incensed. No man had the right to insinuate that he would be prejudiced. He knew he would never bow to public odium.[474]

'This cannot be meant as a serious objection. Let the trial go on,' Impey said.[475]

'Mr Hicky must know he has no right to make this objection,' Justice Hyde chimed in.

This was not actually the first time Impey and Hicky had met. They had known of each other when Hicky was a law clerk and when Impey was a lawyer in England's Western Circuit.[476]

'No popular clamour will ever make me neglect my duty.

I think myself man enough not to be affected with any threats thrown out, and honest enough not to let any prejudice affect my conduct,' Impey told the Court.

Hicky's objection was overruled. But Hicky had more objections to make.

When the Court moved to pick the jury, Hicky objected to any Company servants sitting on the jury. He believed they would all be biased like the grand jury.

Impey suggested a compromise, allowing both Hicky and Hastings' lawyer, Henry Davies, to object to any jurors before they reached a full twelve-man jury. And if they did not have enough jurors then they would go through those that had been rejected.

With that compromise, the Court swore in the jury.[477]

Henry Davies opened the prosecution. Today, he told the Court, he would try the first of Hastings' three counts: the article in which Hicky's writer called Hastings, Clive's 'miserable successor'.

Davies read the article to the Court. He believed he had a straightforward case. Precedent was on his side. All he needed to prove was that Hicky printed the paper and that Hastings was the one libelled.

'Two points will be for your consideration, whether Mr Hicky published this paper and whether the successor of Lord Clive means Mr Hastings,' he told the jury.

Because libel in the eighteenth century was defined as any printed matter whose content could breach the peace, a printer could be sued for libel on almost anything.[478] Furthermore, printers were responsible for their writers' articles, meaning that they could be sued just for printing an article, even if they had never seen its content.

Most important of all, judges, not juries, determined libel. The jury's sole job was to determine who printed the article and who was libelled. Once the jury determined these points, the judges would determine if the words contained malice. If the words contained malice then the printer was guilty of libel.[479]

Thus, to find Hicky guilty, Davies only had to convince the jury that Hicky had printed the article and that the words 'miserable successor' meant Hastings.

'Can anything be more contemptuous than the words "miserable successor"?' Davies asked the jury, and then looked at Hicky, adding, 'He says also that Mr Hastings has reduced the name of Britons to "contumely and contempt".'

Davies then held up Hicky's satiric playbill to the jury.

'All the mean and paltry arts which have been used in England to cajole the lowest of the people, are repeated here to prejudice a jury of the gentlemen of Calcutta. You are to be intimidated by the abuse on the grand jury in Mr Hicky's paper by the description of slaves, train-bearers, toad-eaters and sycophants. And, to be cajoled as the honest petty jury who have not yet found him guilty, by the description of "liberty boys",' Davies said, hoping to show the jury how Hicky had tried to bias them.

11.05 a.m.

Hicky's attorney, Anthony Fay, began his defence. Fay began by cross examining Hastings' witnesses.

He argued that the article may have referred to the military commander at Midnapore, Major Allan Macpherson, not Hastings.

'Do you not think the words "miserable successor" might as well be applied to the military officer who commands in Midnapore?' he asked Thomas Motte, the chief of police.

Fay's plan was to prove that the article could have referred to anyone as Clive's miserable successor. If he could cast enough doubt on who the article referenced, the jury would not be able to determine beyond a reasonable doubt that the words 'miserable successor' meant Hastings, and Hicky would be acquitted.

But Motte was certain. Miserable successor could only mean the person who held Clive's position as Governor-General, and that was Hastings.

'I do not think it can be applied to the military commander in Midnapore. The successor must mean the person now in possession of the place Lord Clive held, because he uses the word disgraces the seat in the present tense,' Motte replied.

Fay asked the next witness, Charles Wilkins, the Company's printer, the same question.

'Do you know of any other person beside Lord Clive that may answer the description of "the Immortal Clive"?'

'I know no other who can answer to the epithet of immortal but Lord Clive,' Wilkins replied.

'May not there be some other person who may deserve that epithet, though your knowledge does not extend so far?'

'Everything is possible, but I know no other,' Wilkins said.

'Why do you apply the opprobrious word "miserable" to the Governor-General, Mr Hastings?' Fay asked, hoping Wilkins would admit ambiguity.

'I have before sworn that the word "successor" meant Mr Hastings and "miserable" must be applied to the same person. I do not think the word successor can be applied to the military commander at Midnapore.'

Fay was failing. Not a single witness testified that 'miserable successor' might mean someone beside Hastings.

Still, he kept his strategy.

'I must beg your indulgence,' he stopped his cross-examination and turned to the jury. 'It must require great ingenuity to form these innuendos. There can be no libel where there is not some person reflected on. If it is uncertain as to the person, it is like a random shot that seldom does any execution. It is like an indictment for murder without saying who the person was who has lost his life. It does not appear except by innuendo that the newspaper concerns Mr Hastings—'

'I had rather read my own defence,' Hicky jumped up. 'You do not seem to understand my counsel,' he said, turning to Fay.

Hicky had enough. It was clear the issue was not who was Clive's miserable successor. The issue was freedom of the Press.

'My newspapers have been arbitrarily stopped at the public post office. I was taken by above two hundred constables and peons and without any ceremony dragged into a stinking prison under the same roof with thieves and murderers,' he said.

Then he turned to Impey.

'Sir Elijah Impey, Lord Chief Justice of the Supreme Court and Superintendent of the Sudder Dewanny Adaulat. The best security of the press is an honest and disinterested jury.'

His defense was simple yet radical. He claimed he was the victim of tyranny and despotism, and he had a right to print that no man, or no Company, could take away from him.

'The mere writing, printing and publishing is no proof of guilt. The malicious or seditious tendency must be proved. Otherwise, they ought to acquit the defendant. If an Englishman now speaks truth he is immediately prosecuted for a libel,' he said.

His goal was to convince the jury that they had the right to determine malice and libel, not the judges. He cited the famous case, *The King v. Henry Sampson Woodfall* in his defence. Woodfall's case bore striking resemblance to his own. The King had sued Woodfall for printing a letter—written by none other than Philip Francis (under a pseudonym)—threatening insurrection if another journalist, John Wilkes, was not released from jail. To everyone's surprise, the jury bucked a hundred years of legal precedent and refused to find Woodfall guilty, finding him guilty of 'printing and publishing only'. By finding him guilty of printing 'only', they implied that Woodfall did not mean malice. Thus, by determining malice, they took away the judges' power to determine libel. The trial ended in a mistrial and Woodfall walked free, becoming one of the most famous editors in England.[480]

Hicky argued that Woodfall's trial should set the precedent for his own, and that his jury, like Woodfall's, could determine malice, and thus libel.[481]

Hicky then argued that he did not mean malice. He began his closing speech with the story of Parson Prick, a Protestant minister, who around 1585 delivered a sermon against Catholicism. Prick recited a passage from *Foxe's Book of Martyrs,* a book that recounted the brutal murders of Protestants by Catholics, and the divine retributions that followed. One of these Catholics who suffered divine retribution was a Mr Greenwood. According to Foxe, God struck down Greenwood for his sins. 'Great plagues' were inflicted on Greenwood and 'his bowels fell out of his body by the terrible judgment of God,' Prick said.[482]

Yet, in a strange odyssey of fate, this same Greenwood happened to be present at Prick's sermon, and very much alive. Greenwood was actually a Protestant, and seeing himself called a 'papist', he sued Prick for defamation. Surprisingly, when the case came to trial, the judge found Prick not guilty because he had only related someone else's story and did not mean malice when he said it.

Hicky argued that Prick's trial set the precedent that retelling someone else's writing did not constitute libel. As an editor, he hoped the jury would recognise that he had only reprinted someone else's letter and did not mean malice.[483]

Hicky stopped abruptly and rested his case, leaving his fate to the jury, hoping that they would protect his freedom of speech and the freedom of the Press.

1.22 p.m.

Impey gave his guidance to the jury in the dripping mid-day heat.

He clearly indicated they should find Hicky guilty and that Davies' interpretation of the law was correct; that the jury's sole job was to determine if the article referred to Hastings. Whether it was malicious, whether it was libel, was his right to determine.

'The defendant Hicky stands indicted for a malicious and false libel. In this heat, and at this time of day, I will not trouble you with more than is absolutely necessary. If the paper has not the meaning which the drawer of the indictment puts, you cannot find him guilty. You are to enquire whether in common understanding the meaning is such as is alleged, not whether they might possibly have had some other meaning. Whether the paper is criminal or not, whether it is libel or not, is not for you to determine,' he said.[484]

2.57 p.m.

With these words, the case went to the jury. All eyes were on them as they filed out to their private room.

The jury's foreman returned fifty minutes later and told the judges that they were unlikely to agree on a verdict soon. With that, the jury adjourned to Justice Hyde's house for further discussion.

The jury sat through the afternoon. They sat through the evening. They sat through the night.

The freedom of the Press stood on the line with no end in sight.

The Verdict

I am treated illegally and cruelly.

– James Augustus Hicky, Petition to Elijah Impey,
19 June 1781.

9.50 a.m., Wednesday, 27 June 1781.
Supreme Court House.

The jury returned to declare their verdict in open court.

Not guilty, they said.

The Clerk of the Crown read their names one by one. 'Gentlemen of the jury, hearken to your verdict as the Court has recorded it. You say the defendant is not guilty of the misdemeanour whereof he stands indicted and so you say all.'

Two of the jurors had starved out the other ten. They had made an informal decision at Hyde's house. But only now, finally, had they come to their verdict.

Impey could not believe what he was hearing. He was transported into a violent rage. Despite the obvious evidence, the jury had found Hicky not guilty. They had usurped his power as a judge.

'[I will] not suffer such a verdict to be recorded, it being directly and positively in the teeth of the evidence,' he told the jury's foreman. He demanded they reconsider.

But the foreman said he would not be intimidated.

'I well know the nature of the oath I have taken which requires me to do justice between the parties, that is between the Sovereign and the prisoner at the Bar. I have not hastily, nor without due consideration, formed my opinion, nor should I lightly change it, or be threatened into giving a different one,' he said.

Nevertheless, the jury went to their room for a few minutes.

They returned with the same verdict.

Not guilty.[485]

Despite all odds, Hicky had won. He had proven that it was possible to protect the Press against the most powerful people in British India. It was a tremendous victory.

But he still had three more trials to go.

Hicky had his second trial this same day, on Hastings' second charge, for his article where he called Hastings an 'all Despotic' 'Great Mogul' with erectile dysfunction.

This time Hicky faced a different jury. No record remains of this trial, except the verdict:

Guilty.

Hicky still had two more to go. He was not done fighting yet.[486]

H I C K Y's
B ENGAL GAZETTE;
OR THE ORIGINAL
Calcutta General Advertiser.

A Weekly Political and Commercial Paper, Open to all Parties, but influenced by None,

| 66 | From Saturday April 21ſt. to Saturday April 28 h 1781. | No. XIV |

NOW IN THE PRESS
AND
SPEEDILY WILL BE PUBLISHED
BY J. A. HICKY
AT HIS PRINTING OFFICE.

THE New Bye-Law properly diſcuſſed, defined and diſſected, Paragraph by Paragraph, fully Explained by the cleareſt comments taken from the higheſt Legal and conſtitutional Authorities, adapted to the meaneſt Capacity. Which will prove a very neceſſary Pocket Manual, not only for this, but ſucceeding Generations, to ſhew how carefull our Wiſe Anceſtors have been to protect us, our Lives, Liberties, and Properties.

To the PUBLIC.

THE great demand for the Original Bengal Gazette has induced Mr. Hicky to Publiſh them in Volumes, which are now to be had bound or unbound at his Printing Office in the Radda Bazaar.

Continuation of CICERO's celebrated Oration, before the ROMAN Senate againſt VERRES, one of the Roman Governors in Sicily in Aſia Minor.

AN opinion has long prevailed, not only here at home but likewiſe, in FOREIGN Countries both dangerous to you, and pernicious to the State viz. That in Proſecutions MEN of WEALTH are always ſafe however clearly convicted. There is now to be brought upon his trial before you (to the confuſion, I hope of the propagators of this Slanderous imputation,) one whoſe life and actions condemn him in the opinion of all impartial perſons; but one who according to his own reckoning, and declared dependance upon his Riches, is already acquitted, I mean CAIUS VERRES.——One whoſe conduct has been ſuch that in paſſing a juſt ſentence upon him you will have an opportunity of re-eſtabliſhing the credit of ſuch trials, of recovering what ever may be loſt of the favour of the ROMAN PEOPLE; and of ſatisfying FOREIGN STATES and KINGDOMS in ALLIANCE with us, or tributary to us, I demand Juſtice of you, Fathers upon the ROBBER of the PUBLIC TREASURY, the OPPRESSOR of ASIA MINOR, and PAMPHYLIA, the invader of the rights and Priviledges of ROMANS, the ſeourge and curſe of SICILY; If that ſentence is paſſed upon him which his Crimes deſerve, your authority Fathers will be venerable and ſacred in the Eyes of the Public, but if his GREAT RICHES ſhould blaſs you in his favour, I ſhall ſtill gain one point viz. To make it apparent to all the World that what was wanting in this caſe was not a CRIMINAL nor a PROSECUTOR; But JUSTICE and adequate PUNISHMENT.

"He makes no ſcruple publickly to declare. That in his opinion they alone have reaſon to fear being called to account, who have only amaſſed what is ſufficient for themſelves. That for his part he has prudently taken care to ſecure what will be ſufficient for himſelf and many others. Beſides, That he knows there is nothing ſo ſacred, but it

"may be made free with, nothing ſo well ſecured but it may become at, by a proper application of Money."—He has accordingly ſaid that the only time he ever was affraid was when he found the Proſecution commenced againſt him by ME; left he ſhould not have time enough to diſpoſe of a ſufficient number of PRESENTS in proper hands. What does his QUESTORSHIP (the firſt Chiefſhip he held in Aſia) what does it exhibit but one continued Scene of oppreſſive Villainy, a Province robb'd and reduced to FAMINE.——The Employments he held in ASIA MINOR, and PAMPHYLIA, what did it produce but the RUIN of thoſe unhappy Countries.——In his laſt HIGH EMPLOYMENT he acted over again the Scene of his former Queſtorſhip, bringing by his bad practices, thoſe whole SUBSTITUTE he was into diſgrace, and then deſerting them. The miſchiefs done by him in that unhappy Country (SICILY) during his Iniquitous Adminiſtration are ſuch, that many Years under the wiſeſt and beſt of Praetors will not be ſufficient to reſtore things to the condition in which they formerly were, no Inhabitants of the remote parts of that ruined Country has been able to keep poſſeſſion of any thing but has either eſcaped the rapaciouſneſs or been neglected by the ſatiety of this unfeeling univerſal plunderer. Thoſe who wiſhed to be in alliance with the Roman common wealth, have been wantonly treated as Enemies, and theſe his atrocious Crimes have been committed in ſo Public a manner, that there is no one who has heard of his Name either in ROME or ASIA, but could reckon up his actions.

Oh Liberty!—Oh Sound once delightful to every ROMAN Ear!—A Sacred priviledge of Roman Citizen-ſhip!—Once Sacred—now trampled upon!—what, then, is it come to this? Shall an inferior Magiſtrate (a Governor) who holds his Power of the ROMAN People—in a Roman Colony act in this licentious Manner,—Shall neither the Majeſty of the ROMAN COMMON-WEALTH, or the fear of the JUSTICE of his COUNTRY, reſtrain or puniſh the Impious Avarice and licentious Tyranny of a Monſter who in Confidence of HIS RICHES, thus acquired, Strikes at the ROOT of LAW, AND LIBERTY, and ſets Mankind at defiance?—— I concluſe with expreſſing my hopes that your Wiſdom and Juſtice CONSCRIPT, SENATORS will not by ſuffering the Atrocious and unexampled Inſolence of CAIUS VERRES to eſcape due puniſhment, leave room to apprehend the danger of a fatal ſubverſion of Authority, and introduction of General ANARCHY AND CONFUSION IN THE EMPIRE.

After Reading and duly pondering the afore recited Speech of the immortal CICERO (which is both genuine, and as nearly tranſlated as the Idioms, of Different Languages will admit) let us only ſhift the Scene in imagination and by the powers of Fancy Conceive SICILY (as deſcribed by Cicero, to be the CARNATIC.——

The PEOPLE of ROME the INDIA PROPRIETORS, or the ENGLISH NATION at large.——The CONSCRIPT SENATORS—the ENGLISH PARLIAMENT.——

CICERO in the Perſon of Ed. Bourke,

the E. of SHELBURNE Mr. T. PITT, Mr, Dunning. And CAIUS VERRES as a ſeem Type of SIR THOMAS PILLAGE.——
The native honeſt powers of Sympathy confirm the horrid Picture.——

To the Printer of the Bengal Gazette.
SIR.

THE wiſeſt meaſures that have ever been purſued by any Government, were ſurely thoſe of the Britiſh Parliament, when under the reign of a wiſe Prince, and the Adminiſtration of a Patriotic Miniſter, the Majority of it's Members were elected by the free ſuffrages of the People, how did the Nation flouriſh under ſuch Rulers, how were it's Enemies cruſhed? and how did they ſink under the Wiſdom of its Counſel, and the Magnanimity of it's Fleets and Armies? But Alas! Alas! inſtead of that glorious ſpirit of Freedom which then fired our Souls, how are we fallen off? how are we ſunk?——Yet we have ſome conſolation in finding that notwithſtanding the conſtitution is now ſo very Rotten, we have a few Members in the Houſe choſen like that glorious Majeſty, by the free and uncorrupted voices of the Cities and Counties, ſuch are the Men whoſe Councils ought to be attended to, and ſuch are the Men who will open the Eyes of the Nation; awake it from that lethargy into which it is now moſt miſerably fallen, and expoſe the Abſurdity, folly, and iniquity of that plan of Deſpotiſm, ſo eagerly purſued and ſteadily ſupported by that corrupt part of the conſtitution, the head of Placemen and Penſioners, Members of paltry, venal Boroughs Men who have purchaſed their Elections to betray their Country, theſe are the wretches who now form the Majority, and who now Govern the Empire, and theſe are the baſe Slaves who will overthrow the moſt beautiful Structure ever raiſed by the Art of Man, planned by the utmoſt Stretches of human wiſdom, the works of Ages, but Imperfect, as all human inventions muſt be and therefore ſtill capable of Improvement, which was its original animating principles to remain entire, might in the end nie to be even the Admiration of ſuperior Intelligencies.

CATO.

A HINT AT A DISTANCE TO THE *Proprietors of India Stock.*

MOST ſeriouſly is to be apprehended, that the Great Moguls, inattention to the immediate and poſitive orders of the Divan, will be productive of very fatal conſequences to this Tottering Empire.—— Upon his acceſſion to the Muſneed, and for ages before, the Hookam of that great Body was the grand ſpring by which every Department here was actuated, and the Diſmiſſion of his immediate predeceſſor for a deviation from their will, tho' cauſed by great neceſſity, ſhould have been a caution to him, that in the Hour of their reflection they will not forget the Contempt with which he has treated their orders. As he throws off his ſubordination to them, it muſt be expected that Officers of Abilities who are placed in independant Commands, will if they find it for their purpoſe hold themſelves no longer answerable to a Government that he conducts as tho' it was his by inheritance. Men of high spirit and abilities, at a distance from the Capital, and habituated to give the Law around them, will have the merit of very great forbearance, if with such an Example before them, they should submit to return to a private station, and tho' there is not a Man of them but would obey the orders of the Divan, if they were properly communicated to them, they are assuredly no longer Dependant upon his will, than they chuse to continue so. If the Four and Twenty, should at a Period not very distant, find, that this blessed, Mahratta War has Erected into petty Sovereigns, their own Servants, they have only themselves to thank, for not having fallen upon some certain method of knowing that their orders are literally, immediately, and religiously enforced. Beware of a combination of the tendency of Lepidus, with Anthony, and Octavus, think of their proscription, and reflect that you have all of you Connections in this Country, that are more or less dear to you, whose throats are perhaps devoted to the wild Chimeras of a Madman.

Cassius.

Cadez July the 9, this morning failed the Combined Fleets under the Command of Don Louis de Cordova, consisting of 22 Sail of Spanish, and 9 French 6 Frigates and 4 Smaller Vessels.

August 5th, Sir James Wallis in the Non-such, has taken the French Frigate Le Belle poule of 32 Guns 12 Pounders Commanded by the Chevalier Kergarion and 275 Men. The Capt. and 24 Men were killed, the second Capt. with Several Officers, and Men to the amount of 50 were Wounded. The Non-such had 3 Men killed and wounded.

August 15th, a large Fleet of Ships of war of Russians, Danes and Swedes came into the Channel, and soon after the Russians consisting of—Ships of the Line and 2 Frigates came into Portsmouth.

In the Begining of July, the Emperor of Germany, under the Character of Count Falkenstine, visited the Empress of Russia at her Capital and stayed there several days, He left Peterburgh on the 28th, Proceeded to Riaga from whence he was to go to Metac Lethwana, and Siventa into his Dominions in Poland and from thence returned to Veinna.

In the Month of August the King of Sweden spent several days at Spa, under the character of count Hague.

The swallow from Bengal arrived in the shannon on the 29 of July.

The Romney on the 8 July had taken and carried into Lisbon the Pearl, a French Frigate of 18 Guns and 158 Men commanded by the Chevalier De Greignon.

Monf. De Terney's Fleet arrived at Boston on the 20 June, the consisted of 9 sail of the line, and 5 Frigates.

August 31st French Frtpates taken.

	Guns.	Men.	
Le Artoes	40	450	taken by Romney
La Belle poule	32	275	taken by Nonsuch
Le Legere	36	—	Destroyed by do.
La Capreceufe	32	318	taken by Prudent
La Nymphe	36	300	taken by the Flora
La Pearle	18	135	taken by Romney
Mauselar	12	80	by Southampton
Le Jenne Lisa	12	44	taken by the Huffar
Le Renard	12	44	
		220	1649.

Vinna August 2d, the Emperor is expected here the 10th of this Month.

Berlin August 5, Prince of Prussia will set out tomorrow for Peterfburgh.

Ships taken by the Company.

	Captains.
Lord North	Wil. Hamtly,
Queen	Peter Douglas
Lathara	John Prince
Henchinbrooke	Ar. Maxwell
New ship	Ar. Morris
Do.	Sam. Roger
Do.	James Ogilvie
Sybella	Thos Walker
New ship	Nath. Paul
Do.	C. Gregorie
Do.	James Rees.

Sir Hugh Pallafier is appointed Governor of Greenwich Hospital,

August 15th, the Nymph Frigate of 32 Guns, and 290 Men commanded by the Chevalier De Romain (who was killed in the action taken) by the Flora of 36 Guns Capt Peer Williams after a fierce Engagement, the Nymph had 63 Men killed and 131 wounded.

September 1st, The Parliament was this day dissolved by Proclamation and the writs made returmable the 31st. of October.

EVERY Man that Dedicates his time to Public affairs as a G——r ought, to begin betimes (if it is possible) to divest himself of self and Consult, the Force of his own Genius, the activity of his mind and his assiduity, before he embraces so difficult and so important an Employment as the management of a Rich and fertile Country; In general we esteem Philosophers as the highest Rank of Sublunary Beings that what harm does a Philosophers do to society, even should his Opinions be erroneous, he seduces at most but a small number with regard to objects which in themselves very little contribute to their felicity or otherwise, in most other degrees of life the want of great Knowledge and abilities is less dangerous or felt.—But if a Man who has the immediate and Arbitrary direction of affairs, makes a mistake in his Politicks? if he draws false Conclusions? or which is equally hurtful to the state; blindly follows the impulse of his own Ambition to the risk and almost Ruin of a once flourishing C——y.—(Flourishing at least until he had the management of affairs) ought such a Visionary to be permitted to proceed on? Look at the measures he has been pursuing.——His Military Detachments at a vast expence, for

what? will Stone walls pay the C———y the immence sums layed out in the taking of them; We fight our Enemies — (Made such indeed by the folly of our measures here) Some hundred Miles from our Presidency, at the same time we are obliged to bribe those to Peace, who are at hand ready to invade those districts from which We draw our only Resources.   ALECTO.

A Practitioner in Physick having boldly undertaken to remove the cause of a slight indisposition, which a certain body of Merchants complained of praying upon their Bowels, first prevailed upon these unthinking Men to make daily exertions of strength beyond their abilities to perform, while he prescribed the most extravagant and wild experiments on their constitution, by which he has brought on a Consumption and violent Fever, attended with a total indifference to their total Ruin, their nearest connections having at last irresolute folly and bad consequences resulting from a conduct so contrary to reason, have formed the generous resolution of taking their Friends out of the guidance of such a Man, who has imposed so grossly upon them, it is confidently reported that they will prosecute him for evident misapplication of their relations Money, particularly for large sums which were recovered from some large Estate, which had fallen under their direction and which this Practitioner had the Management of, the very thought of such an enquiry has given this Gentleman so violent a pain in his Head, and lowness of Spirits, that it is imagined he will endeavour to change the Air, and that he will prefer Germany for many reasons, but particularly as he may assure himself of the most friendly reception from his Relations in that Country, to whose friendship and attention to please him in his most sanguine wishes, he has already had such convincing proof of, that he cannot entertain a doubt of the continuence of them.

Mr. HICKY I have to desire you will give this a place in your Paper, as the Relations of the Merchants at a great distance may not have heard of their Friends indisposition and you will oblige——a Relation.

The Coast News came too late this Week for Insertion.

JACK PHAETON,
(A Character)

JACK was never famous for endowments of the mind, but has by some late manœuvres made himself more exquisitely ridiculous than people thought Folly would have urged him to; in the Career of a long life. Oh! he is the most precious Coxcomb that affectation in a gamesome mood ever exhibited for the entertainment of Laughter, I can hardly, hold my sides when I think of his excentricities Jack's whole Ambition is to shine in the public Eye, by making a figure, far superior to his Circumstances, such Beings as he surely have no pretensions to the appearance of a Nobleman, and the monthly Receipt of—— is certainly, no adequate fund for the support of such Prodigality; his whole income in possession, and expectancy is known to be much under the Standard of Mediocrity, yet he is nettled to a very fashionable Vehicle, Jack frequently strikes in one of a structure singularly whimsical; and drives away in a very pompous manner; to do otherwise would be vulgar, this he does with such Attendants rustic Pageantry as great y to increase the mock grandeur of the scene. He whirled off yesterday in the afternoon in his Phaeton followed by his Gens d'arms, and I really imagined from the aspect of things, that he was not only going to tranfport himself to a distance from Town, but intended a nocturnal Journey for the sake of expedition.——I was wrong.—Jack came home at eight on militaire covered with dust and litterally crowned with Laurels for he decorated his Hat with Leaves plucked in a pleasure Garden.——Upon enquiry I found, that he had only been to pay a visit to a wealthy Banyar, near Town in order to fill him and suffer Neighbour's smith went at his Splendor. In this manner Jack distinguishes himself. By what dexterity he prevents his Creditors, who are certainly numerous, from being impertinent, no body who knows can conceive but some think that time will instruct him in Lessons conducive to a more prudent Carriage, demeanor.   CENSOR.

Mr. HICKY,

ALTHO the securing of the French inhabitants of Chandernagore in Consequence of the flagrant breach of Public Faith committed by those of Pondicherry, is in the General opinion a prudent and a necessary measure, and altho the House in which they are confined (highly exceptionable as is the Plan of it) certainly affords them more spacious and airy accommodations than in any other in which they could be kept either in the Fort, or in, or near Calcutta, yet as it was built for a common Jail (tho hitherto not used as such) and is called by no other name, I fear that that very circumstance, seeing Mankind are in matters of much more consequence governed by no weightier motives) may prove a pretext in the hands of the French Nation for exercising a severe retaliation on such of our Countrymen as may hereafter fall into their hands. Whoever asserted the measure in question, was not, I am persuaded, aware, of the consequences it may produce. It is not very likely that the French will have a similar reason for confining our Prisoners, as the Government of this place at Present his. An Enemy however, it cannot be supposed, will embarrass themselves with making nice distinctions, it will be alledged, that contrary to the engagements of Government, and to the practice of civilized Nations, we had torn the peaceable Merchants of Chindernagore from their Wives, Familys, and dearest connections, had dragged them to Calcutta, and committed them to a Prison destined for the reception of Felons; that this was done without our having alledged delinquency on their part nor, after the had taken the Oaths of Allegiance to our Government, the breach of which had never been imputed to them; that if Lieut. Colonel and Captain in the Service of the King, had shared the same fate, which nothing but a breach of their Parole (and that was not alledged) could Justify. In relatiation of all which, I think it highly probable, that many of our unfortunate Countrymen, may hereafter experience, all the horrors of a loathsome——Dungeon. Altho prudence may dictate the restraining of these People, enough does not, their confinement in the new Jail Room, I am persuaded, might be found for them, in the Cantonments of Barrampore, even after the return of the 3d. Brigade to that place, for they do not, all ranks included, amount to more than forty. If not, they could be sent to Monghser or Dinapore, and a very slight guard of Seapoys would, from the remotiness of these places, suffice to take care of them. At any rate, it may be future mercy to ourselves, to remove them fro'm the Jail (merely because so called) to any other place not liable to that objection.
                    I am   Sir
Your humble Servant   Antigallican.

Bombay News.

BOMBAY all in an uproar, and the Merchants in the Pains's for the safety of their Properties, as the English Flag in distress, there is Block up, upon Block up, and Britannia in Tears, for the Disgrace brought upon the English Flag by that truly brave, active, and Amiable Sir of Neptune Sir Edward Darby. Altho no Ta,

CALCUTTA.

THAT hopeful Spring of Divinity young Dunderham blixham Smack, the famous Pheaton Driver, Entertained the Congregation last Sunday very unexpectedly with a Learned discourse on the ORIGINAL BENGAR Gazette.—— A Matter so New and extraordinary from a Pulpit so famed for AFFECTED piety and Christian MEEKNESS, surprized the Congregation not a little.——suprized his Congregation not a little.—— Sir Barney Grizzle, being fond of strange Characters, Acted the Part of PEEPING TOM having conceald himself behind the Curtin in the Organ Loft, to enjoy the secret pleasure of hearing the Bengal Gazette Directed, by that Croyd'card Apostle in EXEBIO, and Barneys Learned College, OBADIAH BROAD-BRIM alias Peter Nimmock, the Author of the Deceased Monitor assisted at the Bellows in order to testify his gratitude for the Gospel Types.
Mr. HICKY is obliged to postpone the remaining part of Mr. Kiernanders allowance until a more convenient opportunity, to which will be added a specimen of Mr Messinks Veracity.
List of the French Prisoners going in the Neptune.
1st Classe. Culan, Dupare, Bu Moulin, Compagnac.
2d Classe. Trouche J. Rio, Verron, Faviet

Mr. HICKY,

WE Congratulate the public, and you, on the late Reformation, in delivering letters at the post Office; the public should consider themselves indebted to you for the useful hint, given in your paper some time since, respecting it. Convinced, and converted, by the force of your powerful arguments, we now with pleasure behold, regularity, and Order, taking place of confusion, and disorder; a Desk placed at the Door, to prevent saucy intruders from sitting about, perhaps purloining their Neighbours letters, yet we observed three or four prim self sufficient looking Chaps, insolently tossing the Letters about; who I suppose forced their way by some unfair means, against the content of the Clerks, who were (to do Justice) very diligent, not only in keeping others out, but in serving those that came. We know the names and Characters of those three or four (little) great Men, that I presume must have intruded themselves into the Office, we shall take no Notice now of it, but if ever we see such rudeness and Impertinence practised again, three or any other may depend on having their behaviour properly offended.
As the Gentleman to whom we owe this reformation deserves our thanks, we shall now only hint, that a proper half door, with a board to delive the Letters upon, and a strong Iron bolt; would compleat the matter.

Reflect for a few Moments on the Conduct of the Industrious SURVEYOR under the Bye-Law.

HOW exceeding vigilent, and attentive he has been to the Interest of the Public, and how sparingly he has disfurnished their Property, with what Ingenuity He continues to faint it, and you will hereafter observe the plausibility with which he will retire.—As yet nothing has been done in the Scavengers way.——The all Powerful Surveyor even has the Lenity to engross that, such is the strenuous measure of these worthy Commissioners which have been so judiciously selected for the vile offending of the Public fund.——I dica till I see you when a further discussion of meeters shall take Place.   Anti Jobb

Mr. HICKY.

THE striking similarity between the ruinous System of Politics that has been adopted by the Ministry at home, and the leading men here, must occur to every one by which we have drawn the vengeance of not only the most of the Powers of Europe but also of a great part of our own now but well known in this country, that of every Individual, and in this country, that of every Individual,

By this the Glory of Great Britain must shortly be obscured unless a change of measures takes place, and a speedy stop is put to that universal corruption which pervades every department of public affairs at home and abroad. It is truly lamentable that while Interest prompts to the practice of this perverted reason hath rendered it into a System to be defended also in Theory to subvert which a severe shock must be felt.—— Let us not be lulled into security here, Bengal is our support, Here are the springs and Sinews of War, in short our existance in this region depend on it, Let us not expose ourselves to the risk of loosing it on any account.——I am afraid at the Mauritius by this time, they must be appraised of the State of our force here, which will be so confiderably weakened by the assistance afforded to Madras, as well as by the seemingly faulty distribution of the other parts of it is universally allowed that in case of Invasion a small body of Cavalry would be indispensibly necessary, and yet we have two Regiments lying inert at a great distance (where in case of emergency others could be readily procured) on the account it is said merely of private emoluments incredible dictu.——Would they not be better employed with those large detachments of the Army that are liable to be destroyed by the enemy [without a single blow When our force is withdrawn from Bengal may not a formidable enemy rush in like a torrent, which meeting only with gentle asperities in its progress, is by them stimulated with a greater degree of expediay to the end of its course.——Then the Inhabitants of Bengal, when your golden dreams are fled, will you lament your supineness, your negligence and corruption, which shut the Mouths of every intelligent Man on this interesting subject.

Public Notice is hereby given.

THAT on Tuesday the 1st. of May, will be sold by public Auction by Mr. Donald, at his Auction-Room near the Court House, the Houses and Grounds undermentioned.
All that Brick Dwelling House, Godowns, and Compound, part of which was lately occupied by Mr, Duncan Attorney at Law, and the other part now occupied by Mr. P. Cantwell, the whole Premises Standing on four Biggahs of Ground and upwards.
A Lower-roomed House and Compound containing Twelve Cottahs of Ground, with one upper-room over the Gateway detached from the other Buildings, which formerly belonged to, and was Occupied by Mr. Chas. Weston; The Premises may be viewed at any Time before the Sale, and the Title Deeds inspected on Aplication to Mr. Donald in whose hands they now are.
Conditions of Sale.
For Sicca Rupees the amount, Purchase to be paid within 15 days of the Time of Sale, and on payment, Possession of the Premises will be given, on Failure they will be fore-told, and the first Purchaser obliged to make good every Loss that may arise on the Resale. A Rupee earnest to be paid to bind the Bargain.

EUROPE LETTERS.

SEVERAL addressed to Mr. Francis Baugh seen at the opening of the Pockets, brought by the Dartmouth, Rochford, and Lively not having been received, he supposes a Friend has taken, and trusted this to a Servant, any Information will conser an additional obligation on Mr. Baugh; If pecuniary Inducement can prevail, he offers 500 R's. for the Delivery.

To be SOLD.

AT Mr. Levetts distillery the best Oil, and New Rum 27 per Cent cheaper than is sold in Calcutta.
And the best table refined sugar at Mr Huggins, and Cantwell, Batavia and Country Arrack at Mr. Levetts Distillery at adequate rates.

On the present Mode of Dress. Humbly Inscribed to a certain fair Damsel.

IF Eve in her Innocence, could not be
blam'd,
Because going naked, she was not asham'd;
Who'er views the Ladies, as Ladies now dress,
That again they grow Innocent, sure will
confess;
And that artfully too, they retaliate the evil,
By the devil once tempted, they now tempt the
devil.
                                        Tim.

A SONG.

COME push about the Bottle, my Bucks
let's be brisk,
Let's toast the fine Girls, that grace India's
Soil?
Here's a health to the matchless, and pretty
Miss C—pe,
All Beauties to her, are no more than a
foil.
           Chorus-- Here's a health &c.
Since our brave General, is gone to Coro-
mandel,
To give Hyder, Ally a pretty tight bang-
ing;
He'll send them away scampering Pell
mell
So Bub my dear Boys, here's a health to
Miss W—
                        He'll send &c.
Bring us some Loll Shrub, charge your glasses
lip high,
Do you hear you attendants who stand in
the Entry?
Since life is a Jest, we'll drink till we
die,
So here's to the Beautifull and lovely
Miss C—y.
                        Since life &c.
May the Bashaws, who wear Wigs with
three Tails,
And all the under Strapers, like knowing
Tom-Wadler;
In the next Fleet for England, pack off with
wet Sails,
So here's to the Dens, and enchanting
Miss S——r.
                        In the next &c.
May S——h in the Army, who enjoy double
Posts,
Be sent to the Tweed, to live upon
Salmon;
Or the next Expedition, pack'd off for the
Coast,
While we remain here, and drink to
Miss H——d.
                        Or the next &c.
May the partial be unsuccessfull, in all ranks
of Life,
And may English hearts never know, a
moments Sorrow;
Huzza! Huzza! my bright lads heres to a
handsome Wife,
And smoke them that won't fett till Sun-
rise to morrow.
                        Huzza! Huzza! &c.

Mrs. MANN.

BEGS Leave to acquaint the Ladies
and Gentlemen of the Presidency,
that She has just received a neat Assort-
ment of China Goods, imported by the
Ship Rumbold.
N. B. A great Variety of Madras,
and Pulta Chintzes.

To be SOLD.

A Spot of Garden ground, Consisting
of one Baggah and four Gottahs
near Cossey-pore pleasantly situated on
the Banks of the Ganges, with a good
Carriage Road.

For particulars please to enquire of
Mr. HICKY at his Printing Office in
the Radda Baazar, at Calcutta.

NOTICE.

IS hereby given to the Gentlemen of
the settlement and the Public in general that Mr. Robert Harvey's Godown in
the Radda baazar, opposite Mr Guthries
is now open for the sale of the following
Articles viz.
The best Country Rum wholesale and
retail, in Puncheons, Pipes, and Hogs-
heads, at one Rupee fourAns. per Gallon
wholesale, and one Rupee 8 An's. retail. Fine Old Rum at 2 Rupees per
Gallon, fine double, and treble refined
Loaf Sugar, Manufactured at Sookfagur,
and equal to any made in Europe Calculated to answer the end of sweetning,
without, depriving the Tea of its Flavor,
Sugar of this excellent and agreeable
quality has been long wished for in this
part of the World.
The very finest transparent Sugar Candy
at 30 Rupees per Maund. Patna piece
Goods, raw Silks &c. and a variety of
other articles. All Gentlemen favoring
Mr. Harvey with their Commands, may
depend upon his exerting every endeavour to give them satisfaction.

TURNBULL, MAC'INTYRE, and
DAWLEY.

BEG Leave respectfully to acquaint
the Ladies and Gentlemen of Calcutta, that their Investment of China
Goods imported in the Rumbold, is now
exposed to sale for ready Money, and
upon the most reasonable terms, at the
House formerly Occupied by Mr. Slight,
near the Court House.

To be LETT.

A House in the Loll Baazar belonging to Mr. Henry Grant, For
further particulars please to apply to
the proprietor.

To be SOLD.

BY Mr. Fivey at his Shop in the
Rada Baazar the following Articles
Imported by the Ship Neptune.
Sweet Oil in Bottles, Vinegar in do.
Mustard, Pickles in Qr. Case's or Bot-
tles, Olives in ditto do. Rasberry and
Cherry Brandy in Pint Bottles, Fronte-
niac, Europe bottled Porter, Hams,
Rusia Dear Tongues, Old Danish Claret,
Knife Cases Compleat with Spoons &c.
Gentlemens Tool Chests, Ink Stands,
Glauber Salts, Camp Kettles, and a Va-
riety of China, Madras, and other Goods.

ALL PERSONS.

HAVING any Claims, or demands
on the Estate of Capt. George
Davies, of Artillery, on the Madrass
Establishment, lately deceased, are desired forthwith to send an account thereof to Doctor Chas. Allen at Fort
William, sole Executor of the said Capt.
Geo. Davies, and all persons indebted to
the said Estate are requested immediately
to pay the same.
Fort William April the 14th 1781.

ALL PERSONS,

WHO have any demands on the
Estate of Mr. William Justice

---

deceased, are requested to send an account of them to Mr. James Miller one
of the Executors. And all Persons indebted to the said Estate, are requested to
discharge their respective Debts, without delay.

To The PUBLIC,

ALL Persons having Demands upon
the Estate of the late Tho's Kirkman Esq. deceased, are requested to send
an Account thereof to Mr. Fred. Wilson Administrator on or before the 1st
Day of May next ensuing; and all Persons indebted to the said Estate, are requested to pay in their respective Debts
to Mr. Wilson as speedily as possible.

THIS IS TO GIVE NOTICE

THAT on the 30 day of April next
will be sold on the Premises, by
Public Auction, and to the highest Bidder, all that Capital upper-roomed Mes-
suage situated in the Kusaulee Baazar,
late in the Occupation of John Evelyn
Esq. The House contains 5 Rooms, 2
Halls and a Verando above stairs with
good lower apartments and uncommonly
good Out-houses, Stabling, Coach-house
&c. besides a row of Brick Boutique
shops which terminates the Premises to
the Eastward, the whole standing on
One Begah and 17 Cottahs of Ground.
The above Premises belong to the Estate of the late Tho's Kirkman Esq.
deceased and stand Mortgaged for
18,500 C. Rs. and Interest from the
25th Nov. 1778. The Person who shall
be the highest Bidder at the Sale must
sign to an agreement evincing the Purchase, and must be at the expence of
and procure his own Conveyances, and
must Pay the Purchase Money on or
before the 1st Day of June following.
On which Payment being made,
the Premises will be delivered up to
him.
The premises may be veiwed and the
Title Deeds seen, by applying to Mr.
Fred. Wilson the Administrator.

The LOTTERY
for the Harmonic House

BEING nearly filled up Messrs. Stark
and Robertson request that the Subscribers in Calcutta, will meet at Nicolls
and Creightons Tavern, on the first monday of June next, between the Hours of
10 and 11 in the forenoon, to appoint
a Committee to superintend the Drawing
of the Tickets: Likewise request that the
Gentlemen who are not in Calcutta, will
give Orders to their Agents here, to Pay
in the Subscription Money to Messrs.
Stark and Robertson, and to receive their
Tickets previous to that Meeting.
Calcutta 19th April 1781.

To Be LETT.

A Lower-room'd House within a
large Compound and proper out
Offices near the Council Chamber. For
particulars enquire at the PRINTING
OFFICE.   March 30th, 1781.

The fourth page of *Hicky's Bengal Gazette*, 28 April, 1781.
Image: Courtesy of the University of Heidelberg.

THE
INDIA GAZETTE;
OR,
CALCUTTA PUBLIC ADVERTISER.

Saturday, December the 2d, 1780. (No. 3.)

The MONITOR.

[No. 3.]   Saturday Dec. 2, 1780.

Tempus fugit.

THO' the rapid flight of Time has been complained of from the earliest Ages, and it ever has been allowed to be the only thing, which never could be recovered when once lost; yet the generality of Mankind seem as prodigal of it, as if it could be new fabricated at pleasure, and waken not from the delusion, 'till they are on the verge of changing it for Eternity. A reflection of this nature was occasioned the other day, on reading the following beautiful lines of Shakespear.

" To-morrow, To-morrow, and To-morrow
" Creeps in this petty pace from day to day,
" To the last syllable of recorded time;
" And all our yesterdays have lighted fools
" The way to dusty death."

MACBETH, Act V.

I could not help thinking also, tho' Time was strangely trifled with in most parts of the World; yet that my Countrymen were particularly lavish of it in India; squandering it away with a profusion even beyond what they did in the other three quarters of the Globe; and that the heat could not be justly pleaded as an excuse, it being much exceeded in many other places where we have Settlements; at least what it is in Bengal.

The subject seemed worthy of attention, and I wished to be able to account for the depredation: Without a suspicion of flattery; it may be said, that in proportion to the number, there are as many (if not more) British Subjects of real genius, and Scholastically cultivated in Asia, as are to be met with, either on the other side the Cape, or in the Western regions; and yet with too many of them, how shamefully are their forenoons lounged away on Couches, or passed in the most trifling conversations, with an anxious wish for Dinner time! which proves the prologue to an afternoon's nap; and then with dressing, two or three chillims, visiting and supper, they make shift to rub thro' the rest of the day: Again on the other hand, when there is *a real call for Duty*, the Writer believes he may venture to assert, that the British Nation cannot boast Subjects in any part of the World, who have exceeded those in the Eastern Regions, for vigor of mind, activity of body, or a spirited ambition to merit Praise.

How shall these contradictions be accounted for? perhaps the following may a some degree do it.

The great intercourse we are obliged o have with the Natives (who have not nly indolence depicted in every word

and action, but whose morning and evening prayer, might with great reason be supposed to be "Teach me O guardian genius how to procrastinate") which generally commences at a time of life that it is not usual to make the most just reflections on Men and things; and the very few Channels there are for displaying any superior qualities or accomplishments, and of course opportunities of exciting a spirited emulation; Perhaps the Monitor may be so fortunate to prove one, not only by affording an opportunity of exerting superior abilities to his Correspondents, but by these loose hints stimulating abler heads to treat the copious subject in it's full extent. Doubtless the mind cannot be expected to be constantly on the stretch, any more than the body incessantly in labour; but the instances of either being exhausted by excess of application, are few indeed, in comparison of the numbers that are enervated or relaxed by the contrary. The Writer wishes he could persuade some of his Readers every Morning to write down the transactions of the preceding Day, for one Week; not reading it over 'till the whole is finished, and then favor him with the same; which might perhaps in some degree prove how far the accusation of trifling away our time is justly founded, or the contrary: But he shall close this days work, by publishing the Letter mentioned in his first, returned by Pericles.

Mr. MONITOR.

Inest sua gratia parvis.

'THE Origin of Printing in Europe,
' and the great revolution in the
' Literary World (the consequence of it)
' from Savage Ignorance and Superstition,
' to general Philanthrophy, Urbanity and
' rational Theology; is so universally
' known, that many Strictures thereon
' would be tedious and un-interesting:
' 'tis enough to say, that by this great Pa-
' rent and Nurse of Wisdom; this faith-
' ful Monument and Depository of the
' accumulated knowledge of Philosophy,
' Arts, Sciences and Experience, of An-
' cient and Modern times; Mankind, and
' not a few narrow minded jealous, jug-
' gling Fanaticks, freely enjoy those trea-
' sures of Wit and Genius, that were for-
' merly doomed to perpetual and cruel
' imprisonment, within the strong bars
' of Cloistered Cells.
' To this glorious Art of Printing, is
' due the fall of Tyranny, that savage
' Monster, whose Iron Hand enabled our
' ferocious Ancestors to crush humanity
' and benevolence, (then the feeble but
' lawful off-spring of Justice and Truth)

' who insensible to the calls of compas-
' sion and the more tender feelings of the
' human Heart, marked their progress
' to wealth and power by the foulest
' crimes and most atrocious murders; the
' mock Ministers of Religion, adding to
' the black Catalogue of Public guilt,
' by staining their impious hands with
' human Blood, in the name of the Om-
' nipotent.
' Daily Publications and a continual
' Multiplication of Copies, present to
' numberless minds (which would other-
' wise remain uninstructed) matters so
' interesting, ingenious and useful; that
' the understanding becomes improved
' almost without perceiving it.
' But as there's no good without it's
' concomitant evil, the freedom of the
' Press tho' one of the strongest fences of
' Public Liberty, is often converted into
' a destructive engine of Public oppression
' and Private wrong; the number and ex-
' cellence of many Public and Periodical
' Prints in England, do honour to the
' genius and knowledge of our Country;
' yet, the malignant Spirits of detraction,
' calumny and falsehood, is too palatable
' to the ill-natured and envious (a very
' numerous class in every Community)
' not to be received with complaisance
' and avidity. How many needy Wits to
' supply the cravings of penury, or the
' necessities too often consequent on their
' extravagance and intemperence; or
' wicked Men, who are envious of merit
' and ability that they could never imi-
' tate, make an hungry meal on mangled
' Characters, in direct opposition to
' truth and humanity, very often actu-
' ated by passion; which may easily be
' discerned by a judicious Editor, and
' should never be indulged.
' Tho' I make no doubt of your judg-
' ment and capacity in the choice and
' arrangement of subjects, still I hope
' that a few friendly hints will not of-
' fend.
' TRUTH, the knowledge of which
' is the perfection of the understanding;
' should be the primary object of an ho-
' nest and skilful Publisher; the opposite
' vices, *Ignorance* and *Error* the two
' great maladies of the mind, should be
' as much as possible guarded against. In
' attempting Characters or indulging Sa-
' tire, too much delicacy and caution
' cannot be used, left by the former the
' domestic happiness of *worthy* Indivi-
' duals should be wounded, and by too
' strongly colouring the latter (the com-
' mon defect of Satire) you should offend
' against the laws of decency. Religion,
' and Politics, always were and ever must
' remain the grand sources of contenti-
' on in the World, whilst Men differ in
' opinion, which will be the case, as
' long as Mankind is composed of the

The front page of the *India Gazette*, 2 December, 1780. It was printed jointly by Bernard Messink and Peter Reed until Reed left the newspaper in early 1781, after which Messink printed it alone.

Image: Courtesy of the British Library.

The Supreme Court House on the right, and the Writers Building on the left, were the centre of the British East India Company's government. The Writers Building is still standing today. Painted by Thomas Daniell and published in *Views of Calcutta* (1786).

Source: Norman R. Bobins and S. P. Lohia Rare Books Collection.

Warren Hastings, circa 1783-1784.
Source: Yale Center for British Art.

Elijah Impey, 1776.
Source: Victoria Memorial Hall, Kolkata.

Hastings' Impeachment Trial, reprinted in Hutchinson's *Story of the Nations* (pg. 196).

James Augustus Hicky's lawyer, William Hickey (no relation), circa 1785.
Source: Yale Center for British Art, Paul Mellon Collections.

Johann Zacharias Kiernander, circa 1770–1772. Reproduction of an engraving by Charles Imhoff.

Source: Bengal Past & Present, Vol. 10, 307.

Kiernander's Church overlooking Lal Dighi in the center of Calcutta. Painted by Thomas Daniell and published in *Views of Calcutta* (1786). Source: Norman R. Bobins and S. P. Lohia Rare Books Collection.

Warren Hastings' Belvedere Estate, near the site of Hastings and Francis' duel. Painted by William Prinsep (1838).

Old Fort Ghat in Calcutta on the Hooghly River, where most new European arrivals would have landed. Painted by Thomas Daniell and published in *Views of Calcutta* (1786).

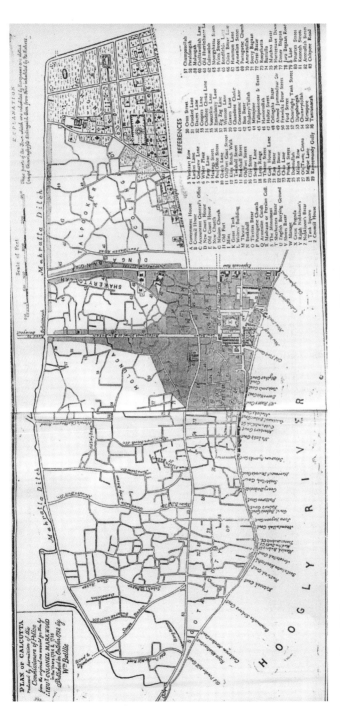

REFERENCES

A Government House
B Council House
C Accomptant General's Office
D New Court House
E Old Court House
F New Church
G Mission Church
H Old Fort
I Mint
K Great Tank
L Writer's Building
M Nunnah
N Bankshall
O Tirretta Bazar
P Portuguese Church
Q Armenian Church
R Madrassa or Persian Coll.
S The Monument
T Writer's Bazar
U English Burying Ground
V Shears Bazar
W Poper Gola
X Great Pergola
Y Rajah Nobkissen's
Z Nudea Monson's Bazar
1 Tank Square
2 Council House

3   Vaukaut Row
30 Cross Street
31 Coolad Lane
32 Dacres Lane
33 Cospos Lane
4   Wher Plaat
5   Hings Street
34 Chekee Chick Lane
35 Superchin Lane
36 Emsaukary Lane
6   Post Office Street
37 Zig Zag Lane
7   Clive Street
38 Wessuen Lane
8   Gisk Lane
9   Old Fort Ghaut Street
39 Granu Lane
10 Tank Street
40 Chandor Ghoke
12 Kim Fench Walk
11 Baukhall Street
41 Gooranne Street
13 Taukdar Street
42 Bus Bazar
14 Portague Street
43 Shakey's Tollah
15 Old Fort Street
44 Mirapore
16 Crik Street
45 Tallpoolerster & Bazar
17 Sova Lane
46 Hassanpool
18 Loil Range
19 Theater Street
47 Chinabbazar
20 Bok Bazar
48 Colingha Bazar
21 Clib Bazar
49 Cooley Bazar
22 Cok Lane
50 Fenwicks Bazar Street
23 Popek Street
51 Ford Street
24 Dobeullan
52 Cowringhy
25 Midden Row
53 Dingabazgnh
26 Old Tauen, Conna
54 Chutaryollah
27 Rajah Nobkissen's
55 Munarpore
28 Magze Lane
56 Tunisuteah
29 Baypossmody Gully

57 Champaltullah
58 Pawabngah
59 Mohungah
60 Chatkawallah
61 Old Harrinbaree La.
62 Calcoozbb
63 Kroquethana Row
94 Price Street
65 Bandelslah
66 China Bazar Lane
67 Hunnman Lane
68 Armenian Street
69 Armenian Church
70 Amrutullah
71 Soory Bagaun
72 Crux Bhara Bazar
73 Booyghatta
74 Rantulla
75 Manchue Bazar
76 Moorys Divoe
77 Deor Bagaun
78 Jura Bagaun Road
79 Luer Street
80 Paurees Street
81 Keereh Street
82 Arrentullah Street
83 Chitpore Road

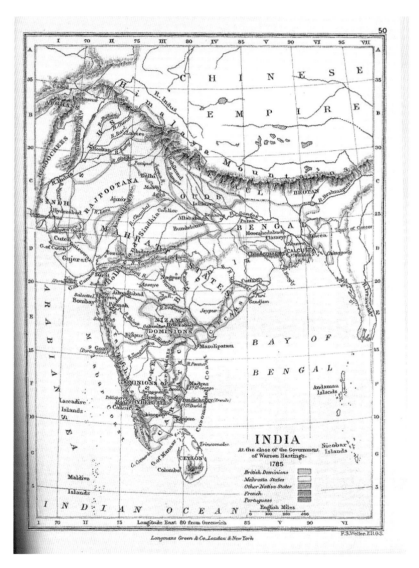

India during Hicky's time, 1785. The British territories are in red, and the Maratha territories in yellow (by S. R. Gardiner, 1892).

Kiernander v. Hicky

What the Devil cannot do himself, he doth through his instruments. But, if God is for me, what is it that men or Devils can do to me? Let them roar and brawl with all their fierceness, my innocence will save them all.

— Kiernander to Reverend Friedrich Wilhelm Pasche, 5 February 1782.[487]

Thursday morning, 28 June 1781. Supreme Court House.

Hicky planned to cause chaos again.

The Court tried to swear in a jury, but he objected to juror after juror. He accused one of being unfit to serve because he was Hastings' friend. A second was Impey's. A third held a lucrative Company post under Hastings. A fourth he even claimed had been bribed to find a guilty verdict.[488]

He accused one potential juror, John Rider, of being prejudiced, having said he would find him guilty if he were on the jury.

Impey said he needed proof.

'Prove that Mr Rider said so. Call those who told you.'

'Mr Watts told me so; but he is not now in court. If you give me time I can prove it,' Hicky said.

Watts had helped Diemer write his letter and had fled Calcutta because of unpaid debts. He could only come if the Court gave him immunity.

Impey refused.

'Do you mean to put off your trial? Call your witnesses,' he said, frustrated

'I have another objection to Mr Rider. He is very intimate to your lordship's family. He buys caps and millinery for Lady Impey,' Hicky said, changing his tack.

'This is the highest degree of insolence, but in the situation in which you are, I do not know how the Court can punish it. Let the words be recorded,' Impey was furious now.

'I don't mean any insolence,' Hicky said. He looked up at Impey.

'I might as well at once plead guilty as have that sycophant upon my jury. He will do just as you direct him. He is absolutely at your beck and at your disposal. The man has no soul: a corrupt, sordid, contemptible toad eater of the Chief Justice, with whose wife he is tolerably familiar, plain as is his person and deficient as is his understanding. Besides, he is running about the town all day long peeping into every Europe shop in order to buy frippery for that said favourite lady.'

Impey sneered as the court erupted in laughter. No sane man would have insulted the Chief Justice like that, or insinuated that someone was so close to another man's wife.

'No man that heard the words can doubt they were meant for insolence,' Judge Hyde chimed in.

'If you didst not mean insolence, thou must be the most stupid ignorant wretch that ever was heard,' Impey said.

'Everything a poor man says is insolence. If Mr Rider does not buy caps for Lady Impey, at least she never wears anything but what Mr Rider approves,' Hicky said.[489]

11.53 a.m.

Finally, both sides agreed on a jury. Judge Chambers came in, late as he often was.[490]

Hastings' lawyer, Henry Davies, opened Kiernander's prosecution. He read Hicky's article, *For the good of the MISSION*, and then laid out the charges. The first that nearly Hicky's entire article was a libel, the second that only Hicky's claim that Kiernander sold types to Messink for 'filthy lucre and detestable avarice' was a libel.

Davies examined his first witness, Christopher Meyer, the young man who had read the article to Kiernander. Davies chose the same strategy as at the last trial. He again tried to convince the jury that their sole job was to determine whom the article referred to, and that the judges were responsible for determining malice.

'Who do you suppose to be meant by "his being influenced by the considerations of filthy lucre and detestable avarice"?' Davies asked Meyer.

'I understand Mr Hicky means that Mr Kiernander can be influenced by any consideration,' Meyer replied.

'In what sense do you understand the words "to the Charitable good Will of this pious Samaritan"?' Davies asked.

'I understand he means to praise him by calling him a pious Samaritan,' Meyer said, not understanding the irony.

Davies tried again.

'Do you understand it meant to praise Mr Kiernander as a pious Samaritan, or in what other sense do you understand it?'

'I understand he says here in the paper in praise of him, but means to dispraise him,' Meyer understood now.

'What do you understand is insinuated by the question, "whether the Annual profits and advantages of the said Church have proved more or equally profitable, as the building of Godowns or Warehouses on holy consecrated public Ground to be Occupied without scruple by the pious and immaculate Board of Trade?"'

'Mr Hicky means Mr Kiernander built godowns to let to the Board of Trade.'

'What do you understand by the "Ecclesiastical Farm"?'

'I understand the Church Fees.'

'Now Sir, by that question, "whether those Dues or Fees do not of legal Right belong either to the Orphan Fund, or to the joint and Capital Stock of the Charitable Society," to whom do you understand Mr Hicky means to insinuate the Dues and Fees belong?'

'I suppose he means Mr Kiernander.'

Hicky cross-examined Meyer.

He asked Meyer if Kiernander had any assistance suing him, insinuating that Chambers had advised Kiernander to sue. This would have violated the judge's impartiality and, if proved, might end his trial as a mistrial.

'Now, sir. Fix your eye upon me. Look towards me, being the prisoner, and towards the gentlemen of the Jury. Now sir, lay your hand upon your breast by virtue of the Oath you have taken in this honourable court. Look round in the course of the sun and see if you can see any person in this court whom you heard advise Mr Kiernander to bring on this prosecution?'

'No sir,' Meyer replied.

Hicky asked again.

'Did you never hear he was advised by any great person in power to bring on this Prosecution?'

'No sir,' Meyer said again.

Hicky pressed his point when he cross-examined Meyer a second time.

'How often have you rehearsed your lesson, and who was your schoolmaster or instructor in the explanation of that paper?' Hicky asked Meyer, implying that Meyer might be perjuring himself.

'My schoolmaster from whom I received my education?' Meyer asked, confused.

'No, Sir. That is not meant,' Hicky said, and stopped, letting the insinuation lie that Meyer's testimony had been coached.

Davies examined his next witness, Thomas Adams, hoping to prove without doubt that Hicky's whole article was a libel on Kiernander.

'What do you understand to be meant there to be "influenced by the considerations of filthy lucre and detestable avarice"?' Davies asked Adams.

'Mr Kiernander,' Adams said.

'What do you understand is meant by the words "to the Charitable good Will of this pious Samaritan"?'

'I think it is meant ironically.'

'Who do you understand is meant to have "built Godowns on holy consecrated places"?'

'Mr Kiernander.'

'Who do you suppose is meant to have let them to the Board of Trade?'

'Mr Kiernander.'

'What do you understand is meant by the "Church Fees and Ecclesiastical Farm"?'

'The fees that arise to Mr Kiernander from being head of the church.'

'Who do you suppose is meant there to have "appropriated to himself the church dues and fees"?'

'Mr Kiernander.'

'To whom do you suppose the dues and fees ought of right to belong?'

'It is insinuated by the paper that they belong to the orphan fund.'

'When he says that "the Legacies left to the sole use of the Orphan Fund and to the Charitable Society have lapsed to the present Incumbent", what is the sense you understand to be meant to be conveyed by that passage?'

'I understand it meant that the present incumbent Mr Kiernander had appropriated them to his own private use.'

Davies stopped his examination, confident he had proven that Hicky's entire article referred to Kiernander and no one else.

Davies then brought Kiernander to the bar.

'What is your profession?' he asked.

'I am a clergyman and a missionary, and I was ordained such in 1739, and in 1740 was sent out by the Society for Promoting Christian Knowledge. I have served eighteen years in the Mission at Cuddalore on the coast. And from the year 1758, I have been here,' Kiernander said.

Davies launched his examination point by point.

'"Whose Eve of Life is fast verging to the shadow of Death— Whose Silver head bows down loaded with the blossoms of the Grave, and whom the Sepulchre is yawning to close upon". Whom doeth he mean by *whose*?' he asked.

'I suppose he means me. Here I stand, and I answer the description.'

'What motives does he charge by "filthy lucre and avarice"?'

Kiernander dropped a bombshell. The types he gave Messink were not the Society's types at all, nor were they consecrated. They were his own and he could do what he wanted with them, even sell them for profit.

'Mr Hicky's meaning plainly is from the whole context, that I have been influenced by filthy lucre and avarice to sell the types belonging to the Mission. But they did not belong to the Mission, they were my own property, consequently. I had right to do what I pleased with them.'

Davies continued.

'In what sense do you understand was meant by "the pious Samaritan"?'

'He means it ironically to defame me by saying that I am not a pious man and unlike the pious Samaritan'

'What do you understand is meant by the question, "whether the Annual Profits of the said Church have been more or equally profitable to Mr Kiernander, as the building of Godowns or Warehouses on holy consecrated ground"?'

Kiernander said he never built or rented any godowns to the Company nor had he ever made money off his Church. Sometimes he even spent his own money to support it.

'Mr Hicky's meaning is plainly this: that he insinuates I have received annually profits, dues or fees from the Church for my own advantage, which I have never since I built it. I have continually supported it from year to year in whatever article has been wanted. The only article which I can say, can be looked upon as an income to the church, is the charitable collection in the church on the last Sundays of every month, on great festivals, and sacrament days. This money so collected is regularly every time, and every farthing of it, brought to the mission account to answer the charges of the mission, partly alms for the poor. I have received nothing from the collections. Now *this* Mr Hicky says must equally have been a benefit and advantage, as that of building godowns and warehouses on consecrated ground, which I never did, nor let any such godowns to the Board of Trade.'

'What do you understand by the "Dues and Fees of the Ecclesiastical Farm"?' Davies asked.

'I understand he meant that I receive dues and fees of the

Church. There is no Ecclesiastical Farm, I do not know what he can mean but the Mission or the Church.'

'What do you understand to be meant by the question, "whether the legacies of Captain Griffin and other Legacies left to the sole use of the Charitable Society have lapsed to the present Incumbent"?'

Kiernander said there was no money left in Griffin's legacy by the time it reached the Mission. When Griffin's boat had been seized at Bombay, Griffin successfully argued that seizure fell within the terms of his insurance. But his insurers in England disagreed and sued to recover their money after he died. When the court in England ruled for Griffin's insurers, Kiernander, as the executor of Griffin's estate, was required to pay them. This reduced Griffin's estate so much that there was not enough money left to pay beneficiaries, let alone leave any money for the Mission.

'And this he charges me with appropriating to myself,' Kiernander added.

'"And there shall arise wolves in sheep's Cloathing"?' Davies asked.

'He means me to be a wolf in sheep's clothing. I charge anyone to give it another meaning.'

Kiernander paused.

'I have missed one thing. He says that many other legacies that have lapsed to the present incumbent for those many years ... If there should be more legacies bequeathed to the mission, I know nothing of them ... If Mr Hicky would be so good as to search the records of the Court, to inspect all the wills and testaments made within these fifteen or twenty years, and find out more legacies for the church or the mission, he will lay me under great obligations to him.'[491]

Finally, Davies wanted to confirm that Kiernander made the decision to sue by himself.

'Were you advised by any great man, or do you undertake this prosecution of your own accord?'

'Entirely of my own accord. I am so deeply concerned in it that I could not avoid it,' Kiernander said.

Davies finished his examination, confident he had proven the entire article was a libel.

Now it was Hicky's turn. He cross-examined Kiernander, trying to prove that he never meant malice, and that Kiernander had been motivated by lucre and avarice to sell types.

'Mr Hicky never meant you any harm. You are a good and holy man. You have not many years I hope between this and heaven. Pray sir on the virtue of your oath, did you ever sell any types to Mr Messink?'

'No, I have not sold him any types. I first lent him part of my types. Afterwards I made him a present of them, but they were my own.'

'You say upon your oath they were yours?'

'Yes.'

'From whom did you buy them?'

'I wrote to the Secretary of the Society for Promoting Christian Knowledge. At my request he purchased them and lent them out for me.'

'Oh did he so! We shall soon find out something further. What year was that in?'

'To the best of my remembrance, two years ago.'

'By what ship?'

'I don't remember.'

'Did you ever give out that these, or was it given out by any of your people, that these types were from Tranquebar?'

Kiernander said he got the types from the Society in England.

'The types I gave to Messink I had from England. But as he talks of Tranquebar, Mr Messink desired me to procure for him a set of old types and a press from Tranquebar. Those I procured. They are arrived and received.'

'Did the Society ever send out to you any types for the use of the Mission?'

Kiernander was adamant the types he sold were his own. What he did not mention, and what Hicky might not have known, was that he and the Mission were the same thing. He had never given the Mission to the Society.

'No. Not one single type for the use of the Mission. But if I have types of my own, may I not be allowed to make use of them for the benefit of the Mission?'

Hicky was getting nowhere. He turned his questions to see if anyone had suggested Kiernander sue him. Just like earlier, if he could prove that Judge Chambers had encouraged Kiernander to sue then his trial might end in a mistrial.

'No doubt, Mr Kiernander, your inclination might lead you to carry on the prosecution against me. Did you never understand either by message or insinuation, that it would be agreeable to any gentleman in this settlement that you would carry on this prosecution against me with vigour?'

'No gentleman whatever, no person whatever or however, insinuated the least of such a thing to me. I was under unavoidable necessity to do it. I am very sorry Mr Hicky, it gives me no pleasure to prosecute a man. But the reason is unavoidable. My character is not only at stake, but the credit of the Mission and the honour of the Society, who consist of upwards of 900 members of the most eminent personages in England and other countries too. All these are injured. I am still more sorry that Mr Hicky should suffer himself to be so much imposed upon, (by whomever it may be I don't know) to print a libel against me of these contents.'

'Mr Kiernander, supposing that you were informed (I don't suppose you read it yourself) there was such a letter in the paper, don't you think as a clergyman that it would have been more becoming you to send a message to me, and I might have told you who was my author?'

'I have more reason to expect you would acquaint me of your information before you put it in your paper. You have done the same as if you had put me in a cart of infamy and have sent me round the whole world to all nations.'

'Mr Kiernander, had you been on the best terms with me, upon neighbourly terms, and never gave me any occasion to harbour a bad opinion against you, you might have expected it, as I have done on many several familiar cases before I published anything against them. Did you not send me a manuscript copy to print an almanac and asked me the price? The same you had done the year before at Madras was sixteen pages for which you gave.'

'I sent you an almanac and inquired the price for printing. The answer was brought and the price was so extravagant that I did not choose to do it.'

'What was the price?'

'It was too much.'

'How much?'

'One rupee for one almanac.'

Hicky turned to the jury.

'That almanac consisted of thirty-two pages. The one he had printed the year before was half the size for which you gave six fanams (half a rupee). Do you think there is any harm in telling an innocent story?'

He told the court that Kiernander had given away almanacs for free to spite him and that was why he sold Messink types, to harm him.

Impey interrupted.

'Take care Mr Hicky, are you going to prove express malice?'

Impey questioned Kiernander, asking if anyone suggested he sue Hicky.

'Have you ever been advised by any judge on the bench to commence the present prosecution?'

'No person whatever on the bench or anywhere else ever advised me to prosecute Mr Hicky,' Kiernander said.

'Have you ever, with regard to myself, ever seen me since the commencement of this prosecution?'

'No, I have not till last Tuesday in Court.'

'Did you speak to me there?'

'No, I did not. Nor to any judge on the bench.'

'Has any person connected with me ever insinuated to you that it would be agreeable to me that you should prosecute Mr Hicky?'

'No.'

'My brother Chambers desired me to ask Mr Kiernander to recollect what passed when Mr Kiernander came to him in distress on this publication?'

'I did. But the purpose of my coming was about the lawyers as they seemed to be afraid to undertake my cause on account of Mr Hicky. I wanted to know whether I could be advocate in my own cause. And somebody told me I could not prosecute criminally and civilly, which I thought I could do. Besides, I had been advised to put off the criminal prosecution entirely, for I was told it was not right in a clergyman, but I found it was unavoidable.'

3.05 p.m.

Hicky began questioning his witness, Robert Harvey. He hoped to prove that his words were not malicious because Kiernander already had a bad reputation and thus nothing could hurt him.

'How many years have you known Mr Kiernander?' he asked.

'I have known Mr Kiernander about nine or ten years,' Harvey said.

'Did you never hear in that time anybody say a heavy word against him?'

'I cannot charge my memory with it.'

'Did you never tell me yourself that he was an oppressive and cruel unfeeling man?'

'I once repeated an affair to Mr Hicky which concerned myself.'

'Did you not insinuate to me that you would wish the world to know the cruelties he had exercised to you?'

'I cannot charge my memory I ever did.'

Unable to prove Kiernander's bad character, Hicky spoke to the court.

'My meaning was simply to show from the character he had before, nothing in this paper could hurt him.'

He then called his star witness, Johann Christian Diemer. With Diemer's testimony, he hoped to prove beyond a reasonable doubt that Kiernander had sold the Society's consecrated types.

He asked Diemer if he knew if the types belonged to the Mission. Diemer was silent.

He asked again if the types belonged to the Mission. Diemer was still silent.

Diemer stayed silent to any questions. He looked frightened and stared about the Court House. The judges dismissed him and he ran out of the Court House. His hat fell off his head and an audience member threw it behind him as he flew down the steps.[492]

Hicky composed himself. His star witness had failed him. He had not proven that Kiernander sold types for lucre and avarice. And he had not proven that Kiernander was advised to sue him. His trial was looking bleak.

4.50 p.m.

The jury returned after only ten minutes and delivered their verdict:

Not guilty on the first count.

It was a surprise but it made sense. The reason was a technicality. The jury believed that not all Hicky's words were directed at Kiernander, particularly the phrase 'ecclesiastical farm', which they believed referred to the Company's priests. Thus they could not find him guilty on this count.

Guilty on the second, narrower count.

The jury believed that his calling Kiernander a 'pious Samaritan' motivated by 'filthy lucre and detestable avarice' was a libel.[493]

Hicky may have escaped a full guilty verdict but he had still been found guilty. And he still had one more trial to go.

A Man Among Dregs

> As for the poor they utter their complaints to the wind, the
> seat of [Justice] is by far too remote from them, for their
> tales to be heard.
>
> – Anonymous Contributor, *Hicky's Bengal Gazette*,
> 30 June 1781.[494]

9.32 a.m., Friday, 29 June 1781.
Supreme Court House.

Almost no records remain of Hicky's fourth trial.

Davies opened the prosecution and read Hicky's article, A HINT
AT A DISTANCE TO THE *Proprietors of India Stock*, which called
on the Company's officers to mutiny, and maybe even launch a
coup because their 'throats' were devoted to 'wild chimeras of a
madman'.[495]

'This libel calling on the whole army to mutiny is much worse
than erecting the standard of sedition in one camp. The other part,
though it might injure Mr Hastings in the opinion of the people
in England, and is therefore very deserving of punishment, is not
of so enormous a nature as the part of the paper concerning the
Company's military's officers,' he said.

Learning from his first failure, Davies switched tactics and
argued that not only did the article refer to Hastings, it was explicitly
published with malice. So even if the jury was unpredictable they
would still find Hicky guilty.

Still, he reminded the jury that it was the judges' responsibility to determine whether Hicky printed with malice, not theirs, and they should respect that tradition.[496]

Hicky stuck to the same arguments too. He again cited Parson Prick. He told the jury that he, like Prick, did not create the libel. He only reprinted it and thus he should be acquitted.

Impey summed up the case to the jury. He made his contempt for Hicky clear.

'Mr Hicky, a man among the dregs of the people, keeps sepoys at his house,' he said.

The jury debated for forty minutes and then returned. This time they sided with Davies and agreed that the judges had the right to determine libel. They pronounced their verdict:

Guilty of printing the article.

Impey pronounced the judges' decision.

Guilty of libel.[497]

Hicky and Davies wrangled for leverage and the terms of his punishment over the next few weeks. Hicky argued that his advocates had been intimidated, but when his advocates said they had not been intimidated, the Court dismissed his claim. Davies argued that Hicky had aggravated his libels by printing the satiric playbill and distributing special edition extraordinary gazettes the day of the first trial.

Impey agreed with Davies. He told the Court he believed the freedom of the Press was no freedom at all, but actually enslaved people by intimidating them.

'This is the boasted liberty of the press, the produce of a real slavery. Mr Hicky threatens those who prosecute him. Mr Kiernander swore he had great difficulty to get any lawyer to undertake his cause,' he said.

'It is now a very complicated case of crimes and misdemeanours and contempt. I have not yet considered the case to be ready to give judgment. If my brothers are prepared they will say so,' he continued.

'We are not,' Chambers and Hyde replied.

'Then the court will take time to consider the sentences ... and in the meantime the prisoner may derive some benefit for the delay. For probably the prosecutor, when he moves for judgment, will consider what does or does not proceed from Hicky's press in the meantime. And certainly it is no disadvantage to the prisoner. For three or four months will elapse between this day and the adjournment, which will certainly be a very small part of the imprisonment he must expect.'

Impey struck his gavel.

'Let the sessions be adjourned to the first day of the next term, Let the prisoner be remanded.'[498]

Hicky stood in silence. He said not a word.

His trials were over. Or at least that's what he thought.

PART III

PERSEVERANCE

Singh's Rebellion

The whole People of Bahar were wavering, those of Patna would have been the first to have cut our throats.

– William Young, Member of the Patna Council, 11 October 1781.[499]

Two o'clock, Thursday afternoon, 16 August 1781, Banaras.[500]

After Hicky's trials ended, Warren Hastings travelled over a thousand miles to Banaras to put down a rebellious vassal. He had come to punish Chait Singh, the raja of Banaras, for being late in paying tribute to the Company, and for having not sent troops for the war effort as demanded.

Hastings had spent a fruitless two hours looking for an interpreter to speak to Singh when he received an urgent letter from an officer guarding Singh's palace. He opened the letter and read that a mob was gathering outside the palace, and the officer's sepoys did not have a single round of ammunition among them.[501]

Hastings looked up from the letter. A look of horror spread across his face. He asked again if there was anyone who could translate for him. But there was no one.

'If we cannot find anybody to write the letter, it is best to send a verbal message,' his Resident suggested.[502]

Hastings turned to a messenger, saying that if the mob attacked, he would punish Singh.

'If any blood is spilt, European or sepoy, the fault will be considered as his and that he will answer for it,' he said, telling the messenger to repeat this message word for word.

The messenger rode off. Hastings hoped that his threat would be enough to quell the mob.[503]

But it was already too late. The mob began scaling the walls and trees and jumping into the palace to free Singh, drawing swords and shields from hideaways as if drawing buckets from a well.[504]

The slaughter began.

The messenger was the first to go down. A scimitar was run right through him. The lieutenant-in-charge followed, cut down trying to defend himself with a sword. The sergeant was next, his arm was hacked off and he fell unconscious. The sepoys went down in droves, surrounded, outnumbered three to one, and with no ammunition.[505]

Dead and wounded sepoys piled up in the gateway and the square inside as the world turned to black with the sound of death.

Singh escaped in the chaos, climbing through a wicker gate overlooking the river, wrapping turbans around his waist and rappelling over the edge of his palace walls. He landed in a boat as his men rowed him across the river to safety.

By the time the Company rescued its wounded the next morning, Banaras had exploded in rebellion. Thousands from the countryside marched to Singh's side, killing any Europeans they could find, cutting off their heads and dumping their bodies into the river. They even killed the Indian servants of Europeans. When they found Hastings' boats they put his servants to the sword. The survivors they tied back-to-back before throwing them into the river alive.[506]

The whole countryside descended into revolt.[507] Hastings scrambled to put down the rebellion, but a few days later, Singh's men ambushed a detachment of Company troops, slaughtering them in the dense slum of a village outside Banaras. Over one hundred were killed and many more wounded, and it was said the captain's head was carried on a spike through the streets of Banaras in triumph.[508]

Only then did Hastings realise the true magnitude of events. The next day, he was told that Singh's men were planning to attack in the dead of night. With the river blocked and almost every road out of Banaras patrolled, Hastings had only one place to run: the fort of Chunar, just up the river. He packed his belongings, got into a palanquin, and with his guard and attendants, made a run for it. By a stroke of luck, he took one of the only roads Singh's men were not patrolling, having left only hours before the attack.[509]

Singh's men could be heard singing on the road behind him:

> *'Hatee pur howdah ghora pur zeen,*
> *Juldee jao, juldee jao, Warren Hasting!'*
> (Horse, elephant, howdah, set off at full swing,
> Run away, ride away, Warren Hastings!) [510]

Over the next month, Hastings holed up in Chunar Fort and, like moving chess pieces on a board, ordered every available man to Banaras to put down the rebellion.[511]

But it was no easy task. The Company army was in chaos. The soldiers' pay was over four months late. One battalion of sepoys refused to march.[512] Another abandoned their English lieutenant, leaving him to his fate surrounded by rioting villagers.[513] A third pointed their bayonets at their captain's chest and threatened to kill him unless he paid them.[514]

Despite the disarray, Hastings was able to amass enough loyal men to counterattack over the next few weeks. Slowly he squeezed Singh's rebellion, conquering fort after fort and pushing the rebellion farther away from Banaras. By the end of September, a little over a month after it began, he had crushed most of the rebellion, forcing Singh to flee the region. Only a few small pockets of resistance remained.

Hastings celebrated the victory, ordering a triumphant proclamation to be distributed to the people of Banaras. He warned them that resistance was futile, that the Company would always be victorious. That if they submitted, they would be treated well, but if they rebelled, they would receive his wrath.

> How deep has been [Singh's] ingratitude to his benefactor! How unwarrantable his rebellion against the Company! And what must be the resentment of the Company, and of the whole English nation, when they hear that a Rajah, so avowed by them,

attempted the life, and cut off the followers, of that very Governor
General [who had hoped] to recall the Rajah to his duty, and to
get him to assist the Company in the present war; a war very
expensive to the Company ...

   The English, renowned over the earth for their good faith,
have upon that principle towards their friends, as well as from
their bravery against their enemies, became the most powerful
nation in the universe! And we, as their representatives in these
provinces, should be unworthy of our situation, if we were less
ready to support and reward the fidelity of those attached to our
government, than to punish those who attempt to insult it.[515]

Unparalleled Insolence

Be assured the House is on Fire and I really think the Mischief will begin in Oude (Awadh).

– Philip Francis, 2 November 1780.[516]

Late August 1781. Munger, Bihar.

Chief Justice Elijah Impey wiped the sweat off his brow as he looked over this small town on the river Ganges, halfway between Calcutta and Banaras. His sweat glistened and glowed, and came in shining waves like the ocean. It was one of the hottest monsoons he had ever witnessed.[517] The town of Munger felt like a furnace.

He opened a letter from Hastings, pulling it slowly out of the ink quill it had been secretly hidden in.[518] He unrolled it. The first paragraph had been ripped off—perhaps during transport— but the message was clear. There had been a terrible rebellion in Banaras and he would need to stay put.

'The recital is too painful to me for the repetition of it,' Hastings wrote.

'Do not think of coming,' Hastings added.[519]

Impey had been on his way to see Hastings and had spent the first months of what should have been his vacation working to set up his Adalats, *courts*: appointing judges, translators, pundits, muftis, qazis, sheriffs, and setting salaries, punishments, and rules for an entire justice system. His Adalats would be the first and last stop for people seeking justice, and he would be the sole person to hear appeals. The Supreme Court would now be irrelevant for most people in Bengal. Cases that would have gone to it would now go to him alone.

Impey's wrist hurt and his hand shook as he drafted a reply. He wondered what it was that caused his arm to fill with tremors, or that caused the numbness in his hand. His symptoms were spreading, too. His feet tingled when he walked or bent his neck, and he found it difficult to feel objects. Unless he returned to England soon, he feared he would join his many colleagues in the grave.[520]

He had brought his doctor, his servants, and his sixteen-man personal guard with him. He had also brought his family. They, too, had suffered, and that made him think about going home, if not for himself, then for them. His wife, Mary, was often so sick she was bedridden and unable to sit up. She had four children in seven years in India and just had a miscarriage. His daughter, Marian, had constant fevers and diarrhoea and was often close to death.[521] He worried another year in India might kill them.

Yet he had come so far. He always knew he would return to England eventually, but not yet. Not as long as he had his Adalats. He had finally achieved the ambitions he had so long desired. The extra salary helped cover costs like sending some of his children to school in England, munshis to teach him and his wife Indian history, religions and languages, and an exotic bird, animal, and art and curio collection, amounting to over 300 paintings by local artists.[522] His lifestyle came at a heavy cost, but the Sadr Diwani Adalat helped cover it.

Impey had become so much happier ever since the appointment. He no longer had to worry about checking the Company's oppressions now that he was working for it. 'I have the happiness to acquaint you that Harmony is perpetually restored between the Court and the Governor-General and Council,' he wrote to his brother.[523]

When he learned that Parliament was considering legislation to limit the Supreme Court's jurisdiction to the city of Calcutta and drastically reduce its power, he remarked that the legislation would have upset him in the past but now it meant little to him. If anything, it would send more cases to his Sadr Diwani Adalat.

'I am perfectly indifferent with regard to the [Supreme] Court. If the powers of it are thought inconvenient ... Let them with all my heart abolish them. Let them annihilate my power, if they do not injure my reputation,' he wrote.[524] The Supreme Court would be eviscerated, but his own power would increase.

Over the last year he had lobbied politicians in London to let him keep his appointment, starting with close friends like John Dunning and Sir Richard Sutton, lawyers he had met when he was a barrister in England and who were now members of Parliament.

He needed their support. He knew many might say his appointment was illegal, but he was confident most would understand that he was going to make the Company better. 'If I have the support which I am promised, I shall be able to convert these Courts, which from the ignorance and corruption of those who have presided in them have been the worst oppressions to the natives,' he wrote.[525]

He hoped his letters would reach home before Francis could do damage, reminding his friends that his appointment was about public service, not private profit. 'As this met with some opposition from Mr Francis, I think it not improbable that it may be a matter of discussion in England. I request you, to use your influence to support me on it. I do solemnly assure that public benefit has been my main inducement,' he wrote.[526]

He waited for his first letters to have their intended effect before he sent a second round, this time to important members of government in England, members he was less familiar with. He admitted that he had received a salary for the Adalat, but he was convinced they would see that his appointment merited it. Also, if they did not like it, he'd be happy to return the salary. 'If you or any other of His Majesty's Ministers intimate to me, that it is improper, I sh'd return it,' he wrote to the Prime Minister.[527]

Yet he realised that all his hard work convincing politicians in London would come to naught if he did not address Hicky's libels. Hicky's slanders would certainly reach powerful people in England.

He set down to explain his actions. He began writing a massive, twenty-four-page letter about Hicky's trials, his appointment, and

Singh's rebellion. He wrote one draft and then another, dividing and subdividing it into different articles.

Finally he was ready. He sent multiple editions to his friends and to members of government in England.

As he looked down at the black ink scrawled across the page, he wondered if others would be able to read his words. His writing looked like the scribbles on the back of a notebook. But it would have to do.

A weekly paper containing the most scurrilous abuse has been published in Calcutta and as the most inflammatory libels had been published in it reflective to the Governor or his measures, and actually leading to mutiny and sedition: He was advised not by me tho' I think he did right to prosecute. Hicky the printer immediately placed armed sepoys at his door as public Centinels ... The under sheriff frequently applied to me ... that Hicky had armed Sepoys at his house, that he feared force if he executed the Process, and desired to know if he should be justified in taking sepoys with him. I told him he ought to attempt to execute it by his own officers, but if he was opposed he might apply to those who could give him assistance, that the Court could not. He afterwards acquainted me that Hicky himself had come out with a drawn sword ...

Before the trials, the abuse against Mr Hastings vis his paper was more virulent than ever. The judges, the Council, the attorney for the prosecution, the grand jury ... were most grossly abused and on the morning of the trial and the first indictment, printed hand Bills were delivered at the door of the Court House containing the similar abuse and endeavoring to influence the petit jury by promises of popularity if they found a verdict for the Defendant, and by threats of public odium if they found for the Prosecution. I thought the best way to prevent the publication of libel would be to let the judgments hang over during the long vacation, or to intimate to him that his conduct during that time might possibly induce his Prosecution to press a severe or acquiesce in a mild sentence ...

During the trials he behaved with unparalleled insolence and contumacy. He read a most impudent libel in his own defense. This Hicky was a retuchier of Sargent Davy. He went once round the Circuit with him as his Clerk [and was] called the Captain, having belonged to a man of war. He is ignorant and illiterate but supported by a party [loyal] to Mr Francis ...

Hicky in addressing me had stated me Chief Justice of the Supreme Court and Judge of the S.D.A. He occasioned me to state that the Gov. Gen'l and Council requested me to accept the office, my reasons for accepting it, and what I had done relative to the Salary. Hicky's trials were taken down, Mr Hastings wishing they should be printed. The Printing has been deferred because Judgment is not yet passed. The trials are locked in my desk in Calcutta. If I could have yet sent them I would have sent them ...[528]

He wondered why he bore the brunt of Hicky's vitriol. Hastings had given his fellow judge, Chambers, a similar appointment only two months ago, appointing Chambers the judge of Chinsurah, a largely ceremonial position that paid Rs 3,000 a month.[529] Moreover, Chambers was also police commissioner and could pay himself for overseeing the Bye-Law.

Impey thought the reason he was the only one ridiculed was because of personal politics. Chambers and Francis had once been friends and he believed many of Hicky's writers had been Francis' supporters.

I cannot help observing it is very peculiar that I alone am arraigned for acts of the Court done in common with the other judges, that with relative to the acceptance of offices. Sir R. Chambers should not be mentioned who is appointed in the Dutch war Chief Judge of Chinsurah, and tho Sir Robert has taken a more active role in the Ordinance, by getting himself appointed (for he solicited it) a Commissioner ... yet I alone am accused concerning it. The pointing out me in particular makes that this comes from a party to which I have ever been obnoxious.[530]

To his brother and his most select friends, he added one piece of information that he wrote to no one else. He calculated his net worth at £40,000 and then mentioned that at some point after Hicky's trials, Hastings had promised to buy him a seat in Parliament when he returned to England.[531] He believed his fortune and a seat in Parliament would make him comfortable when he returned.

'I believe Mr H will not remain more than a year after me; he has a desire that we shall both be in Parliament and for that purpose furnished me with draft to the amount of £10,000 on his attorneys for the purpose of purchasing two seats, one for me, to take place the latter end of the Summer 1783, and for himself the latter end of the summer 1784,' he wrote.[532]

While in Munger, waiting for Singh's rebellion to be crushed, Impey sent a letter to Judge Hyde, back in Calcutta, about Hicky's punishment. Given that the Court had declared Hicky in contempt for insolent behaviour at the trials, Impey suggested a total of nineteen months in jail and Rs 2,500 in fines, or twenty-four months in jail and no fine if Hicky filed as a pauper.

> Munger, September 20,
> I remain here ... Nothing occurs to me as material in the Court except Hicky's business ... what think you, if his paper (which I have not seen) should not have been offensive since the trial, of three months' imprisonment for the recent contempts, six months for each of the Governor's indictments and four for the Padre's, with a fine of 1000 rupees for each of the Governor's, and 500 for the Padre's, if he lays no affidavit to prove his poverty before the Court, and if he does, to add two months imprisonment for each of the Governor's and one for the Padre's, or shall we remit the contempts?[533]

On October 26 Impey arrived in Banaras. Hastings showed him that he was writing a short book, which he called a 'narrative', justifying his house arrest of Singh. Impey suggested that the narrative alone would not be enough to justify Hastings' actions if they came under scrutiny in England. He also offered to collect affidavits from witnesses to authenticate that it was necessary to suppress Singh.[534]

Impey then travelled to Lucknow, the capital of Awadh. Hastings suspected that the mother and grandmother of the Nawab—the 'Begums of Awadh'—had supported Singh's rebellion, recruiting troops, encouraging sepoys to desert, and supposedly even promising rewards for the heads of any Europeans.

Hastings told Impey to have the Company Resident seize the

Begums' wealth and property as punishment for supporting Singh. If Impey could get the Nawab to agree to seize his mother and grandmother's jewels and possessions, so much the better. If not, the Resident was to seize the treasure himself.

'He wishes it to be done immediately,' Impey wrote to the Resident.[535]

Impey travelled night and day to get to Lucknow, taking with him only his doctor and three or four servants. When he arrived, he got into the Resident's chariot, carrying with him Hastings' instructions.

He spent the next few days collecting testimony that the Begums had supported Singh's rebellion. In all, he collected forty-three affidavits from British residents, Indian officials, and Company soldiers certifying that Singh had rebelled and that the Begums had supported him.[536]

Under the instructions Impey carried, the Company army imprisoned the Begums' eunuchs, shackling and torturing them to reveal the location of the treasure, estimated to amount to Rs 55 lakh.

Hastings then used the treasure to pay his troops, as Impey returned to Banaras and from there to Calcutta.[537]

A Darker Turn

[Hastings] writes that he does not despair of procuring a GOOD PEACE *before he is much older. Procure a good peace Ha! ha! ha! what would he be at? why then go to war!*

– James Augustus Hicky, *Hicky's Bengal Gazette*, 24 November 1781.[538]

1.20 p.m., Monday, 29 October 1781.
Supreme Court House.

Only Judge Chambers and Judge Hyde were present when Hicky was dragged from jail to hear his sentencing.

Chambers read his sentence. Following the instructions in Impey's letter, he pronounced that Hicky would serve twelve months in jail, pay Rs 2,500 in fines—not to mention an unnamed sum in court fees—and be imprisoned until the fines were paid. Perhaps because of their leniency, Chambers and Hyde had settled on this lesser sentence, and did not increase Hicky's punishment for his contempts of Court.[539]

Hicky was dragged out of jail again four days later for more bad news. Hastings would be suing him again, next term, for the article calling Hastings, Clive's 'miserable successor', the same article he had been found not guilty on.

Hicky said he was not guilty and that he had never published a libel, before being dragged back to jail.[540]

Imprisonment did not stop Hicky, and he somehow managed to continue printing his newspaper from jail. He continued to defend the freedom of the Press, but his tone turned darker, his writing increasingly bitter, and his mood more melancholy.[541]

Over three issues, he reprinted selections from the famous *Cato Letters,* written from 1720 to 1723, which condemned the corruption of the British prime minister at the time, and were later widely quoted by American revolutionaries arguing for liberty. One of the letters, titled 'The Right and Capacity of the People to Judge of Government', traced the history and eventual downfall of Greece and Rome, arguing that Greek Democracy and the Roman Republic declined because they were taken over by despots. 'What are Greece and Italy now?' it asked rhetorically. 'Rome has in it a herd of Pamper'd Monks and a few starving lay Inhabitants', while Greeks had become 'contemptible slaves Kept under Ignorance, Chains, and Vileness' by a 'Turkish Monarch'.[542]

Hicky reprinted this letter to warn against tyranny, and argue that it was the cause of the decline of civilisation. Like ancient Rome and Greece, if British India continued to be ruled by despots, then it, too, would decline and fall.

His next article implied that it was already too late for the Company to be redeemed.

He revealed the forgery Clive had committed to help the Company win victory over the Nawab of Bengal—the forgery that was the foundation of British rule. The article compared Clive to Nanda Kumar. Their crimes were the same, yet Clive returned to England a war hero while Nanda Kumar was hanged. The only difference was that Clive was a Company servant while Nanda Kumar was an Indian. Hicky's act of printing this article implied that he wanted people to know that the British had no special right to rule India; their rule was based on nothing but military might and cold steel.

We first committed a successful forgery on a native of Bengal, and gloried in it, though it occasioned his death. Soon after ... a native of the Country, who knew nothing of English laws, is hanged for a crime which we had triumphed in committing. Clive was made a Peer in England though he committed in Bengal the same crime, for which we hanged Nundocomar.[543]

Many in Calcutta must have been shocked to see Hicky publicly blemish Clive's name and question the legitimacy of Company rule. But Hicky did not stop there.

His correspondents accused Hastings of violating the Company's contract with Raja Chait Singh, in which the Company had promised Singh that he would maintain his independence, his tribute would never increase, and no extra demands would ever be made of him. Hastings' demands for extra tribute, and Singh's subsequent arrest, one correspondent wrote, shows 'us how much further we are capable of going in the roads of Rapacity and extortion.'[544] Hicky's writers believed that Hastings' actions amounted to an illegal takeover of what once had been an independent nation.

His correspondents went so far as to sympathise with Singh, explaining that Singh was right to rebel. They wrote that Singh feared for the independence of Banaras and worried that Europeans wanted to control every political office, even ones with the 'smallest profit'.[545] One wrote that the Company was like a harsh master and that Singh, 'soon experienced the unremitting severity of a master whose soul ne'er knew the generous godlike purpose of forgiving'. Would it be surprising then, if Hastings' policies had 'alienated his affections from our Government?'[546]

Hicky's writers also ridiculed their fellow Britishers for jumping into boats and sailing away, abandoning their Indian servants to rebels who would kill them.[547] They claimed this flight was a shameful scene of cowardice. 'What a spectacle,' one wrote.[548] 'Is *this*, Sir, the manner in which we support our friends?' another asked.[549]

One of his correspondents was one of those who had abandoned his servants, and was ashamed of his actions. 'No Europeans ever before made themselves look so little in the eyes of the Natives as we did ... I was ashamed for several days after to look any of them in the face,' his correspondent wrote.[550] His shame, and the shame of those like him, was compounded when they realised what they thought was Singh's army was actually a nearby wedding celebration that had gotten out of hand. The fire from a few straw huts had been magnified into the approach of Singh's rebels.

While Hicky's contributors criticised those Britishers who abandoned their servants, they praised those Indians who helped the British flee even at the peril of their own lives. One wrote that this help was a 'Striking instance of the natural Gentleness of these people'.[551] By describing the help Indian servants gave the British, Hicky implied that Indians were at least as honourable as they themselves were.

If Hicky portrayed Indians as Samaritans and the British as cowards, then the greatest coward in his eyes was Hastings, who he mocked for holing up in Chunar Fort while Banaras descended into chaos. He thought it a disgrace that Hastings and Impey were writing a 'narrative' to justify their actions.

> The [Governor] has not yet thought it safe to venture out of *Chunar Fort*—Alas! How the proofs of our publick faith, wisdom, and strength *thicken* upon us, Good God! That we should be so degraded. All He and His Colleague now want is to *immortalize* their Names, they have just honesty enough to tell the truth to the English Nation—which, God knows the *flimsy* and *elaborate Authenticated Narrative* given.[552]

Through the rebellion, Hicky continued to see himself as the subalterns' voice, and continued to publish subalterns' grievances. Many complained that they had not been paid for months while they saw blatant corruption around them. 'We daily hear of the ... Treasury being full; while we are going on four months in arrears ... we are starving,' one wrote.[553] 'Our Soldiers have not Bread to Eat ... their commanding Officers have reason every hour to apprehend a general Mutiny,' another added.[554]

They expressed their frustration that Hastings' acolytes cared more about their pockets than the army's integrity. One opined that the military had a fund of Rs 10 lakh for emergency situations, but this had been exhausted by largesse and nepotism.[555] One particular army paymaster was rumoured to have drawn off Rs 125,000 for himself. Many subalterns believed corruption was the reason their pay was so late. 'Us poor Lobsters send down our bills of arrears to the Commissary Gen.' only to have them come back months later 'with that cursed red Ink *disallowed*,' one wrote.[556]

It was a painful irony to subalterns that while they suffered, some were making off with the fortunes of a lifetime.

These complaints led Hicky into dangerous territory. Amid the chaos, subalterns used his newspaper to question their loyalty to the Company. 'An Officer … must serve at least Eighteen or Twenty Years, encountering Poverty, and a dreadful climate … what is the reward for so long a service?' one asked rhetorically.[557] Another suggested that unless Hastings paid them, they would not respect him. 'You will then (and not till then) experience the Happiness … of being universally Honour'd Respected and Beloved,' he threatened.[558]

When the army seized Singh's last fort of Bija Ghur, Hicky reported that the soldiers quickly divided the prize money between themselves because they feared Hastings would take it from them, like in the Rohilla War. He noted they were not going to let plunder slip out of their hands again, reporting that the soldiers were shouting, 'The Rohillah prize money prettily shroffed and paid.'[559]

One of his writers wrote that Hastings had actually allowed the soldiers to take the plunder, but then had rescinded that permission when it became known that the prize money amounted to Rs 50 lakh, more than seven times the Rohilla War prize money.[560] Hicky insinuated that the reason Hastings wanted the money back was for new conquests.

> We hear that the [Governor] having in all his Actions no other object in view but the interest of the public, has actually ordered the Captors of Bija Ghur to refund every Rup. of the prize Money so honourably and dearly earned by them, and that he means to Employ It in new Conquests on the Bundlecund Country.—An illustrious Traffic!

Perhaps Hicky's most vicious insult was when one of his correspondents accused Hastings' top commander in Banaras, Lt Colonel William Blair, of dishonourable behaviour. His correspondent claimed Blair had charged Hastings for food and lodging while at Chunar Fort. It was ungentlemanly to give a superior a bill like a tavern-keeper. The supposed bill also insinuated that Hastings' men were drunk and riotous:

The [Hon. Warren Hastings] Esq; G—r G—l ...

To Dieting himself—and Family for 33 days, Feeding Elephants, Camels, Horses, and Bullocks &c. &c. &c. Breaking of Tables, Chairs, Couches, Teapoys, Shades, Decanters, Bottles, and Glasses, &c. &c. &c.

Sicca Rupees 42,000 ...

(Signed) William [Blair]

Lt. Col. Commanding at Chunar.[561]

Wednesday, 16 January 1782, On the river below Buxar, near Banaras.

The cogs of the Company's wheels began to move when this article reached Hastings. Hastings immediately wrote back to his Council in Calcutta.

'I was this morning presented with the Copy of an infamous Libel,' he wrote, ordering them to find Hicky's source and to devise, 'some means of checking a practice so pernicious to the peace of the Community and to the character of every Individual in it.'[562]

It was clear that Hicky was not going to mollify his writing, regardless of whatever actions Hastings took. The only way to prevent Hicky from printing such libels would be to shut his press entirely.

In early 1782, Hastings returned to Calcutta intending to do just that.

Double Jeopardy

*All that know me in the Settlement also know that I am a
very poor Man, not worth a Rupee.*

– James Augustus Hicky to Elijah Impey, 19 June 1781.[563]

Saturday, 12 January 1782.
Supreme Court House.

The Supreme Court began proceedings against Hicky in earnest.
Hastings was now suing Hicky again, on the first article that
Hicky had been found not guilty on.

It did not matter that Hicky had been declared not guilty of
libel for the article calling Hastings, Clive's 'miserable successor'.
Hastings was now suing him in a civil court, not a criminal court.
Where a criminal suit was designed to find someone guilty of a
crime, a civil suit was designed to get money from someone. Thus,
according to British law, Hastings could sue Hicky twice.

Hicky had had the right to a jury before. He had no such right
in a civil suit. His fate would be decided by the judges alone.

Faced with certain defeat, Hicky tried to delay. He
simultaneously asked for a copy of his trial from over the summer,
asked to subpoena an impossible list of witnesses, including
Hastings himself and many army officers, and claimed he could
not find a single lawyer to represent him, saying they were all
either hired by Hastings, or were too intimidated.[564]

Impey refused all Hicky's requests.

'Mr Hicky knows very well that this is not the proper mode
of application. What purpose he may suppose it may answer to

endeavour to raise a clamour I do not know, but that seems to be the intention of this paper,' Impey said.

Next week, Hicky followed with a second claim that he needed to delay his trial because he was sick and had to go to the hammams, the public baths, for his health.

But the judges did not believe him. They sent the sheriff to bring him from jail into court.

He came and did not appear to be ill.

Impey told him that there were two lawyers willing to represent him, as long as he would not interrupt them in trial.[565] Impey also said he could delay his trial if he wanted, as long as he wrote an affidavit explaining why.

Hicky began to write an affidavit, but when he learned that delaying his trial would cost ten gold mohurs—about Rs 160—he said he could not afford it.

'If you can not afford to pay costs, you must make a proper affidavit to be admitted a pauper,' Impey said.

'I would rather the case should now go on,' Hicky said, too proud to plead as a pauper.

Hicky gave his own defence.

He said that he did not mean malice.

'If there had been papers in praise of Mr Hastings or of another certain gentleman in the settlement, I should have inserted them with great pleasure,' he said.

He argued that article calling Hastings Clive's 'miserable successor' was not a libel at all. It was the truth because it had correctly prophesied that sending Pearse's detachment would encourage Indians to rise up and revolt. Hastings' incompetence was the reason the Company's reputation had sunk in 'the opinion of all the native Powers' and why Chait Singh had rebelled.

'The prophecy was proved true, in the massacre at Banaras,' he said.

After he finished, Impey summed up the case. Impey said it was no longer a matter of whether he was guilty but whether Hastings was entitled to damages.

'The only two questions in this case are whether the paper is a libel on Mr Hastings and whether Hicky published it. Mr Hicky is not charged with being the author, nor with knowing who the author is,' Impey said.

As quick as a gavel strike, the judges ruled for Hastings, and ordered Hicky to be dragged back to jail.

The next day the judges announced that Hicky would owe Hastings Rs 5,000 in damages and that these damages would be added to his previous fines. He would also be imprisoned until he could repay them.

Impey said they made his punishment severe because he had libelled an important person. Hastings was entitled to more damages than an average person.

'A libel on a mean person is not the same injury to him as on a person in an high office,' he said.[566]

Still, Hicky did not give up. Just like his trials over the summer, he condemned Hastings and others for corruption and tyranny. He again printed a playbill—by an anonymous contributor—called the 'Congress at Sooksagur' named after Hastings' favourite vacation spot, Sukh Sagar, the *Sea of Delight*, upriver of Calcutta.[567]

In the play, Hastings took the lead as the 'Dictator' and as 'Sir Francis Wronghead', a character in an English play, *The Provoked Husband*, known as an incompetent country gentleman over his head in politics.[568]

Impey was cast as Hastings' tool, a travelling justice taking affidavits to justify anything Hastings wanted. Chambers was a 'Fiscal', a Dutch legal officer—a reference to Hastings' appointing him judge of Chinsurah (which had been a Dutch territory for a while)—too cowardly to take his hands out from under his shirt. Hyde, the only uncorrupted judge, was cast as 'No body', irrelevant and ignored.

Hastings' fellow councilmen also featured. Edward Wheler, who once opposed Hastings along with Francis, featured as 'Ned Silent', a spineless former Francis partisan. The newly-arrived John Macpherson was portrayed as 'Thane', an unquestioningly loyal Scottish lord who would do any duty for his liege. Army contractor Charles Croftes also featured as the lethargic Somnus, the Roman God of sleep, whose profits from his contract somehow vanished.

A special place was reserved for Kiernander, who was cast both as a chimney sweep and as the servile Vicar of Bray, an infamous English priest who served during the reigns of four monarchs and was said to have changed his religion from Catholic, Protestant, Catholic, and back to Protestant again to stay in office. Like a soulless Swiss mercenary, Kiernander contorted and cast away his principles for money. Kiernander was also shown with a consort, Messalina, the wife of the Roman Emperor Claudius, notorious for her sexuality. But due to old age and the decline of his 'abilities', she was looking elsewhere to satiate her desires.

Each character sang a song depicting their position. Hastings starred twice, singing how 'war was his pleasure' and how he was 'weather beaten and shattered', overwhelmed by his responsibilities. Impey sang about how the law was made for little except personal gain, while Kiernander offered his services to do any dirty work for his master, Hastings.

The Congress at Sooksagur

Dictator [Hastings]	In the character of Sir Francis Wronghead crying out, we are on a forlorn hope and must drive on neck or nothing.
Old *** [Impey]	A travelling justice of the peace taking affidavits gratis, with the following motto on his breast, '*Datur pessimo*', [Giver of wickedness] and 'all was false and hollow'.
Ned Silent [Edward Wheler]	A windmill; he wore the habit in which he recanted the errors of the St Franciscan faith: he had a label on his breast, on which was inscribed: 'Good tho' late, if sincere, but seldom sincere when so late'. ...
Thane [John Macpherson]	Appeared in a Highland dress thrumming on the bag pipe. He was overheard whispering to the Dictator, 'Keep all secret, mon, and I'll help thee oot.' ...

Vicar of Bray [Kiernander]	A *Chimney Sweeper*—He came up to the *Dictator* crying *Sweep ho!*—God bless your Honour.—you know I can do great deal of dirty work.—Pray employ me on all Occasions; –particularly in swearing down the printer.—It was remarkable that a mask in the Character of *Messalina* shewed great contempt for her old favourite *sweep*—owing, it is supposed, to the *decline of his abilities*.
Viner [Chambers]	Having lost his own character by his acceptance of a place in May last, came into the room with his hands under his shirt in that of a Fiscal.
Justice Balance [Hyde]	In the character of No body.
Charley Bullock [Charles Croftes]	In the character of Somnus which sat as easy on him as his three lucrative Offices and *losing* contract ...[569]

List of the Performers with the several Songs they Sung

Songs	Performers
Know then war's my pleasure.	By Sir F. Wronghead. [Hastings]
How I am Weather-beaten and shatter'd	Ditto [Hastings]
Gold from Law can take out the sting	By Poolbundy. [Impey]
The Laws were made for the little ...	Ditto [Impey]
'Had I a soul for treach'ry fram'd I ne'er could injure you; For though your Rank no service claim'd Your power would make me true.'	Vicar of Bray [Kiernander]
'Point d'argent point de Suisse.' [No money, no Swiss][570]	Ditto [Kiernander]

Thursday, March 7, Supreme Court House

After this masquerade, Hastings brought four more legal actions against Hicky.

Still in jail, in debt, and unable to bear the costs of his trials any longer, Hicky swallowed his pride and filed as a pauper. He hoped that this would also protect his printing press. British law allowed paupers to keep the implements of their profession because they were seen as the only way the poor could pay back their fines.

The judges permitted his plea. It was a joyous moment. His types and press would be safe. It seemed like he could keep printing his newspaper from jail and defending the right to free speech indefinitely.

> Citizens and fellow Subjects permit me to Address you this day with heart-felt Joy, and lay before you the following lines.
>
> The Hon'ble the Lords the Kings Judges of the Supreme Court ... Having from Mr James Augustus Hicky's Circumstance, been humanely inclined to admit him this 7th Day of March 1782 to plead in *Forma Pauperis* in the defending of four fresh Actions brought against him this Term at the suit of Warren Hastings Esq ...
>
> Every British Subject and every lover of his Country I hope will join with me this day in grateful acknowledgements ... to the Hon'ble the Lords the Kings Judges ... for having crushed and nipp'd in the bud a base and vile attempt made by Mr Davies—to violate and break thro' the Laws of their Royal Sovereign with intent to answer the base and vile purposes (of a few) to ruin and oppress his Majesty's most Loyal Subjects in this distant part of the world.
>
> Thus by protecting the Types, they have protected the Liberty of the subject, and the Liberty of the Press
>
> James Augustus Hicky
>
> Typographer.[571]

After this, Hastings brought yet two more legal actions against Hicky. It seemed unlikely that he would ever leave jail.

On March 23, he printed a desperate address to the public. He had already been confined for nine long months, separated from his family and friends. He promised to continue printing no matter what the future held, no matter what Hastings would do.

To the Public.

A scene of continued tyranny and oppression for near two years having reduced Mr Hicky very much in his circumstances involved him more in debt and [reduced] his business very considerably, tho' he is still immured in a jail where he has been these nine long months separated from his family and friends, at the suit of Warren Hastings, Esq., and where he still expects to remain, as the said W. H. has brought no less than six fresh actions against him this term. Mr Hicky has bore those afflictions as becometh Man and a Christian, and will still bear them with resignation and fortitude ...[572]

The next week, with no explanation, the judges reversed their decision to protect his types. Impey ordered the sheriff to seize his printing press and his types. The sheriff raided his home and shop, taking his furniture, press, types, dining ware, clothes, and even his family letters. Everything Hicky owned was gone in an instant.

Two weeks later, all his belongings went up for auction.[573] The Company's printer bought everything he owned for one sixteenth its value.[574]

Hicky's Bengal Gazette was no more.

Hicky had been silenced. Yet his case and his complaints, in his own newspaper, would be conveyed to the foot of the throne of Great Britain.

Back to Britain

Shall I tamely submit to the yoke of slavery, and wanton oppression, no my Case and complaints, in my own Newspaper shall be convey'd to the foot of the throne of Great Britain.

– James Augustus Hicky, *Hicky's Bengal Gazette*, 25 November 1780.[575]

Midnight, Friday, 19 October 1781. Off the coast of Dover, England.[576]

Philip Francis stared longingly at the black coastline of England, the fresh ocean breeze on his face, wondering what to do next.

It had been a long, lonely, dangerous journey home. He had only learned at the last moment that his mistress had decided to take a different ship. To add to his discomfort, his ship, the *Fox*, had been stopped by news that Spain had joined the war against Great Britain. A journey that had once been dangerous had become hopeless without a convoy home. He had waited four boring months on the windswept island of St Helena before returning to England.

He was convinced the Company was tottering on the edge. Its economy was ruined, its treasury was empty, and its wars were never ending. 'My Lord, India is on the Verge of Destruction,' he wrote to the prime minister.[577] With Hastings in control of the Company, he was convinced there was nothing to stop it from being run into the ground.

But he had not given up. If he could no longer fight Hastings in India, he would fight him in England. 'If, by one gallant Exertion more, I can do a public service, I have still Newes enough left to make the attempt. If not, I will take care at least to finish my part handsomely, and to be consistent to the last; to gather up my Robe and fall with Decorum,' he wrote.[578] He saw it as his mission, his one last duty to the nation, to expose Hastings, and he would do this by writing for the newspapers in England, and for Hicky.

His strategy was to use the Press to turn public opinion so far against Hastings that Parliament would be compelled to do something. He wrote pamphlets and articles, essays and letters, all against Hastings.[579] Most of his articles were anonymous, making it difficult to track down what he actually wrote. But some are known to be by him. In one article, he accused Hastings of disobeying the Company's directors' orders with 'impunity'.[580] He even paid a ghostwriter to write a book accusing Hastings of starting the Rohilla War because he had been bribed. The book promised that Hastings and his coterie would be judged by history. 'Time will prove ... that their cobweb pretences will vanish like smoke before the sunshine of right and reason,' it read.[581]

Anonymity had another benefit. It gave the appearance he was widely supported. In letters to friends in India, he wrote vaguely that 'the press groans under an Infinity of publications', making no mention he was a reason the press groaned. He pretended he had nothing to do with the ghostwritten book. 'In answer to a thousand lies,' he wrote to Council Member Edward Wheeler, 'I declare to you, most solemnly, that I never did employ or authorise him, directly or indirectly, to say or to do anything for me.' Secretly, he paid over £1,000 of his own money to fund the ghostwriter.[582] It was all part of his grand strategy to flood the Press while denying ever being involved.

And so, he also sent information to Hicky, anonymously. He gave instructions to his companions in India to publish articles on his behalf. 'I will endeavour to send you some Pamphlets by the Ships,' he wrote to one friend.[583] 'Pray forward this Intelligence to George Shee with the Newspaper and Pamphlets' he wrote to another.[584] 'I shall send you all the Pamphlets I can pick up about India Affairs,' he wrote to a third.[585]

In some cases he had to explicitly say that information was *not* to be sent to Hicky. In one letter, he mentioned some personal details of meetings with politicians. He told the Company's Advocate General, and his ally, Sir John Day, not to tell Hicky of his actions. 'Observe that this letter is only for the private *ear* of Lady Day and yourself (you understood Irish, and can explain the expression), and not to be published by Hickey,' he wrote.[586]

To his most trusted friends, Gerard Ducarel and Edward Hay, he wrote his instructions in cipher. In one letter, he had some secrets to pass along, possibly to Hicky. 'Let it be known to our friend,' he wrote, and then added a string of numbers, '117. 38. 48. 19. 10. 75. 100. 76. 83. 60.'[587] These numbers were his secret code, and men like Ducarel and Hay—who was the secretary for Hastings' Supreme Council and possibly one of Hicky's sources— were like his secret agents. Little did he know that *Hicky's Gazette* would be long gone by the time any of his writing reached India.

Using his leverage as a former Supreme Council member, he began lobbying politicians. Above all, he met with the Member of Parliament whose committee was responsible for investigating the Company, Edmund Burke.[588]

On 6 December 1781, Burke's Committee called him to testify for an upcoming report they were writing on Hastings' Supreme Council and the Supreme Court. Francis answered many questions, but he focused his testimony on Hastings' appointment of Impey to the Sadr Diwani Adalat, which he considered the most obvious example of their corruption. He said he had 'not a doubt upon his mind that the appointment was illegal'. 'A lucrative office, revocable at pleasure, creates dependence, and can create nothing else,' he said.[589]

After he finished his testimony, he was convinced he was making progress. There might even be enough political will to recall Impey.

'Depend upon it that 39 [Impey] is a condemned man,' he wrote to a friend.[590] 'The Chief Justice, as far as I can perceive, stands Extremely ill in all Quarters. It is not very unlikely that the House of Commons may address the King to remove him, and that perhaps may not be the End of his Punishment,' he wrote to another.[591] To a third, he added that Burke's upcoming report, 'on the Purchase and Sale of Sir E. I. will be as black as ink can make it.'[592]

He was delighted when Burke's first report came out. It was every thing he hoped for, and was a stunning indictment of Hastings and Impey, accusing them of gross corruption and collusion.[593] It claimed they had 'mutually abandoned their Principles,' made a 'mockery' of justice and 'dissolved' all trust in government. It predicted that Impey's appointment would result in more tyranny and oppression as people were forced to rely on Impey alone for justice. Finally, it recommended that Impey be recalled to England to answer for his 'Abuse of Office'.[594]

A few days after the report came out, Francis chanced upon Hastings' representative, Major John Scott, in a bookshop in London. He shook Scott's hand, as if greeting an old friend, gleefully smiling because he was winning the war of words against Hastings.

'Well Major, have you done writing of me yet in the Papers?' he asked.

'Yes Sir, if you have done writing at Mr Hastings, not otherwise,' Scott said.

Francis said he would write no more, but he did not mean it at all.[595]

He was confident that this was just the beginning of inquiries into the Company's corruption. 'If there be faith in men, these inquiries will go to every thing done in Bengal ... if there be justice on earth, some criminals will be punished,' he wrote.[596] 'It cannot be very long before I see the final effect of my endeavours,' he wrote to a second.[597] 'There is no power in this Country [that] can save Mr Hastings,' he added to a third.[598]

As winter turned to spring, he grew closer to Burke, bringing notes and papers for Burke to read. He showed Burke all the documents he had on Hastings, from the Rohilla War, the Poolbundy contract, Impey's Sadr Diwani Adalat appointment, to the army contract and more. He became the star source for Burke's Committee. 'I have undertaken a vast Task; but with your assistance I may get through it,' Burke wrote to him.[599]

Success came quickly. In May, the House of Commons passed resolutions to recall both Impey and Hastings to England.

But not at all went to plan. While no one objected to Impey's recall, Hastings' allies in the Company's government called an emergency meeting and refused to accept the House of Commons' recall, saying Parliament did not have this authority over the Company. Then, before anything more could be done, the Prime Minister died. Political events were also on Hastings' side. Disrupted by defeat in the American Revolutionary War, England underwent five different prime ministers in two years.[600] There was not enough stability to continue proceedings against Hastings, even had there been enough political will.

Francis and Burke prepared their materials as best they could. Burke outlined the charges while Francis filled in the details. 'I have sent you the first scene of the first act; the Rohilla War. You will make it what it ought to be,' Burke wrote to Francis.[601]

Driven by their desire to see Hastings impeached and determined to be on the right side of history, they pursued their goal regardless of politics. 'My business is not to consider what will convict Mr Hastings, (a thing we all know to be impracticable) but what will acquit and justify myself to those few persons and to those distant times which may take a concern in these affairs,' Burke wrote to Francis.[602]

Even if it took a while, retribution was coming.

His Lying Tongue

One day or other, after so many dark clouds, I hope the Sun will shine clear again.

– Johann Zacharias Kiernander to Friedrich Wilhelm Pasche. 5 February 1782. [603]

Thursday, 20 June 1782, The Mission

Kiernander looked out from the foggy brightness of his church windows. In his hands was his newly printed book, *The Tryal and Conviction of James Augustus Hicky.*

Everything he had gained, everything he had done over forty-two years—twenty of those in Calcutta—was now in question because of Hicky. His book would answer those questions.

Through dedication and perseverance, he made his Mission, his school, and his business flourish. He had bridged cultures, endured hardships, and survived war and privation. He had built buildings and acted as an investment manager. He had even converted five Catholic priests to Protestantism and shepherded a 300-strong congregation.[604] He had led and guided his Mission even as his assistants fell sick and died. He had done much of this alone, struggling to establish something from nothing.

But all this was under attack.

Hicky had dragged his reputation through the streets of Calcutta as if carrying him in a cart of infamy for the whole world to see.

He had thought he had cleared his name by suing Hicky. He now realised that his trial was only the start. The rumours about him had expanded and multiplied without end: that he was Hastings' tool, that he had been motivated by lucre and avarice to sell sanctified types, that he had stolen from the orphan fund, that he had embezzled Griffin's legacy.

He now realised that though Hicky's newspaper was gone, the allegations remained. He was saddened and surprised that many still believed the lies that Diemer fed Hicky.

'I must for some time suffer much more from Diemer's false Tongue than any one can imagine: his bad and most malicious slanders here being of the greatest Prejudice to the Mission; the total Ruin of which, he studies with all his ability in laying,' he wrote.[605]

The lies had taken an emotional and financial toll on him. As was standard practice for the time, the Supreme Court had charged him fees to sue Hicky. All he had gotten was the satisfaction of seeing Hicky in jail, while Diemer, the true author, walked free.

'For this Lawsuit I have paid the Lawyers' Bills with 742 Sicca Rupees. The fine of 500 Rupees from Hicky, the King received. I got nothing. Thus innocence must suffer a double punishment. First it must suffer Reproach and Infamy, and Secondly it must pay very dear for a very faint and insufficient Protection. And the Author who is most guilty, more than the Printer, escapes with impunity,' he wrote.[606]

But now he thought he had found the end to all his suffering. His book would answer them all.

It was small, only a short thirty pages, but he saw it as the ultimate proof of his innocence and his great defense against the Devil and the Devil's instrument: Diemer.

'We are surrounded on all sides with Devils and their instruments, how can we expect Peace with them?' he wrote in his book.

The answer was to wage war.

The core of his argument lay in the first few pages. He outlined why he had sued Hicky: to set the record straight, not just for his reputation but for the reputation of his Mission. He hoped 'to give the publick a clear Idea of the matter,' he wrote.

He rebutted Hicky's allegations one by one, printing official certificates to show he had never offered to sell or rent his

Mission, never rented warehouses to the Company, and never embezzled Griffin's legacy. 'It does not appear you ever made any offer of the Mission Church for Sale or hire,' the Supreme Council certified to him. 'No Godowns have at any Time been hired from you,' the Board of Trade added. 'I received back from several of the Legatees of the said Deceased in India a rateable proportion of their Legacies,' wrote one of Griffin's executors. He believed that these certificates proved his innocence beyond doubt.[607]

Although he did not mention it in his book, Kiernander privately accused one of the Company's priests of renting godowns on consecrated land to the Company, complaining that Hicky had probably confused Reverend William Johnson's warehouses with his own. 'His godowns and warehouses built in the English Burial Ground in Calcutta, have since, by the order of the Governor General and Council, been pulled down to the foundations, and lay now in a heap of Ruins,' he wrote.[608]

Despite the certificates in his book, he still could not disprove some of Hicky's most important claims, so he asked the Society to send him further certificates. He asked them to write a letter or invoice saying he had bought the types he gave Messink and Reed with his own money, and another that he had never solicited money to build his church. He needed the Society to help him prove his innocence. 'Of all this the Society can give the strongest Evidence,' he wrote.[609]

Kiernander worried that Society might never reply to his letter. He had been too embarrassed to show his receipt for his types in court. In former years, the Society's secretary had written formal receipts for all shipments. But the only invoice they had given him for the types was a note written on a scrap of paper.

'Had the Society's secretary signed his Name to that amount of Remittances for 1779. I could have produced it in the Supreme Court of Judicature, and plainly proved that I had paid for those Types with the amount of my Salary for that year. But I was ashamed to produce in the Court, such an account, which looked as an insignificant Scrap of Paper, being no Name Signed to it, and which would have been of no Credit,' he wrote.[610]

Although Kiernander left Diemer unnamed in his book, to those who knew him, he left no doubt that Diemer was his target. He expected Diemer to burn in hell for eternity for leaking information to Hicky. His book's last words were a quote from the bible: 'ALL LIARS SHALL HAVE THEIR PART IN THE LAKE WHICH BURNETH WITH FIRE AND BRIMSTONE.'[611]

He sent copies of his book to the Society and to his professors at Halle. He hoped they would see how he had suffered at Diemer's hands.

You will see by this, how busy the lying spirit has been ... In the first question, which Hicky put to him to answer, about the Types whether they did not belong to the Mission, Diemer stood mute and trembled, and could not speak a single word. Wherefore the judges dismissed him, and there was no further notice taken of him. My wish was that he could have spoken out what he had to say, and what he no doubt had before told Hicky, and made him believe. But he could not bring out a single word. What the Mission and I have suffered by his lying Tongue is not so easily to be imagined. God is a just judge, and His time of judging will come. I was quite blind, and age made me weak, that in all human probability, the Grave seemed yawning to receive me. He thought this was the Time to triumph over me. But, thanks to God, just a little before the Court opened, I received my sight again, and God was pleased to restore me, after that, to better Health. I could be present at the Court to face my enemy and answer for myself.[612]

With his book printed, he thought he could finally move on.

Over the next few years he shifted further from missionary work to business ventures. He began to tackle new challenges with renewed vigour. His improved health and spirits from his recovered sight gave him the ability to work again. 'I now enjoy a better state of Health, than I have for these fifteen years past,' he wrote.[613]

With money from his existing real estate empire, he appears to have assisted many of his son Robert's building projects. He acted as Robert's financial backer, taking out loans at 12 per cent interest to finance construction. He likely planned to increase his investment in real estate to take advantage of Calcutta's high rents.

He had also deepened his role as a philanthropist and money lender. He sent money to missionaries at his old home of Cuddalore, and, when the missionaries at Tranquebar and Trichinopoly lost money through risky investments—one of their missionaries had been jailed for debt—he offered bail and paid their debts.[614] He also lent money to others and charged interest, including to one missionary, Bernard Philip Berkemeyer, to whom he lent Rs 2,820 at 10 per cent interest.[615]

His school and printing shop also seem to have prospered. His Mission Printing Office made forays into Arabic type. Without competition from Hicky, he monopolised printing and selling almanacs.[616] He continued to import many typesets from Europe through the 1780s and resell them around Calcutta.[617]

But his Mission withered as he focused on business. English society began to abandon his church.[618] Concerned with pride, he began fabricating reports back to the Society to mask the size of his shrinking congregation. He claimed adherents that never existed and baptisms that never occurred. His report in 1786, for instance, claimed that in one year he baptised thirty-six children, eight adult Muslims, ten Hindus, and two of unknown caste. He claimed he had performed the marriage rites of thirteen, converted fifteen Catholics, and had 147 English and 119 Portuguese congregants. In reality, it was all false. A later audit revealed that there was no English congregation, and only a small Portuguese congregation, with no Hindu or Muslim converts.[619]

As the years wore on, he began to grow suspicious that the Society was trying to suppress him. At first he noticed Diemer had received several letters from the Society while he got none. Then his salary had stopped coming. To add insult to injury, the Society's annual reports still officially stated that he was being paid.[620]

'Diemer has had his salary for nothing these 2 years and 3 months for doing nothing but Mischief. And the labourers here in the Mission must live upon the Air,' he complained. He began to reconsider his old vow to transfer ownership of the Mission to the Society. 'The Church, the School and other Mission Buildings must go to Ruin, and it is thrown away to no purpose. The Congregations that are gathered must be forsaken. How can I in these circumstances execute the Deed and make it over to the Society for the Mission?'[621]

In his stubbornness, he began to entrench himself in his Mission. Relations with his assistant, Johann Gerlach, once cordial, began to slip. They snapped when he forced Gerlach out of the Mission House because he wanted it for himself.

'I will live and die in it,' he told Gerlach.[622]

Gerlach left the Mission in 1784, leaving Kiernander without the head of his printing office and without his most loyal assistant in the school. He asked the Society for replacements. 'All my good intentions are frustrated,' he wrote.[623] 'I lose now a good and most faithful fellow Labourer in the Mission.'[624] He thought Gerlach had only left because of his constant headaches. He did not realise that Gerlach had grown increasingly unhappy, and had even written to Halle that they should never send any more missionaries, because it would 'condemn them to live in misery'.[625]

Diemer left India near the end of 1784. Kiernander celebrated when he heard that Diemer's son died on the voyage to England and Diemer's father-in-law rescinded money given for taking care of the boy. He thought the death of Diemer's son was divine retribution against Diemer, to whom money was God. He immediately wrote news to the Society.

'Diemer's God was lost … The character he has left behind at Calcutta, is in several Respects, of the worst Kind … it is the opinion of many, that he was the Cause of the Death of his wife, and how he afterwards lied with his slave girls is most talked of. One of them he carried home with him, and two others he provided for, by giving them to other Gentlemen here to live with them,' he wrote.[626]

In August 1784, Kiernander finally received the Society's reply to his book.

He was shocked. He had expected the Society to confirm that he bought the types with his own money. Instead, their letter— which no longer exists—only told him that he should not have sent so many copies of his book because it would be shameful for the outside world to see such division between missionaries.

He wrote an angry reply four months later. He would not see himself admonished by the same people who should support him. It was his duty as a Christian to stand up and fight the Devil. He would stand his post till the last drop of blood ran through his veins.

> You say, 'There was no occasion to send so many of Hicky's Trial—it is better not to make Known such Things.' Perhaps, as the admonitory Letter to me is almost equal and the same with Hicky's Libel, you will have me suffer all to be fixed upon my character.—NO, Never.
>
> That passive Tameness, which submits, without struggle to every violent encroachment and Insult, forms no Part of Christian Duty ... It is to give the Devil his own will and let the World do as they please. It is absolutely impossible to support the purity and Dignity of Christian morals, without opposing the wicked world and the infernal agents on many occasions, even though we should stand alone to support the Combat. We must not make ourselves guilty of the mean Spirit of Cowards and the fawning affect of Sycophants. A truly good mind renounces no just Right from Fear. It gives up no important Truth from apprehension of Danger or any Trouble whatsoever, nor will it ever yield to Flattery. A firm mind, a manly spirit, a fixed Principal of Truth and Honesty guided by the Divine Spirit, must hold the Reins of all our actions. And this is my Resolution through God's gracious Aid, to stand to my Post and not desert it as long as a warm Drop of Blood runs through my Veins ...
>
> I have not been favored with a single letter from the Society with any of the ships that have arrived this year 1784. And must therefore be silent. No more now. Through divine aid and mercy I am
>
> Reverend Sir,
> Your Most O. H. Servant
> J. Z. Kiernander
> Calcutta, December 10, 1784[627]

With this letter, there was no going back. He burned all his bridges.

He never again received a letter from the Society. As if to emphasise his isolation, the only things he got from them over the next few years was some stationery and a block of cheese.[628]

He could not understand why the Society had abandoned him, their most faithful missionary.

The only reason he could conjure was that they had been infected by Hicky's libels too. Maybe the two men he usually communicated with at the Society, Friedrich Pasche and Michael Hallings, were conspiring to silence him because they were Diemer's friends.[629] 'The Society's management of their missions, of late, has been directly opposite to what it always has been in former years,' he wrote.[630]

His fears came true when he heard that Diemer was in London attending the Society's meetings. 'Diemer ... has made the Society believe that it is in vain to send out another missionary, because as long as I am alive nobody could do any good,' he wrote.[631]

Over the next few years he became increasingly frustrated with the Society. He desperately wanted to prove his innocence and desperately wanted them to believe him. 'What I have requested of the Society in my Preface to Hicky's Trial and Conviction for his Libel, is all this Time not complied with as yet. Favour I do not ask, but suffice is my due,' he wrote them.[632]

Finally, he gave up asking for support and began thinking of going to London himself to talk to them in person. 'Matters are now such as make this step absolutely necessary,' he wrote in one letter.[633] 'Let me have a fair Tryal, and an opportunity to answer for myself. Here I am, and ready to answer, at least I hope you will not condemn me unheard,' he added in another.[634]

Yet he wavered. When his last assistant, Bento de Souza, died he knew he could no longer go to London. Other than his son, he was all alone in his Mission.

'If I, and my Son, should go now, the Congregations, will, till my return, be left forsaken,' he wrote.[635]

By September 1787, he had given up on going to England entirely.

But it was not because he would be alone. Calcutta's housing bubble had popped like a swollen balloon. Housing prices were falling fast, in some cases losing over 90 per cent of their original value. Highly leveraged, with most of his capital in construction, no one would lend him money to weather the storm.

'It is a difficult matter to get money here from any one,' he pleaded, 'few or none will credit my Draft.'[636]

Abandoned by the Society, grieving the death of his last assistant, and at risk of losing everything he had ever worked for, his life had never seemed darker.

'I am now in the midst of the Darkness of a dismal night,' he wrote.[637]

But it was about to get much worse. The end of the Mission was nigh.

Impey's Recall

My office naturally raises me many enemies.

           – Elijah Impey to his brother Michael,
                    5 February 1782.[638]

Thursday, 8 August 1782, Calcutta

Impey held the first of Burke's reports in his hands.

The words flew by.

'Mutually abandoned their Principles'

'All Trust in any Branch of Government is dissolved'

'A Degradation of the Court'

'Abuse of Office in India'

'They ought to be called Home'

'Return to England'

'Must be questioned in Great Britain'

He also held one of Francis' letters. It accused him of taking a cut of the Poolbundy contract.

Boiling anger welled up inside him. He composed himself and immediately began to think of what to do. He asked Archibald Fraser and Fraser's subcontractor to testify for him. They deposed that he had never profited from the Poolbundy contract.

'Sir Elijah Impey has not, nor has any other person on his behalf or in trust for him, received directly or indirectly any profit, reward or emolument whatsoever,' Fraser said.

'Not one rupee thereof had passed through the hands of the said Archibald Fraser,' the subcontractor added.

Then Impey began writing.

'You will not be surprised at my anxiety to refute the insinuations,' he wrote, adding others had been given appointments and no one had seemed to mind. 'Two of the Counsellors ... have been appointed openly by the East India Company Commander in Chief of the Forces in India with considerable salaries, and have received and enjoyed those salaries. I could not imagine ... that the acceptance of an Office, of great trust, and real business tho' with a Salary could be deemed illegal in me.'

And even if his Sadr Diwani Adalat appointment was illegal, he said he had never taken the salary, but kept it in sealed bags in his house in case anyone objected. 'I had scruples from other motives against applying the Salary to my own use until the whole circumstances of the Business should be perfectly known in England,' he wrote. [639]

He closed up his letter and gave it to Hastings to send to the Company's directors.

Over the next few months he wrote to important people in England to back up his claims. He was adamant he had never made a profit from the Poolbundy contract.

'I call God most solemnly to witness I have not benefitted by it or ever do or did expect to be benefitted by it directly or indirectly,' he wrote to the Prime Minister.[640]

With these letters, he hoped the matter would come to an end. But he did not hope too much. In the face of Francis' venom and Burke's ability he worried all he wrote would 'do little good'.

His fears came true on October 29, when Hastings forwarded him a letter that the House of Commons had resolved to recall him to England.[641]

'I am not fond of being the Conveyancer of ill News; but I know your anxiety upon a certain point, & think you will be less hurt by this early Communication from me, than by being told abruptly of it, & perhaps in public by others,' Hastings wrote.

The next week, he resigned from the Sadr Diwani Adalat. In a way, he thought going home might actually be a good thing. He would finally see his old friends again. And his family would get better. His wife was pregnant and ill. He and Fraser had sat up for three nights with his youngest daughter as they watched her suffer from diarrhoea and dehydration.

'This is real truth. I have undergone great fatigue, compiled a laborious code, restored confidence to the suitors and justice and regularity to the courts of justice, and settled the internal quiet of a great empire, without any reward, and for my recompense shall have lost my office, reputation, and peace of mind for ever,' he wrote.[642]

'Whatever now may be the case I shall bear it with fortitude and even a degree of exultation; all that I fear was the loss of the good opinion of those friends whose judgment I held in esteem,' he added.[643]

On 27 January 1783, he received his official recall letter.[644] And in December that year he boarded a ship and left for England.[645]

Finally, he was going home.

Letters from Birjee Jail

Great and afflicting as those hardships really have been, and still will continue to be, I have never complained of them, nor do I complain now.

– James Augustus Hicky to Elijah Impey, 17 January 1783.[646]

September 1783, Birjee Jail, Calcutta[647]

William Hickey had just come back to India after four years in England when he received a letter from an old client begging for help. He was enjoying every moment of his life back in Calcutta: his mansion in the centre of town, his servants, his palanquin, even his live-in Italian hair dresser.

The letter bore a name he had not seen in years: James Augustus Hicky. Just like before, this letter was also penned from jail, but this time it was from the brand new Birjee Jail. Curious, he set off to see what had happened to his old client.

Birjee Jail was in a very different part of the city from the common jail. Instead of bathhouses and taverns, the common jail was surrounded by an expanse of grass, green like the sea with the monsoon rain. Instead of nooses on display, he saw Calcutta's most fashionable residents parading their chariots on a shimmering horse-race track. Instead of thieves being whipped up and down the square to the beat of a tom-tom drum, he heard only the quiet of the wind.

He rode up to the jail, its eleven-foot brick walls rising over the Maidan like a fortress in the ocean, and greeted the gaoler.[648] Inside he was welcomed by the same old smell of urine and faeces. The same old drunken prisoners walking around the yard, shackled and fettered. The same poor conditions.

Then he spotted the cell he had been looking for.

Inside was James Augustus Hicky.

'I am most iniquitously and unjustly confined. In me you behold a victim to arbitrary power, illegally exercised,' Hicky ranted. 'As those despots found they could not crush me by open, fair and legal means they without scruple or compunction had recourse to the most diabolical machinations to effect their wicked purpose and complete my ruin.'

William shifted uncomfortably, a pained look growing on his face.

'They first tampered with and finally actually bought over the High Sheriff of Calcutta to their interests; that at their instigation and under their instructions that public officer had been base and infamous enough to pack a jury,' Hicky continued, his anger rising.

'The scoundrel Chief Justice and his equally abandoned and unprincipled partner in iniquity, Warren Hastings, aided by the villain of a Sheriff, managed matters so as to suit their sinister purposes. A petit jury consisting of despicable wretched tools and dependents [was] summoned. Fresh Indictments were preferred, True Bills found, and finally, to the eternal shame and disgrace of twelve Englishman, they returned in each of the three cases a verdict of guilty, notwithstanding the evidence given was precisely the same as upon the former occasions,' he said.[649]

Hicky explained that he had been in jail ever since his first trials in 1781. Without his printing press and types he had been unable to earn a single rupee. In jail, with nothing to do, he grew desperate. He began selling food and necessities to other prisoners for money. But by Christmas he began to despair. He had to give up the small brickhouse he was renting for his children, and since then, they were living in his cell with him, 'pining away under the contaminated air of a filthy jail'. The man in the next cell was an abusive drunk who harassed him and his children, yelling obscenities no matter what small kindnesses Hicky showed.[650]

In June, he had had a glimmer of hope. Hastings had decided to forgive part of the fines. Because his sentence was technically over, the only thing keeping him in jail were his remaining fines. If he could pay them off, he would be free.

But before he could do so, three of his money lenders learned he might be leaving jail. They all submitted their claims for his money, wanting to be first in line.

He spent two months worrying how he could scrounge the money, and considered giving up everything he owned as collateral. He still had to pay Kiernander's and the Court's fines. He thought that maybe the judges would pity him and forgive these as well, so he petitioned them.

> Your lordships Petitioner has been confined in upwards of two long years—and sixteen long months of that time has been deprived of the means of earning one Rupee for the support of his family (being Twelve in Number) and that their only subsistence during that time derived from the produce of a few bills which happily he had by him—on which himself and his said family lived all the above mentioned time.
>
> That in the Month of June last Mr Hastings did generously forgive your Petitioner his part of the fines and that your said Petitioner was at that time in hopes of obtaining his liberty ...
>
> It is very common in England not only to give some part, but the whole of the fines, but also to reduce the length of the Term of Confinement, your Lordships Petitioner most humbly presumes that the power of freeing him from those fines, so forgiven by Mr Hastings rests with your Lordships, and that it entirely lays in your Lordships Breast to forgive him the said fines, which he hopes your Lordship will on account of his little helpless children, and his very long confinement.
>
> Your Lordships Petitioner has done all in his Power for a Month past to raise the Amount of the fines, on the Mortgage of his Garden but he finds it impossible on account of the great scarcity of Cash.
>
> Your Lordships Petitioner most humbly requests your Lordships kind answers to this humble Petition, and your Lordships Petitioner will as in duty bound, Ever pray.

Birjee Jail,
August 11th 1783
James Augustus Hicky[651]

He followed up this petition with a second, and then a third, and waited nervously for a reply.[652]

A week later, Impey's clerk, James Forbes, came to jail and told him that the Court would not forgive his fines.[653] He would still need to pay them if he wanted to leave jail.

All his hopes were crushed.

He felt truly alone now. He wrote one final letter pleading to have his fees forgiven if he stripped his family of their furniture and sold everything he had at auction.

Now every dawn of hope is fled, nothing but a gloomy picture of Horror, Confinement, and Distress, appears before his distressed imagination—And the only recourse your Lordships' Memmorialist has, is to implore the assistance of God to give him patience and Fortitude to stand the shock, which your Lordships' Memmorialist received last Sunday night, when Mr Forbes delivered him your Lordships' Message! ...

Give your Lordships' Memmorialist leave to ask your Lordships one simple and harmless question—Is it possible my Lords that you, who are all Fathers of Children yourselves can be void of feelings for a man in his situation, separated from his Little helpless infants, for upwards, of two years and are now at that age where they ought to be sent to school, but it is not in the power of your Lordships' Memmorialist to pay for it ...

One only request more your Lordships Memmorialist has got to make, which is that as he is now stripping of his family, of the necessary furniture which they had got about them, that when they are sold at outcry, and the Money paid to the Clerk of the Crown, that he will no longer be detained in jail by any other Demands upon him relative to this business—How deplorable would be his case, stripped of his Furniture, that he has long work'd for, and the Money that it brought, and yet still be kept in Jail. He hopes your Lordships has no intent of this kind—if you should, he hopes your Lordships will let him know, before he pays in the Money, that he may keep it for the support of his Family.

And your Lordships' Memmorialist will as in duty bound, ever pray.

Birjee Jail

19th August 1783.

Jas. A. Hicky [654]

The judges never replied to his plea.

'I agree with you in thinking that it is not necessary to send any written answer to Mr Hicky,' Chambers wrote to Hyde, adding in a following letter, 'I do not see how we can relieve his distress.'[655]

Hicky made one final plea for his freedom, writing a public address to his supporters for help. But only a few gathered.

'Only five gentlemen attending the meeting so summoned (every person being more or less fearful it should be known they were disposed to aid a man whom the Governor-General and Chief Justice had devoted to destruction), the matter dropped,' Hicky told William.

Now he had no hope, no way out, and no future. There was nothing more to do, other than to wait and die.

'Thus I am immured in a loathsome prison for life, for all patriotism and public spirit is fled from this quarter of the globe … Here, after a confinement of upwards of two years, I am doomed to terminate my miserable existence, gradually sinking with a broken heart to the grave.'[656]

Freedom on Christmas

I suffered in patience; I did my duty when I could; I waited for better and more lasting means, no act or word of intemperance escaped me; no meanness of submission ever afforded my assailants the triumph, even of a moment, over me ... My antagonists sickened, died, and fled. I maintained my ground unchanged.

– Warren Hastings to David Anderson,
13 September 1786.[657]

Sunday, 26 December 1784, Calcutta

Hastings read the abstract of an Act of Parliament—known as the East India Company Act of 1784—with disgust.

It was an Act that would regulate the Company and would strip away his power. It would make him answer directly to the British government, and would put British ministers in charge of policy in India, not him.

It had its origins in a bill Francis and Burke had drafted the year before.[658] Worst of all, this act was written by the Prime Minister himself, a man he had thought was his ally.

With politics going against him in England, Hastings saw no future for himself in India.

'It has destroyed all my hopes, both here and at home ... I feel my mind warmed with a sense of personal injury,' he wrote.[659]

Moreover, he feared he would soon be recalled to England for impeachment because of Francis and Burke. He had seen the shame Impey had faced on receiving a recall letter in 1783. He did not want to incur that shame himself.

The act made him think that leaving India would be a good thing. His wife had left a year ago because of frequent illnesses. All he wanted was to be with her again. He still remembered watching her ship as it disappeared over the horizon from Calcutta.

'I will not repeat all the Workings of my Mind; but will only tell you that in every Situation of my Life I am continually reminded of my Loss. I feel the want of you,' he wrote her.[660]

Ever since he had shut down *Hicky's Gazette*, he had never really had the power he coveted for long. The new men on the Supreme Council had foiled his plans of conquest, had stopped him from vassalising the Mughal Empire, and had nearly forced him to sign a humiliating peace treaty with the Marathas.

He wrote his final letter to the Company's directors with disappointment, that this was the way he was being treated, after serving the Company faithfully for over three decades.

> I do not part from it with indifference. I owe to my ever honoured employers the service of my life, and would with the devotion of a heart animated with the highest sense of gratitude offer it even with life ... I have the honour to be, with the greatest respect and attachment, honourable Sirs, your most obedient and most faithful servant.[661]

He began closing up his affairs and getting ready to go home. As he did so, his thoughts wandered to Hicky.

One of his last acts was to order the Supreme Court to forgive the rest of Hicky's fines and let Hicky go free. He had his attorney tell William Hickey—who had become the Court's undersheriff—to release Hicky from jail.

William was there at the beginning. Now he was there at the end.

For the first time in years, Hicky was free.[662]

Hicky's punishment had ended. But Hastings' was just about to begin.

Hastings formally resigned and sailed home in February. As he watched the shore of Bengal disappear into the distance, he contemplated his many long years of service and all he had accomplished.

He thought England would thank him.[663]

How wrong he was.

Disgrace

The charges will gibbet their characters to all eternity.
— Philip Francis to George Shee, 4 December 1786.[664]

Friday, 17 February 1786, London

Edmund Burke launched his attack on Hastings in Parliament, making a motion in the House of Commons that certain documents relative to Hastings' rule should be presented to the House. Later, in April, Burke presented twenty-two charges for impeachment against Hastings. Each charge was for a separate issue, covering everything from accepting bribes, giving corrupt contracts, extorting and imprisoning Chait Singh, seizing the Begums of Awadh's treasures, and engaging in wars of aggression. The same charges that Hicky had made against Hastings.

The charges were read in front of the full House. Hastings' representatives arranged for him to defend himself, thinking that the power of Hastings' oratory would sway Parliament to drop the charges. On May 1, Hastings addressed a crowded House of Commons in what was to be one of the most important moments of his life.

In an exhausting speech that lasted almost two days and two nights, Hastings answered each charge individually. He said that there was nothing wrong with conquering the Rohillas. 'They had only to pass the Ganges to their countrymen on the other side of it,' he said.[665] Nor was there anything wrong with punishing Chait Singh or seizing the property of the Begums of Awadh.

Their support of Singh was 'the grounds of ... the consequent confiscation of their treasures,' he said.[666]

Furthermore, he said that giving contracts, like the Army or Poolbundy contracts, to his friends and subordinates was the reason the Company had survived the wars. 'The very existence of the empire in Bengal depends upon our army,' he said, adding that these contracts had been performed fairly.[667] 'The [Poolbundy] contract was concluded upon fair and reasonable terms' and was 'faithfully and honestly performed,' he said.[668]

His most important point was that everything he had done, he had done for the Company. 'Every measure I pursued had for its object the defence of the Company's possessions,' he said, adding, 'I shall never regret the services and sacrifices which I have made to my employers, and to my country.'[669]

By the time he finished, Hastings was confident that the public would see he was the victim of a political vendetta, confident he had proven he was innocent on every charge.

'It instantly turned all minds to my own way,' he wrote.[670]

How wrong he was. Most of Parliament left rather than listen to him speak for two days. His speech was panned in the Press as boring and pedantic, and many noted that he never actually addressed many of the issues, implicitly admitting he had broken the law.

While Hastings was convinced of his success, the House of Commons debated the charges over the next few weeks and through the next year. By May 1787, they found grounds for impeachment on seven of the twenty-two charges, including the charges on contracts, bribes, the treatment of Chait Singh, and the Begums of Awadh.[671] The impeachment proceedings would go to the House of Lords, where Hastings' fate would be decided.

Impeachment proceedings against Impey began around the same time. Burke gave control of Impey's impeachment to a young Member of Parliament, Sir Gilbert Elliot. On December 12, Elliot presented six charges against Impey: using the Supreme Court to have Nanda Kumar executed, accepting the Sadr Diwani Adalat appointment, taking affidavits against the Begums of Awadh, and three counts of illegally extending the Supreme Court's jurisdiction.[672]

The Sadr Diwani Adalat appointment was considered one of the most obvious examples of Impey's corruption. Yet the Nanda Kumar charge was considered the most important because Nanda Kumar's execution ended investigations into Hastings' corruption, so Impey pleaded and was granted the right to have it heard first. After three days of debate, and after the Prime Minister surprisingly publicly defended Impey, the House of Commons voted on 9 May 1788 to acquit him 73 to 55. With his acquittal on this first charge, the prosecution fell apart, despite a brief attempt to renew it. No other charges were pursued.[673]

Impey's impeachment trial was only a shadow of what awaited Hastings. On 15 February 1788, Burke began Hastings' impeachment in front of the House of Lords. The trial captured the public's attention. The Queen, princesses, members of the House of Commons, the House of Lords, and many spectators were present as Burke launched into stunning oratory.

Burke walked to the centre of the stage, stood in dramatic silence for a minute, and began. He spoke for four days, denouncing nearly the entirety of Hastings' rule in damning terms, and saying that Hastings should be found guilty not just because he was a national disgrace to Great Britain, but because he hurt the lives of millions who lived under his rule. He claimed that the people of both England and India would finally get their vengeance on a tyrant.[674] His final words were an indictment of everything Hastings stood for:

I impeach Warren Hastings, Esquire, of high crimes and misdemeanours.

I impeach him in the name of the Commons of Great Britain in Parliament assembled, whose Parliamentary trust he has betrayed.

I impeach him in the name of all the Commons of Great Britain, whose national character he has dishonoured.

I impeach him in the name of the people of India, whose laws, rights, and liberties he has subverted, whose properties he has destroyed, whose country he has laid waste and desolate.

I impeach him in the name and by virtue of those eternal laws of justice which he has violated.

I impeach him in the name of human nature itself, which he has cruelly outraged, injured, and oppressed, in both sexes, in every age, rank, situation, and condition of life.[675]

As the trial progressed, Hastings watched with horror as he became a spectator to his own proverbial hanging, powerless in a legal process that unfolded before his eyes.[676] The trial moved slowly as Burke and the other prosecutors presented evidence and called witnesses. Overwhelmed by the amount of evidence they had to present, by the end of 1788 Burke and his prosecutors had only covered two of the many charges: Chait Singh and the Begums of Awadh. By May 1791, they had decided to finish their prosecution, having only covered two more charges, bribes, and contracts, leaving the others untouched.

Hastings and his counsel offered their rebuttal over the next two years. After that, Burke gave his reply to the rebuttal. Public interest waned as the trial wore on. Many began to pity Hastings as he sat through endless proceedings. Hastings seized on the public mood and repeatedly tried to throw out the case or speed it up, while Burke hoped to outlast him and drain his finances.

On 23 July 1795, after over eight years of draining parliamentary action, Hastings' impeachment finally came time to vote. The trial had lasted so long that a third of the Lords who had attended its opening had died. Only twenty-nine Lords declared themselves present long enough to be eligible to vote.

One by one they stood up, put their hands on their breasts, and declared their judgments. They acquitted him on all charges by large margins.

Hastings bowed and left the hall. The trial was over.[677]

Hastings had found vindication for his rule. But he found none for his reputation nor his fortune. He had spent almost his entire wealth on lawyers' fees, and had fallen so far in social standing that he was considered nearly criminal among his peers.[678]

Yet, he thanked those who had supported him, most of all his friends in Calcutta, where his heart remained, and for whom he had fought for his entire career.

To the British Inhabitants of Calcutta

19th June 1796

Gentlemen ...

There was a time in which the authority of my public office derived a considerable support from the influence of your good opinion of the manner in which it had been exercised. The knowledge of your sentiments, publicly and authentically expressed on the day of my departure from Calcutta, contributed largely to support my credit with my countrymen in England, when, but for this and similar aids, it must have sunk under the pressure of accusations heaped upon me without number ...

When I parted, in the year 1785, from that community to which I had attached myself by an intercourse of many years, and by various relations, my heart sorrowed for the separation, but consoled itself with the hope ... that I might still devote what remained of the active portion of my life to the advancement of your welfare, with that of the State on which it depended. I have been disappointed, and have painfully, though patiently, borne the disappointment ...

To the Almighty Disposer of human events, I humbly and fervently offer up my prayers for your prosperity, for the prosperity of British India, and for the ease, content and happiness of the inhabitants of it who have a more immediate and indispensable claim to its protection!

I have the honour to be with the most grateful and indelible attachment, Gentlemen,

Your much obliged and faithful servant,

Warren Hastings[679]

After the trial, Hastings retired to a quiet life at his estate, Daylesford, finally achieving his childhood ambition to return his family to the status it had lost. He spent much of his remaining fortune building a massive new mansion on the property.[680]

'God knows there were periods in my career, when to accomplish that, or any other object of honourable ambition, seemed to be impossible, but I have lived to accomplish it,' he said.[681]

He was able to attain contentment watching the small stream that passed his estate, thinking of what he accomplished for the British Empire.

Downfall

When Mr K. should die, and be indebted, his House and School would be sold according to the English Laws, as certain, as 2 times 2 is 4, because it is his private property.

– Johann Christian Diemer to Gottlieb Anastasius
Freylinghausen, 26 December 1782.[682]

Thursday, 30 October 1788, Society's Headquarters, London

A letter from Calcutta sat on the secretary's desk, sealed and written on cloth paper. It came bearing urgent news.

Kiernander had gone bankrupt and lost everything.

The sheriff had seized his property, his houses, and anything under construction, and had auctioned it off for fire-sale prices. All Rs 400,000 he had invested in real estate was gone in an instant. One house he spent over Rs 40,000 building sold for only Rs 5,000.[683] The sheriff went so far as to even seize other people's property that had been entrusted under his care and which he had mortgaged.

His Mission was the only thing saved. A wealthy Company servant, Charles Grant, bought it for Rs 10,000, a tenth of what he had spent building it.[684] The buildings he had fought so hard to keep his own, to live and die in, were all gone.

To George Gaskin, Secretary of the Society

March 7, 1788.

Reverend Sir,

[Kiernander's] work, like his Substance, has been smouldering away for several years ... Many indulged rancour against Religion itself, under pretence of rendering Hypocrisy true. The whole settlement was in a flame against him ... He now lives in infamy and misery, as instance of the Vanity of the World and of the Deceitfulness of Riches.

You will doubtless require of me his real Character, and as I have no passion to gratify but the Love of Truth, I shall attempt to give you it in few words. It plainly appears that Mr Kiernander has intermeddled with worldly things, to the great injury of his Character as a Minister. His time, Talents and attention have been too much employed in this way. The consequence to the Mission is what might have been expected. It has not prospered, neither are there any sincere or honourable fruits of it among the Heathen. And this defection and manifest departure from the Lines of his Duty, have rendered both the Zeal and Truth in the Eye of all men problematical ...

P.S. In the Society's printed accounts of their Mission in Bengal, I observe reports of adult Heathens, instructed and baptized. Since the Mission Church came into my hands I have met with no persons of the above Description. None attend publick worship. Nor do I know of one real Convert to Christianity from either the Bengalise or Mussalmen ... Mr Kiernander does not understand their language to teach in it, and they do not understand either English or Portuguese sufficiently to be understood. Besides, as soon as they are baptized there is no more heard of them but in the Society's accounts. I intreat you, Sir, not to suffer this Fact to operate against the Missionaries on the Coast, who deal truely with the Society ... They are true Labourers and have real Fruit. Mr Kiernander, to keep pace with them, has often, I fear, made his Reports too splendid.

D. Brown.[685]

Although Brown's letter confirmed the Society's suspicions, Brown chose not to divulge the series of unfortunate events, bad investments, and outsized risk that led Kiernander to this point. What was undeniable, Brown wrote, was that Kiernander had engaged in worldly affairs, and this was why his Mission had collapsed. He had become an example of the deceitfulness of riches and the hypocrisy of religion.

Events out of Kiernander's control had brought him to this point. In 1784, drought and famine struck the country upriver of Calcutta. Even though Calcutta was sheltered from the brunt of the distress, the events triggered a collapse in the city's housing market.[686] Finally, in September 1787, at the height of the collapse, heavy rain and violent winds struck Calcutta, causing flooding and damage to buildings. Those who invested their savings in real estate could no longer support themselves. Kiernander watched his wealth vanish before his eyes.[687]

The Society debated what to do over the next few months. One person saw opportunity in Kiernander's troubles: Diemer. He had been sitting on the Society's board and asked to be sent to Calcutta again.[688]

But Hicky's libels had a long reach. Many remembered Diemer's involvement at Hicky's trials, and few wanted to see him return. 'If he shou'd come, he wou'd disgrace his office, & dishonour the Society, more than Mr Kiernander,' Brown wrote, adding, 'I fear Mr Diemer has spoken more than the truth to the Society, which is very easy to a Person, who is both prejudiced and angry. Foolish Tales, as I have before observed, are by no means sufficient to determine any thing, where one side is only told.'[689]

With the opinion of the clergy against him, the Society refused Diemer's request. 'The chief thing that appears to have been done, by Mr Diemer during several years stay, at Calcutta, was to altercate and jangle with Mr K.,' they recorded in their secret proceedings, adding, 'there is much reason to believe that he neither has the confidence of any of the Missionaries in India, whether English or Danish, nor of the Society's German Connexions.'[690]

The Society began to look for a new missionary to send to Calcutta. Once they found one, they had their secretary write to Kiernander. This was the last recorded letter they ever wrote him. They wanted Kiernander to know their relationship was terminated.[691]

Reverend Sir,
Without saying anything, or deciding, upon matters of Report, or matters of notoriety, it clearly appears, on your own Testimony, as

well as that of other Gentlemen, that you are now to be considered as in a State of Separation from the Mission, and from the Society— that the Church, and premises, instead of being conveyed to the Society, as promised, is absolutely the Property of Messrs Brown, Chambers, and Grant—and that among the Gentile people, there are few, if any, remaining fruits of your Missionary Labour. The Proprietors of the Church, it seems, are piously preserving it, as a Place, where good may yet be done ...

P.S. I cannot help but adding, that very extraordinary particulars have been mentioned here, respecting a considerable share of Property, belonging to a young Lady, now in England, and whom I have seen, which was entrusted to your care, and is detained.[692]

In light of the total collapse of his real estate empire, Kiernander fled to Chinsurah rather than face jail for debt in Calcutta. Yet he was not destitute. The Dutch Governor appointed him chaplain, and he and his son Robert set up a school. Also, their creditors had been unable to seize any property held in his daughter-in-law's name, and this may have amounted to Rs 1 lakh, from which they likely lived comfortably.[693]

But Kiernander was deeply shaken by his default, and decided to dedicate the rest of his life to repentance.

'I will never aspire to a higher Character, then that of a repenting Sinner,' he wrote, adding, 'I plainly see ... my unworthiness, my unfitness, and my manifold failings.'[694]

He reflected on his life in a series of letters, explaining how he struggled against great odds to spread Christianity in India. That he saw war every year from 1740 to 1758. That the Marathas stole his milk cows. That he was alone every time an army approached. That he had only the clothes on his back when he fled to Calcutta.[695] That he struggled to survive on a £50 a year salary.

But there were some things he was not repentant about, such as his business.

'In regard to my having had great dealings with the world, I am exceedingly sorry that I ever should have been brought into an absolute necessity of having any at all. Yet I have never traded in any way whatsoever. Architecture, is the only thing I have, but not without the utmost pressing necessity made use of ... Let then an impartial judge say, what he himself would have done in such a case,' he wrote.[696]

He also denied Hicky's libels. He said he never made money from his Mission, nor solicited money to build it, and had often spent his own money on it. He bought the organ, the church bells, the clock, the gilded cups and the plates himself. He bought the property for the burial ground, the school, and the Mission using his wife's jewels and his own income. 'So all this was my own Property and no one has a Claim upon it,' he wrote.[697]

He also said it would have been impossible for him to embezzle legacies because he would have been embezzling from himself. 'Respecting Legacies and Donations. The truth is, that not one has ever been made either to the Society or to the Mission,' he wrote. Because all legacies were made to 'Mr Kiernander's church,' the money legally belonged to him alone.[698] Thus, even if there had been money left in Griffin's legacy, it was his to spend as he wanted.

He blamed the Society for being the reason he never transferred his Mission. He wrote that he had tried to transfer it in 1780, but later stopped because he felt abandoned. 'Had the Society not forsaken me and the Mission ... all would have been conveyed over to them,' he wrote. Then the great housing collapse made it impossible. 'Not only I, but many Hundred Families more, who had all their Property in Houses and Lands, have been cruelly ruined ... It was my hearty wish and Desire to settle it all upon the Mission, under the Care of the Society; but alas. I could not have my wish,' he wrote.

Lastly, he wrote that the Society had conspired to suppress him and support Diemer, because Diemer was friends with some of them. 'In Pasche's correspondence to Halle, I can see that he endeavours to cast all the Blame upon the Society, in order to clear himself,' he wrote.[699] 'Mr Pasche's main aim was, to protect his friend Diemer, who was the author of the Libel,' he added in another letter.[700]

But this was all behind him now. He did not care about worldly affairs anymore. He only cared about preparing himself for another world. 'I am better and happier engaged. And I thank God for it. I have a school where I am to a better purpose imployed. I have a Church ... I now begin to live in my proper and most delightful Element, and have nothing else to do, but to prepare and qualify myself for the happy Duty required of me,' he wrote.[701]

Kiernander slipped into obscurity in his old age. By the time he returned to Calcutta in 1795 he had few friends left in the city that had once been his home. He had outlived almost everyone he knew, even his son Robert, who died in 1791.[702] To many, he was just a memory. A mark on the history of the Church.

'I rather wish that I may be forgotten ... I am now left among a new Generation who know me not, and to whom I have not the Honour to be Known. But I hope soon to see my former Friends and to renew our Friendship forever,' he wrote.[703]

On the morning of 28 April 1799, he slipped and fell after getting out of bed. The fall broke his thigh and he died on May 10, at age 88.[704]

Despair

But as I am now a very old man should I die here my children must beg through the streets of Calcutta.

– James Augustus Hicky to Warren Hastings,
13 November 1793.[705]

Saturday, 22 October 1786, Calcutta

Over ten months after Hicky was released from jail, he tried to restart his newspaper.

But he was a broken man, and his newspaper appears to have failed within months; no records appear to survive of it.[706] His conflict with the Company had put him thousands of rupees in debt. But he had never given up his sources. He had kept their identities secret to shield them from prosecution. But now, years later, he felt slighted. He felt that he had suffered for nothing. He at least wanted recognition.

When he learned that one of his correspondents, William Young—probably the author of the letter titled 'A By Stander', one of the articles for which Hicky was tried for libel—was about to leave India, he blackmailed Young, threatening to release Young's letters if Young did not pay. He had expected Young to thank him for protecting his identity, yet Young had ignored him. Had he given up Young's letters, Young would have gone to jail, not him.

Sir,
Of all the men on whose account myself and my family have been ruined, there was not one in whom I had a firmer reliance for an indemnification than on you, or at least for some act of friendship.

Is it not a very hard case, Mr Young, that a man who has acted so faithfully and honourably by others as I have done, lost upwards of eighty thousand rupees, bore a confinement patiently for two long years and three months and by the seizure of my types have been rendered incapable of earning one rupee for my family for upwards of four years, and in consequence thereof am at this instant overwhelmed with debts, and myself and helpless family reduced to the most excruciating indigence; is it not very hard I say Mr Young that such a man should be ungenerously treated.

Had I given up your papers, and all those which are now in my possession, I would not have been detained in jail a week, nor been obliged to pay the very large sums of money which I have paid; the publication of my paper would have continued, and I might have made a very considerable addition to my interest and to my fortune.

The criminal prosecution, and the civil actions would in that case have been brought against the authors, and the fines and damages given would have [been] enormous, for they would have been in proportion to the fortunes of those who they were given against, and would beside have proved the total ruin of those persons in the Honourable Company's service for ever.

You have Mr Young I understand been led astray by insinuation that the manuscript copies had been seized which is false, not one was seized. I have them all at this instant, and you shall see them, if you will call on me. How often has the following advice been given me whilst in jail:

Take care of them papers Hicky, Young is a worthy generous fellow, and will make you ample amends hereafter when you give up the papers. This advice Sir came from your own intimate friends and acquaintances—and God best knows how faithful and secret I have been to you and all those for whom I have suffered, and still continue to suffer. As I have taken a copy of this letter, I request that you will keep this by you, as it may be wanting hereafter.

I have done every thing in my power under the most afflicting confinement, and losses to shield you and many others from shame, and perhaps total ruin, and I now see myself most cruelly and ungratefully slighted, in the room of being rewarded, and those who ought to have proved themselves my friends have

proved themselves my greatest enemies. If it should please God
that I should live to publish the Bengal remarks which I have been
writing for some time past the world will see the very worthy
and honourable characters of many which are now taking their
departure from this country as well as those who have been gone
some time past. My friends have within these two last years, often
advised me to bring prosecution against those men on whose
account I suffered, namely those who treated me ill; and I am sorry
to say that they have all treated me ill (one man only excepted).

I am Sir, Your obdt. Servant,

Jas. A. Hicky.

February 28, 1786 [707]

Young called Hicky's bluff and sent the letter to the *India
Gazette*—Hicky's old rival—claiming that he never wrote for
Hicky. The *India Gazette* published Young's and Hicky's letters
after Young was already safely away on a ship to England.

To the Editor of the India Gazette,

Sir,

I think the accompanying letter which I received only this morning,
tho' dated the 28th Feb. is of so much importance to the characters
of Gentlemen now on the spot, and some who may have left the
country, that it is but common justice to give it to the public, for
my own part, if time would permit, it should be published before
I go, but as that is impossible I leave it with my Attorney to send
it to one or to all the papers, declaring upon my honour, as a
Gentleman, that I never did directly or indirectly write, or cause to
be written, one single line in Mr Hickey's newspaper, reflecting on
the character of any person whatever, and thus leave Mr Hickey
to pursue his own measures.

I am Sir

Your most obdt. Servant

Wm. Young

Calcutta, March 2, 1786

Hicky faced increasing problems with money as he aged. He
still had not been paid for printing Coote's army regulations.
Sinking into despair as he struggled to earn enough for his family,
he began to see deliverance in the regulations.

He had petitioned Hastings for payment after he was freed from jail. But Hastings had replied that since he was no longer leading the Company and was leaving India, he could not order the bill to be paid. Hicky then petitioned Hastings' successor, John Macpherson, sending Macpherson a bill for Rs 43,514. He pleaded that he needed the money to feed his children and send them to school.

> It is now three years since the Seizure of your Petitioner's Types which has reduced him and his helpless family (having three small children) to most distressed indigence, your Petitioner therefore most humbly prays that your Honour will take this his hard case into your humane Considerations and order his Bill to be paid that he may (as far as lays in his power) stop the mouths of Clamorous Creditors, Cloathe his little Children, and send them to School.

After months of not receiving a reply, he sent a reminder. Macpherson replied that he was considering his bill.

But nothing appears to have happened for the next three years, after which Macpherson left for England, leaving Hicky back where he started. In May 1788, Hicky sent a petition to the new Governor-General, Charles Cornwallis, pleading that he needed the money soon, again for his children.

> Your Petitioner relying on your Lordships well known love of Justice, and the Justice of your Honourable Board, has every hope that your Lordships will take the Justness of your Petitioners Claim under your wise Consideration and order the payment of his bill. Your Lordships Petitioner being in great want of Money at this present time, having a very large family and several small and helpless children to maintain, which he finds a very great difficulty to perform from the badness of the times, and the great scarcity of Money.[708]

Cornwallis replied three months later, asking him to testify before the Supreme Council because the Council was unable to tell exactly how many pages he had printed. Hicky appears not to have testified, perhaps because he was arrested for debt that same month. He posted bail and just barely escaped imprisonment.[709]

Four years later, in 1792, he pleaded his case again. His health was declining and he feared if he did not get his money now, he might never.

He begged the Council's secretary to put his bill in front of the Governor-General.

'I am at the moment unable to walk, set up only supported with pillows,' he pleaded.[710]

Still he received no reply. He sent reminder after reminder. In February 1793, he wrote that he needed the money for his 'young and helpless children'.[711] In April, he added, 'I am at the present moment confined to my room & in the utmost distress.'[712] In June, he begged, 'If his Lordship did but know the one half of the distresses of myself and my children he would soon order my bill to be paid.'[713]

The Council finally wrote back in July. They offered to pay Rs 6,711, a fraction of the Rs 43,514 he thought he was owed. And if he did not like it, the Council added, he was welcome to sue them.

'You are at Liberty to Assert your Claim either in the Supreme Court, or, in any other mode that may seem to you best calculated to obtain the object of your Application,' they wrote.[714]

Hicky was incensed and confused why they offered so little. It had been almost fourteen years since he had been given the contract. Moreover, he had charged less than half of what the Company printers would have charged at that time. That did not even count the complicated brass rule work he had needed for the regulations.[715]

'I wish to be informed by what calculation or Rule it is that the Hon'ble Board has made out so trifling a sum,' he wrote back.

The next week he received a reply that the Council did not feel it was necessary to explain their reasoning.

Hicky's desperation was so great that he even wrote to Hastings for help. He thought about going to England as a surgeon to try and get his children educated in the Blue Coat Hospital charity school. At the same time, he asked Hastings to help him get appointed the deputy clerk of the market of Calcutta. He had not been employed for several years and would do anything for money.

Sir,

I have not had any employment for several years past and am at present much distressed with a very large family, which with repeated and severe spells of sickness, has reduced me very much; I wrote several letters to you since your departure from Bengal but apprehend you have not received them all.

I have been repeatedly told that it was your intention to do something for me and my family before you left Bengal. If so, I hope you will not think me less deserving of your good wishes now, for I can safely say that I have not done anything since that time by which I might forfeit your good wishes. Mad is my place here under government by which I could barely and with frugality support my children. I would intirely give over all thought of leaving this Country. But as I am now a very old man should I die here my children must beg through the streets of Calcutta, as they are by their youth unable to earn their own bread. From these considerations I have been lead to think that I had better endeavour to get my passage home as a Surgeon on board one of the ships of the season and by that means get liberty to Carry my children along with me. I have some friends still living, and should it please God to take me from my children after my arrival in England my friends could get them placed in the Blue Coat Hospital, as I am by being a freeman of the city of London entitled of that indulgence.

There are many places occupied by men who are from sheer Riches and inactivity very unfit for places of the kind. The clerk of the Markett of Calcutta is occupied by a man who has no family, is very old, and very rich. He never goes into the Market being prevented by old age and infirmities. A deputy under him at a small salary would render the inhabitants a very great service, as [they] do at present labour under many impositions, relative to a high price, and bad provisions—As I am thank God (tho' old) one of the activest men in the settlement, the place of deputy clerk of the Market, with a small monthly allowance would enable me to support my family ...

A line or two from you Sir would procure one the place alluded to, or any other, which might enable me to support my family with frugality. Being much pinched for time as the Pacquet closes within the hour I hope it will apologize for the blots on the letter, which happened thro' a hurry in writing.

Wishing you health and every other happiness. I am sir,
With sincerest respect.
Sir, your Obt. Humble Servant
Jas August Hicky[716]

The next two years are lost to history. Perhaps Hicky decided not to return to England. Perhaps something prevented him.

But, by 1795, he needed money more desperately than ever. He wrote the Council one final petition, full of anger and bitterness, pleading for the full sum of his bill.

'There is a demand on me, for a large sum of money, and if I am not able to discharge it before the publication of the last Ship's dispatches I shall be sent to jail,' he wrote.'

He did not want to sue the Council. He doubted he would win. If anything, he had learned that lesson the hard way.

'To go to Law with your Hon'ble Board might with propriety be deemed equally as absurd as if your Memorialist was to strip off his Garments to fight with an Elephant,' he wrote.[717]

The Council refused.

He asked if he could get interest on the Rs 6,711.[718]

They again refused.

'As to Interest you certainly can have no Claim to any as it is your own fault that you did not close with the Proposal and agree to receive the money when it was tendered to you,' the Company's attorney wrote.[719]

Finally, he gave up. On 7 March 1795, he signed the release and got the Rs 6,711.[720]

Hicky disappeared from the records for another two years until he showed up, surprisingly, in the Supreme Court again.

Wednesday, 12 April 1797. Between 10 and 11 p.m.

Hicky was about to go to bed when he heard his dog yelping in pain.

Then he heard a woman screaming.

He got up and ran out of his house.

'What is the matter?' he asked.

'They are in liquor and have beaten my wife,' his coachman said.

'Who has done so?'

His coachman pointed at Khowaji, a passerby, half naked and drunk.

Khowaji had kicked his dog and threw bricks at it, but missed and had hit his coachman's wife instead. When she complained, Khowaji grabbed her by her hair, kicking her and dragging her along the ground.

'Go home,' Hicky approached Khowaji, adding he would bring him before a magistrate if he did not leave.

Khowaji came close to Hicky. Hicky pushed him away and slapped him.

Just then, Khowaji's father came up.

'Why have you thrown down a sober man?' he asked.

'Go home, you are all intoxicated,' Hicky said.

Khowaji's father, Faizullah, came up close to Hicky and put his arms around him as if to hug him.

'I have not struck your son. Go home,' Hicky said, grabbing a stick and whacking Faizullah to let him go.

Faizullah cried out that he was wounded and called for help.

A small mob formed. Twenty to twenty-five men assembled.

'Break into the scoundrel's house,' Faizullah urged them.

'Follow me,' Khowaji called out.

'*Maar! Maar!*' Kill! Kill! Khowaji and Faizullah led the mob chanting.

Hicky turned his back on the mob and walked to his garden, hoping they would go away.

Suddenly, he heard a voice.

'*Khabardār Saheb!*' Watch out Sir! A woman called out

A clay pot hit him on the leg. Then a brick knocked off his hat. He turned his head. Another brick passed by his cheek, almost cutting him. He ran into his house and grabbed his sword.

He returned to find the mob had broken his gate and were grabbing bamboo sticks from his garden. Khowaji's brother, Jumaun, led the crowd up his steps, carrying a six-foot-long piece of bamboo as thick as his arm.

Jumaun swung it at him.

Hicky stepped backwards and raised his sword to meet the blow. The twang of steel collided with the thud of bamboo.

Jumaun swung again at his head.

Again, Hicky parried.

Jumaun raised the bamboo back, bringing it around and swinging it down at the other side of Hicky's head.

This time Hicky was not quick enough. The bamboo cut his cheek. Blood flowed into his mouth.

Hicky now realised the extent of the danger. He jabbed at Jumaun with his sword, cutting Jumaun's wrist and knocking the bamboo to the ground, before running into his house and shutting the door behind him. He thought frantically about what to do. Then an idea occurred to him. He rushed to the back of his house with his coachman, helping the man climb out a window, telling him to bring the police.

The mob outside began throwing bricks at his house, breaking pots and water jars and bashing in his windows.

The mob dispersed by the time the police came. Later, the mob's leaders were tried and found guilty of rioting, assault, and trespass.[721]

For one brief moment Hicky was brought into the public light again. Newspapers in London picked up the story, remarking that the trial excited 'no common degree of curiosity' in Calcutta, as people sat in Court, excited to watch a 'very old and well known British Inhabitant, who, many years since, was the Proprietor of the first Newspaper ever Printed in *Calcutta*, or in *India*.'

Hicky again faded into obscurity, until his death in 1802 aboard the Ajax. In 1799 he sent out his last recorded words, a desperate plea to Hastings for money, help, anything.

Sir ...

It would be painful to you to read a long and particular account of the distress of myself and children. Let it suffice that everything which I had has been sold and mortgaged for my unhappy family, and none but God and ourselves know the keenness of our distress ...

Jas. A. Hicky.

December 26, 1799[722]

Notes on Other Characters

Johann Christian Diemer – Returning from India, Diemer spent time in Strasbourg before heading to England, where he was ordained an Anglican priest in March 1790. He returned to Calcutta but died shortly thereafter in 1791, having never achieved his lifelong dream of succeeding in Kiernander's place at the Mission.[723]

Philip Francis – Despite his work setting the stage for Hastings' impeachment, Francis was ultimately not chosen to be a part of the prosecution. He grew increasingly idealistic as he grew old, opposing slavery in British colonies even though it meant he had to give up inheriting a slave-owning estate. He lobbied to become Governor-General after Hastings' impeachment, but was passed over. Embittered, he refused a consolation offer to become Governor of the Cape Colony in South Africa. He died in December 1818, outliving Hastings by a mere four months.

William Hickey – After he gave news to Hicky that he would be free from jail, William met the love of his life, Jemdanee. She died in childbirth after bearing a son. He continued to practice law in Calcutta for many years before retiring to England in 1808. He died in 1830.

Elijah Impey – After his impeachment Impey ran for Parliament in 1790. Although he lost his first election (his opponent paraded around an effigy of Nanda Kumar hanging from the gallows), he was later elected in another district.[724] India ever on his mind, three days after his victory, he petitioned the Prime Minister to be reappointed Chief Justice of the Supreme Court, but was rejected. He later travelled to France to recover money he had invested before the French Revolution, but was detained for three years. He died in 1809.[725]

Simeon Droz – After Hicky's article against him, Droz left Calcutta to become the Chief of the Company's factory at Cossimbazar. Droz later returned to England, where he was accused of corruption for his time on the Board of Trade and for fraud while in Cossimbazar. In the end, the Company dropped its suit against him in return for a payment of £3,000—a fraction of the fraud which he was charged.[726]

Epilogue

Hicky began and influenced traditions of journalism that still exist today. He strongly supported freedom of the Press and opposed corruption and absolute power, sacrificing everything to defend his newspaper. Yet his downfall was the same free speech that he defended. His inability to make a distinction between personal and professional invective led those in power—like Hastings and Kiernander—to sue and suppress him. Even if Hastings had not pursued him so harshly, and even if the Supreme Court's independence had not been compromised, Hicky may still have been found guilty. While many of his articles contained truth, they were often founded on rumour, and some points, especially his claims about Kiernander, remain unproven.

Hicky should be known for his legacy. While his printing press operated for a brief five years, and his newspaper only for two, he set the foundation for future printers in India. He trained printers who would later transform Calcutta into one of the most vibrant literary cities in Asia. The exchange of ideas among his intellectual descendants in business, religion, and education eventually contributed to a literary culture in Bengal that is still strong today.

Two of his assistants, Paul Ferris and Archibald Thompson, founded the *Calcutta Morning Post* in 1792. Ferris later went on to run an important bookselling business in Calcutta, and printed the first illustrated book in Bengali, *Annada Mangal,* written by Ganga Kishore Bhattacharji. Bhattacharji was also the editor of the second Bengali newspaper, the *Bengal Gazette*—perhaps a homage to *Hicky's Bengal Gazette.*[727]

Another assistant, Thomas Jones, went on to found the *Bengal Journal* in 1785—where he was joined by yet another of Hicky's assistants, Richard Tisdale—and later founded *The Times* in 1792.[728] These men went on to train their own assistants, establishing a family tree of printers in Bengal. There are likely others that history has not recorded.

Hicky's influence lived on after the death of his newspaper. A newspaper known as *Bengal Journal* followed in his footsteps. Like Hicky, the *Journal's* editor, an Irish-American named William Duane, had many contacts in the Company army, having arrived in Bengal as a private in the army. Like Hicky, he made his newspaper a forum for disgruntled Company subalterns. Also like Hicky, he was a radical and a strident advocate of the liberty of the Press and the right to representative government where ideas of life and liberty could be aired.[729]

Duane had yet more similarities with Hicky. His aggressive approach soon got him in trouble. When news of the French Revolution reached Bengal, Duane printed a report that Governor-General Cornwallis had died campaigning in South India, citing French royalists as his source. Colonel de Canaple, the leader of the French royalists, demanded Duane publicly apologise for printing mistruths. A heated argument broke out when Duane visited Canaple the next day. Canaple refused to answer Duane's question if he was the one who had started the rumuor, while Duane refused to retract his story.

The Governor-General later returned to Calcutta very much alive. In an effort to intimidate Duane, his soldiers ransacked Duane's house, and attempted to deport Duane from Bengal. Duane filed a plea in the Supreme Court to stay his deportation, but the Court ruled that the Company had the right to deport him because he did not have legal approval to reside in India. A stroke of luck saved Duane: Canaple died nine days before Duane's scheduled deportation and the new French leader wrote to the Governor-General that Duane had been punished enough. The Governor-General nevertheless banned the *Bengal Journal* to prevent future embarrassments.[730]

Undaunted, Duane founded a new newspaper, *The World*, that

same year, promising to abstain from controversy. Despite his promise, *The World* quickly became a hub for radical politics. Duane openly supported the French Revolution at a time when the British were at war with France and he allowed disgruntled subalterns to use his newspaper to organise, publishing articles suggesting they form committees and lobby the Commander-in-Chief to redress grievances such as the lack of promotion opportunities.[731]

The Governor-General again tried to intimidate Duane. Duane's subscribers and advertisers were pressured to stop patronising his paper and the police arrested him on a pretence for an unpaid debt. The sheriffs, along with a mob armed with clubs and sticks, dragged him by his hair to the Court of Requests. Intimidation did not stop Duane, who continued printing for the next two months until the Governor-General again ordered his deportation.[732]

In desperation, Duane tried two strategies at once, asking the Governor-General to rescind his deportation while at the same time threatening to publish the army's grievances for the world to see. When the Governor-General invited Duane for breakfast the next morning, he drew Duane into a side room, surrounded him with soldiers, and had him dragged into a jail cell. He then locked Duane in a ship's cabin and told the captain not to let him out until they reached England.[733]

The next twenty years were a dark time for journalism in India. The Company exercised increasing power over the Press as governor-generals used deportation to quell dissent. The editor of the *Madras News* was deported after some 'democratic opinions' in his newspaper.[734] The editor of *The Telegraph* was nearly deported after he published an article accusing Calcutta's sheriff of extortion. He avoided deportation by revealing his sources. The editor of the *Asiatic Mirror* was deported after speculating that Indians could easily overthrow the few Europeans in Bengal if they banded together. In 1799, the Company issued the strictest crackdown yet, deporting three journalists in quick succession and enacting strict new censorship laws.[735]

Calcutta's press soldiered on despite the repression. Over time, with increasing intercultural exchange, printing began to enter

Indian daily life as Calcutta grew. The first Indian-owned presses were founded in the early 1800s. Within only a few decades, Indians rivaled and then surpassed the output of European presses. By 1820, it was estimated that Bengali presses had printed more than 15,000 copies of at least twenty-seven different works. At least sixteen Bengali newspapers were launched between 1828 and 1835.[736] Newspapers became the source of information for Calcutta in the nineteenth century.

Perhaps the most notable of these early Bengali journalists was Ram Mohun Roy, the founder of two newspapers. He, too, had connections with earlier printers, having once been a writer for Bhattacharji's *Bengal Gazette*.[737] Through his newspapers, he helped launch the Bengal Renaissance, a literary and intellectual awakening in the nineteenth century.

The worlds of Indian and European journalism collided with the case of James Silk Buckingham in 1823. A European freebooter and radical just like Hicky, Buckingham established his own paper, the *Calcutta Journal*, and began calling for an end to the Company's monopoly and the 'tyranny' with which it ruled India.[738] Like Hicky before him, Buckingham aired the army's grievances in his newspaper. When he published an article from a subaltern complaining about the lack of promotion opportunities, and an article exposing a corrupt appointment, the Governor-General moved to deport him.[739]

Roy leapt to Buckingham's defense, petitioning both the Supreme Court and King of England that Buckingham's deportation was a violation of civil rights, and later leading a joint Indian-European protest in front of Calcutta's Town Hall.[740] Although Roy's legal challenge was unsuccessful, his protest marked the first time that Indian and European newspapers fought on the same side and the culmination of Hicky's legacy.

Later, Indian leaders such as Mahatma Gandhi and Jawaharlal Nehru turned to the Press to advocate for independence. In many ways, India is still undergoing great change. India currently has over 100,000 newspapers and a total circulation of around 450 million copies per day and growing, making it one of the most vibrant media markets in the world.[741]

Yet not all is bright beyond the statistics. Inequalities remain and high illiteracy persists. Moreover, India's press is only partially free. Interference in editorial content from government and large media owners, online censorship, legal actions, threats from nationalist organisations, and an increase in killings of journalists make for a worrying reality.[742]

India is not alone with such worries. Journalists around the world are intimidated, threatened, or killed for opening issues others would rather have closed.

Hicky is an example of the importance of standing for liberty and free speech. He sacrificed everything to defend the freedom of the Press: his ambitions, his person, and his paper. As he so frequently discussed in his Gazette, where the Press is free, the people are free; where the Press is oppressed, the people are oppressed; and when the Press is gone, the people are no longer protected.

Afterword

The recorded descriptions and dialogue in this book are the result of exhaustive research, and are often printed verbatim with their original formatting based on the letters and writings of the individuals within. However, the dialogue in this book is derived only from those who recorded it, and may reflect their biases and motivations. Likewise, unless explicitly referenced, the thoughts, feelings, and emotions of the individuals, as well as the descriptions in this book, are to some extent imagined, based on the remaining records of the individuals in the archives. Sadly, no image of Hicky exists to this day; whatever images that exist on the Internet are not authentic representations of him.

I have worked to portray the individuals in this book accurately, and to represent, to my best ability, the world as they would have seen it. History, especially where it lacks a cohesive narrative, is the product of imperfect recollections. Yet, I hope to have portrayed these individuals in a way acceptable both to scholars, and to the wider public. It is my hope that this story has been factual and enjoyable for all.

Acknowledgments

It is often said that a book is the work of many hands, and that is no less true for mine. There are many people whom I would like to thank. Thank you Tim Wright, Andrew Zonderman and Markus Berger for generously helping me at the Franckesche Stiftungen. Thank you Meghann LaFountain for translating French. To the University of Rochester's Phi Beta Kappa O'Hern scholarship fund, which provided the funding that began my research, and to the United States-India Educational Foundation, which oversaw my Fulbright Fellowship, thank you.

Thank you Irene Cooper, Rick Otis, Ross Dingwall, John Amir-Fazli and Josef Kuhn for your thoughtful edits. Thank you Carol Siri Johnson for joining me on this wild ride into eighteenth century British India; without your help I don't know how I would have finished this book. Thank you Aidan Kiernander for your kind attention and edits. To my parents Mindy and John Otis, and to my family, thank you. Thank you Priyanka Ray for teaching me the most important Bengali words. Thank you Mike German for being a friend and buddy through all these times. To my agent Aanchal Malhotra at Red Ink, and to my editor Karthik Venkatesh, thank you for making my dream a reality.

To my closest friends for encouraging me through these six years of research and writing, thank you. To anyone I have forgotten or omitted, I apologise. You all helped me more than you know.

References

Abbreviations

BL – British Library
AFSt/M – Missionarchiv der Franckeschen Stiftungen, Halle
NAI – National Archives of India
HBG – Hicky's Bengal Gazette
IG – India Gazette
BP&P – Bengal, Past & Present
SPCK – Society for the Promotion of Christian Knowledge Archive, held at University of Cambridge.

All dates formatted Year. Month. Day.
Surviving copies of *Hicky's Bengal Gazette* can be found at:
The British Library,
University of California, Berkeley,
The University of Heidelberg,
The University of Melbourne,
The High Court of Calcutta,
and The National Library of India.

Notes

1. I requested to digitise this issue of *Hicky's Bengal Gazette* three times, my final application burgeoning to twenty-four pages filed in triplicate. I was rejected each time.
2. The Minutes of the Supreme Court. If I could find these records, I would have known exactly what happened in Hicky's trials.
3. P. Thankappan Nair, *Hicky and his Gazette* (Kolkata: S & T Book Stall, 2001), 80-83.

4. There are many errors on Hicky among noted scholars. Vilanilam incorrectly stated that Hicky carried only advertisements on his front page. John V. Vilanilam, *Mass Communication In India: A Sociological Perspective*, (New Delhi: Sage Publications, 2005), 51. Watson falsely claimed that Hicky printed under Hastings' patronage. A. H. Watson, 'Origin and Growth of Journalism among Europeans,' *Annals of the American Academy of Political and Social Science* 145, Part 2 (Sep., 1929): 169. Nandy wrongly stated that Hicky was deported to England in 1782. S. C. Nandy, 'A Second Look at the Notes of Justice John Hyde,' *BP&P* 97, (1978): 30. One author printed a wholly imagined drawing of James Hicky wearing a wig and judge's robe. Arun Chaudhuri, *Indian Advertising*, (New Delhi; New York: Tata Mc-Graw Hill Pub. Co., 2007), 3. Finally, another author wrote that Hicky was born in a place called Colimba in Rockinghamshire in 1745, confusing the name of the ship Hicky arrived in Calcutta on, the *Rockingham*, with the name of the neighbourhood he settled in, Colimba, adding an entirely uncited birth year, and claiming that Hicky retired to England with his family. Jitendra Nath Basu, *Romance of Indian Journalism*, (Calcutta: Calcutta University, 1979), 23-32.

5. As Partha Chatterjee noted, 'Hicky's trial has been, unfortunately, long mired in the numerous stories of scandal and intrigue that form the staple of literature on eighteenth-century Calcutta.' Partha Chatterjee, *The Black Hole of Empire: History of a Global Practice of Power*, (Princeton, N.J.: Princeton University Press), 110-114; Mukhopadhyay, *Hicky's Bengal Gazette: Contemporary Life and Events*, (Calcutta: Subarnarekha, 1988), 123-130.

6. Abhijit Gupta and Swapan Chakravorty, 'Under the Sign of the Book: Introducing Book History in India,' in *Print Areas: Book History in India*, ed. Abhijit Gupta and Swapan Chakravorty, (Delhi: Permanent Black, 2004), 11. The Dutch printed the *Memorie des Nouvelles* in Indonesia, which reprinted stories from Dutch newspapers verbatim. The Spanish published the *Successos Felices* in 1637 in the Philippines, although only one edition is known to have been printed. Green, 'The Development of Mass Media in Asia Pacific,' *International Journal of Advertising* 22, No. 2 (2003): 2.

7. I have only been able to track two of Hicky's children—his family were twelve in number as of 1783—for certain: John Augustus Hicky, who died on 8 July 1809, and Elizabeth Hicky, a child, who

died on 12 July 1787. BL, Add MS 16264, f. 201, Hicky to Impey, 1783.08.11; BL, N/1/8 f.241; BL, N/1/4 f.40.

8. *Calcutta Gazette* 1802.05.06, 1802.05.13 (Accessed in the National Library of India's Rare Books Room). Governor-General Wellesley tasked the ship to bring jute, hemp, vegetables, and nutmeg for the Calcutta Botanic Gardens, but the seeds did not take hold, NAI, Home Public, Cons. 1803.03.10, Nos. 11-15.

9. BL, L-AG-34-27-30, Inventories & Accounts of Deceased Estates, No. 35, 1804.03.09.

10. Mofakhkhar Hussain Khan, *The History of Printing in Bengali Characters up to 1866, Vol. 1*, (unpublished Ph.D. thesis, School of Oriental and African Studies, University of London), 133. Hicky's occupation was listed as a 'printer' in *The Bengal Calendar and Register*, (Calcutta, 1790), 122. Graham W. Shaw, 'A Letter from James Augustus Hicky,' *Library* 6-5, No. 4 (1983): 395-397.

11. BL, Add MS 29177, f. 165.

12. The *Calcutta Gazette* announced that news of peace with France arrived in Calcutta on 9 September 1802, so the *Ajax* certainly sailed before word of peace reached Bengal.

13. *Calcutta Gazette*, 1802.06.17, 1.

14. After leaving Calcutta, the *Ajax* stopped at Madras on its way to Canton. It had a 'fine passage' to China. *Calcutta Gazette*, 1803.01.13.

15. Accounts of procedure for burial at sea taken from Rex Hickox, *18th Century Royal Navy* (Bentonville, AR: Rex Publishing, 2005), 89.

16. The *Calcutta Gazette* recorded: 'Deaths: Lately to the Eastward, on board the *Ajax*, Dr. J. A. Hickey.' *Calcutta Gazette Supplement*, 1802.12.16, 2. Based on this newspaper snippet, historians like P. T. Nair have incorrectly asserted that Hicky died in December 1802. However, since the *Ajax* was on its way to China, Hicky must have died months before news reached Calcutta in December. Given that the *Ajax* reached Canton sometime before mid-November (the *Calcutta Gazette* reported on 13 and 20 January 1803 that the *Betsy* had seen the *Ajax* in China before it left port on 14 November 1802) and assuming a two to three-month delay for news to travel from Canton to Calcutta, Hicky probably died in October 1802.

17. *Calcutta Gazette* 1803.05.10, 2; *Calcutta Gazette*, 1803.05.12, 2.

18. Hicky died intestate, his assets totaling Rs 3,056, about $6,000 today. Some people did take interest in the tools of Hicky's trade,

probably for posterity as well as profit. His former assistant, Paul Ferris, and two others, bought 640 pounds of his type, 44 teak frames for setting type, his press, and all his copies of *Hicky's Bengal Gazette*. Also present at the auction was one of his sons, James Hicky. See BL, L-AG-34-27-30, Inventories & Accounts of Deceased Estates, No. 35, 1804.03.09 and No. 133, 1804.10.02.

19. William Hickey, *Memoirs of William Hickey, Volume 2, 1775-1782*, ed. Alfred Spencer, (London: Hurst & Blackett, 1918), 173.

20. William Hickey must have met James Hicky in November 1777. William Hickey, who arrived in Calcutta in early November, wrote in his memoirs that he had 'only been a few days in Calcutta' when he received Hicky's letter for help. Hickey, *Memoirs, Vol. 2*, 118, 173.

21. *Calcutta in the Olden Time: its localities*, (Calcutta: 1852), 17-18. See also Hyde, *Hyde's Notebooks*, 1778.10.05; H. E. A. Cotton, *Calcutta, Old and New: A Historical & Descriptive Handbook to the City*, (Calcutta: W. Newman & Co., 1907), 336-337.

22. Hyde, *Hyde's Notebooks*, 1788.12.04. (Microfilm in the possession of Professor Thomas Curley of Bridgewater State University. Also accessed in microfilm of deteriorating quality at the National Library of India, and original and digitised forms at the Victoria Memorial, Kolkata).

23. Phebe Gibbes, *Hartly House, Calcutta*, (London: J. Dodsley, 1789), 230-231. Although fiction, *Hartly House*, written in 1789, has been acknowledged to provide valuable information about life in 18th century Calcutta.

24. The common jail could hold up to 170 prisoners with thirty-five guards. 'The gaol was an old ruin of a house, formerly the residence of some black native,' recalled a man imprisoned there. See James Creasy's testimony. Great Britain, Parliament, House of Commons, *First Report from the Select Committee Appointed to take into Consideration the State of the Administration of Justice in the Provinces of Bengal, Bahar, and Orissa*, (London: 1782), Appendix 11.

25. William Hickey's testimony, Parliament, *Select Committee's First Report*, Appendix 11.

26. Ibid.

27. NAI, Home Public, Original Consultation (hereafter O.C.) 1778.09.14, No. 9. The Common jail was, at least, better than Calcutta's other jail, the Hurrinbarry, house of corrections, for petty criminals. The Hurrinbarry was on lower ground than the

surrounding land. When it rained, the prisoners had to stand 'knee deep in water.' The situation of these 'unhappy prisoners' was so 'deplorable such as no Man of common sensibility could be a Witness of [it] without feeling the utmost Compassion for them ... Many of the poor Creatures were quite naked,' Calcutta's Police Superintendents, Thomas Motte and Edward Maxwell, wrote. NAI, Home Public, O.C. 1785.08.30, No. 36.

28. Nechtman, 'A Jewel in the Crown? Indian Wealth in Domestic Britain in the Late Eighteenth Century,' Eighteenth-Century Studies 41, No. 1 (Fall 2007): 73.

29. BL, L/MAR/B/493E(1), Ajax's Ledger (Wages).

30. BL, IOR/L/MAR/B/493B, Ajax's Log, 1772.02.04 to 1773.11.11.

31. Hicky was apprenticed to William Faden, a Scottish printer who owned a printing shop in Wine Office Court on Fleet Street, London. John Sainsbury, *John Wilkes: The Lives of a Libertine*, (Aldershot: Ashgate, 2006), 153; Arthur Cash, *John Wilkes: The Scandalous Father of Civil Liberty*, (New Haven: Yale University Press, 2008), 135-136. Assuming that Hicky was apprenticed as a printer at age fourteen, the usual age, he was likely born in 1739 or 1740. Donald Francis Mackenzie, ed., *Stationers' Company Apprentices, 1701-1800*, (Oxford: Oxford Bibliographical Society, 1978), 122.

32. BL, Add MS 16260, f. 52, Impey, undated [appears to be written 24 September 1781 to Masterman, Harrington, and Dunning]. Justice John Hyde confirmed Impey's claim that Hicky was Serjeant Davy's clerk, writing 'Mr Hicky was once clerk to a learned Serjeant (meaning Serjeant Davy).' Hyde, *Hyde's Notebooks*, 1781.06.29. Given Hicky's timeline, he may have clerked for Davy in one of the most important trials in the 18th century, *Somerset v. Stewart* in 1771–1772, a case that abolished slavery in England. Somerset had escaped slavery but was recaptured, and as punishment, was sent to Jamaica to work on a plantation. Somerset's godparents applied for habeas corpus before the Court of the King's Bench in London. Davy won their case, securing Somerset's freedom.

33. Details of Hicky's early life taken from BL MSS Eur G 118, 233 (William Hickey's memoirs) and BL, Add MS 16260, f. 52. Little is known about Hicky's early life. Historians like P. T. Nair have believed that Hicky came from Long Acre, Ireland, based on the Stationers' Hall printers guild's report stating: 'James Hicky son of William (late of Long Acre, linen weaver) was bound apprentice here on the 5th February. 1754.' It appears equally likely that this

Long Acre was Long Acre Street in London, a road known for makers of horse buggies. There seems to be no place named Long Acre in Ireland. Mackenzie, *Stationers' Company Apprentices, 1701-1800*, 122.

34. For centuries, passing ships left mail under these boulders for others to pick up, forming an informal but effective international news delivery service. See George Walker, *Haste, Post, Haste!: Postmen and Post-Roads Through the Ages*, (New York: Dodd and Mead, 1939) 145.

35. NAI, Home Public, Cons. 1772.12.21, No. 1a.; BL, IOR/L/MAR/B/493B, Ajax's Log, 1772.02.04 to 1773.11.11.

36. Quote from a passenger who took the *Rockingham* the following year to India. Philip Dormer Stanhope, *Genuine Memoirs of Asiaticus, in a Series of Letters to a Friend*, (London: G. Kearsley, 1774), 15.

37. Captain Hamilton demoted one John Cooper for drunkenness and gave another David Mackore a dozen lashes for several days' absence while docked at Bombay. By the time the *Rockingham* was ready to return from India, thirteen of the 131 crew had deserted, and four had died. BL, L/MAR/B/493B; BL, L/MAR/B/493E.

38. Death explained the departure of nearly 80 per cent of those who left the Company in their first ten years of service. Santhi Heejebu, 'Contract Enforcement in the English East India Company,' *The Journal of Economic History* 62, No. 2 (June 2005): 508-509.

39. Of cadets who travelled between 1760 and 1834. Richard Holmes, *Sahib: the British Soldier in India 1750-1914)*, (London: Harper Perennial 2006), 474; For more on illnesses plaguing Europeans, see Peter James Marshall, *East India Fortunes: The British in Bengal in the Eighteenth Century* (Oxford: Clarendon Press, 1976), 218–19.

40. The *Rockingham* docked at Hijli, at the entrance to the Rasalpur River. The *Rockingham* reached Calcutta between 28 and 31 December 1772. The journey between Hijli in Calcutta was usually quicker, but Captain Hamilton waited to unload large amounts of gunpowder before continuing over the sand banks in the Hooghly called 'The Braces'. NAI, Home Public, P.P. 71, and O.C. 1773.01.25; NAI, Home Public, No. 1., O.C. 1772.12.31 and No. 14., O.C. 1773.02.01.

41. These palaces were in the Garden Reach neighbourhood. Eliza Fay, *Original Letters from India*, ed. Walter Kelley Firminger, (Calcutta: Thacker, Spink & Co, 1908), 131.

42. The Fort was finished in 1773. See Charles Edward Buckland 'The City of Calcutta,' *Journal of the Royal Society of Arts* 54, No. 2,765 (1906): 283.

43. According to William Hickey, Hicky had been shipwrecked on the Hooghly. 'The Vessel he thus belonged to was unfortunately wrecked entering the river of Bengal, whereby he lost everything but life; In consequence of this misfortune the Government of Bengal employed him in one of their coasting vessels wherein he speculated in Trade,' Hickey wrote. I have been unable to substantiate Hickey's claim; the *Rockingham* is not recorded to have encountered any misfortune on the Hooghly, although it is possible Hicky may have finished his journey on the Hooghly in a smaller vessel. BL, MSS Eur G 118, 233.

44. Stanhope, *Asiaticus*, 49.

45. J. B. Gilchrist and Thomas Williamson, *The General East India Guide and Vadecum*, (London: Kingsbury, Parbury & Allen, 1825), 81-82.

46. Sumanta Banerjee, 'City of Dreadful Night: Crime and Punishment in Colonial Calcutta,' *Economic and Political Weekly* 38, No. 21 (May 2003): 2047-8; HBG 1780.03.18, 1.

47. HBG 1780.03.25, 2, Philantropos; Eliza Fay, *The Original Letters from India of Mrs. Eliza Fay*, ed. Walter Kelley Firminger (Calcutta: Thacker, Spink & Co., 1908), 165.

48. Bhaswati Bhattacharya, 'Armenian European Relationship in India, 1500-1800: No Armenian Foundation for European Empire?' *Journal of the Economic and Social History of the Orient* 48, No. 2 (2005): 304; Peter James Marshall, 'The White Town of Calcutta under the Rule of the East India Company,' *Modern Asian Studies* 34, No. 2 (May 2000): 313-316; Krishna Dutta, *Calcutta: A Cultural and Literary History*, (Oxford: Signal Books, 2003), 9-32.

49. Stanhope, *Asiaticus*, 42.

50. Subaltern, from the Latin 'subalternus,' meaning below every other.

51. Remittances averaged £12,462 over an average career of fifteen years. Heejebu, 'Contract Enforcement,' 512; Gregory Clark, *Average Earnings and Retail Prices, UK, 1209–2010*, (University of California, Davis, 2011) Table 17; Raymond Callahan, *The East India Company and Army Reform*, (Cambridge: Harvard University Press, 1972), 31-33.

52. Lewis Namier and John Brooke, *The House of Commons 1754-1790*, (London: Boydell & Brewer, 1985), 61.

53. Company servants risked fines, dismissal, or prosecution for their private trade. Yet they traded privately anyways. When the directors once wrote to India to limit private trade, Calcutta's Governor responded, 'If the Company allowed no private trade, their servants must starve.' Chatterjee, *Black Hole*, 9; See also Brijen K. Gupta, *Sirajuddaullah and the East India Company, 1756–1757: Background to the Foundation of British Power in India*, (Leiden: E. J. Brill, 1962), 9-13.
54. Heejebu, 'Contract Enforcement,' 503-505.
55. Company servants often saw themselves entitled to their perks. When the Board of Trade was investigated in 1786, one of the members resigned, saying that 'he would no longer serve under such a set of illiberal men.' William Hickey, *Memoirs of William Hickey, Vol. 3, 1782-1790,* ed. Alfred Spencer, (London: Hurst & Blackett, 1918), 306-310.
56. Callahan, *Army Reform*, 31-33.
57. Marshall, *East India Fortunes*, 225.
58. HBG 1781.05.19, 3.
59. Dennis O. Flynn and Arturo Giraldez, 'Cycles of Silver: Global Economic Unity through the Mid-Eighteenth Century,' *Journal of World History* 13, No. 2 (Fall, 2002): 413.
60. Hicky sued some of his patients when they did not pay after he treated them. See High Court of Calcutta, Mayor's Court Archives: *James Augustus Hicky v. Frederick Charles*, June 24, 1773; *James Augustus Hicky v. Thomas Frowhawk*, September 14, 1773; *James Augustus Hicky v. William Spranger*, September 14, 1773.
61. Some of Hicky's creditors were lenient. For instance, the firm of MacKenzie and Mathew Erskine collected their Rs 1,400 loan many years after Hicky's death. The loan was given on 25 April 1776 and collected on 17 September 1819. BL, L-AG-34-27-65, Inventories & Accounts of Deceased Estates, 1838.
62. Hicky claimed he entered jail on October 20, but the Supreme Court's writ indicates he entered jail on October 22. The Court set bail at Rs 1,110 which Hicky did not furnish. HBG 1780.11.04, 3; High Court of Calcutta, Mayor's Court Archives, *John Natley, Executor of Hester, Deceased v. James Augustus Hicky*, August 7, 1776; July 15, 1777; November 11, 1777 and January 23, 1778.
63. Hickey, *Memoirs, Vol. 2*, 175.
64. Ibid., 173-174.

65. William Hickey's testimony, Parliament, *Select Committee's First Report*, Appendix 11.
66. Hickey, *Memoirs, Vol. 2*, 174.
67. Ibid.
68. Rammody Bysack sued Hicky on 12 July 1776. High Court of Calcutta, Mayor's Court Archives, *Rammody Bysack v. James Augustus Hicky*, July 12, 1776. For more on the Bysacks, see Atis Dasgupta and Subhas Ranjan Chakraborti, 'The Growth of Calcutta: A Profile of Social Dislocations in the Early Colonial Period,' *Social Scientist* 20, No. 3 (Mar.-Apr., 1992): 37. Contrary to the Supreme Court's records, Hicky claimed that his debt was only Rs 4,300. HBG 1780.11.04, 3.
69. Hickey, *Memoirs, Vol. 2*, 174.
70. High Court of Calcutta, Mayor's Court Archives, *John Natley, Executor of Hester, Deceased v. James Augustus Hicky*, 29 July 1778.
71. Hester's estate sued Hicky on 7 August 1776. High Court of Calcutta, Mayor's Court Archives, *John Natley, Executor of Hester, Deceased v. James Augustus Hicky*, August 7, 1776.
72. William Hickey got a writ habeas corpus to bring James Hicky out of prison and into the courtroom for this case. Hicky pled not guilty on 22 June 1778. High Court of Calcutta, Mayor's Court Archives, *John Natley, Executor of Hester, Deceased v. James Augustus Hicky*, 29 July 1778. In his memoirs, Hickey said that this trial (the second trial) came two days after the first.
73. Hickey, *Memoirs, Vol. 2*, 175. Hicky's claim of perjury is possibly referring to Samuel Greenway. Greenway's deposition, in which he argued that Hester did not owe anyone any money, appears struck out in the High Court's records. High Court of Calcutta, Mayor's Court Archives, *John Natley, Executor of Hester, Deceased v. James Augustus Hicky*, July 29, 1778. Although the gist of William Hickey's memoirs tends to be accurate, his facts are often wildly incorrect. Hickey claimed that one of Hicky's debts was for 20,000 rupees, probably an exaggeration. Additionally, I have assumed that *Hicky v. Bysack* came before *Hicky v. Hester* because the first trial involved a 'native of Bengal,' while the second appeared to be against Europeans alone. Hickey, *Memoirs, Vol. 2*, 174.
74. The judges estimated Hicky's 'lodging, boarding, attendance and physick' for Hester cost Rs 4 a day, for approximately 500 days. The judges then deducted this sum from Hester's loans to Hicky. *Hyde's Notebooks*, 1778.07.29.

75. Hicky printed each bill for five annas, or 5/16 of a rupee. NAI, Home Public, Body Sheet, Cons. 1793.02.01, O.C. 1793.01.09.

76. The Regulations were last updated by a previous commander-in-chief, Sir Robert Barker. NAI, Home Public, O.C. 1788.08.22.

77. BL, IOR/P/18/47, Coote's regulations are discussed in consultations from 7 July to 9 August 1780.

78. Nathaniel Brassey Halhed, who later joined Charles Wilkins and became Hicky's competitor, was then the Commissary General. NAI, Home Public, Body Sheet, Cons. 1793.02.01, No. 28, O.C. 1793.01.09; See also J. Duncan M. Derrett, 'Nathaniel Brassley Halhed: Mystic or Maniac? His Association with Joanna Southcott,' *Annals of the Bhandarkar Oriental Research Institute* 60, No. 1 (1979): 229.

79. NAI, Home Public, Body Sheet, Cons. 1793.02.01, No. 28, O.C. 1793.01.09.

80. Colonel Robert Kyd appears to have directly supervised Hicky's contract because Coote left Calcutta on 27 September 1779 to inspect army bases in Bengal and Awadh. Joseph Parkes and Herman Merivale, *Memoirs of Sir Philip Francis K.C.B. with Correspondence and Journals, Vol. 2*, (London: Spottiswoods & Co., 1867), 168.

81. Given that Hicky claimed he had fully printed the proof sheets, and that full contracts included at least nine proof sheets, with 2,135 sheets of paper in each proof sheet, as well as 192 sheets of paper for Coote's personal regulation book, the project would total 38,814 pages (every sheet of paper equals two pages). NAI, Home Public, Body Sheet, Cons. 1793.07.26; NAI, Home Public, Body Sheet, Cons. 1793.02.01, O.C. 1793.01.09. It is possible the printing job was much larger as these were described as the 'first' nine proof sheets. NAI, Home Public, Cons. 1788.08.22, O.C. 1788.07.24.

82. H. C. Wylly, *A Life of Lieutenant-General Sir Eyre Coote K. B.*, (Oxford: Clarendon Press, 1922), 172; NAI, Home Public, O.C. 1795.02.25, No. 22.

83. Hastings personally sponsored Wilkins and Halhed, paying their salaries and the salaries of their assistants and making them the Company's official printers. There is some confusion over whether Hicky or Wilkins was truly the first printer in Bengal. Mofakhkhar Hussain Khan has argued that Wilkins began printing in June 1777 citing a letter from Halhed and Wilkins dated 14 January 1785 to

the Supreme Council that 'it is now seven years and a half since our demand of 30,000 S. R. was approved by the Governor General in Council.' However, this could also mean that printing was solicited in June 1777 and the majority of their book, *A Grammar of the Bengali Language*, was printed from June 1778 to September 1778, since they claimed greatest part of the printing was done in the rainy season. Regardless of who truly began printing first, only a matter of months would have separated them. On 22 December 1778, Hastings made Wilkins 'Superintendent of the Press,' with a monthly salary, office expenses, and a boat to move supplies between Calcutta and Hooghly. Khan, *Printing in Bengali Characters*, 135-136.

84. Parkes and Merivale, *Memoirs of Francis*, 167-169; Peter James Marshall, *The Impeachment of Warren Hastings*, (Oxford: Oxford University Press, 1965), 178.

85. NAI, Home Public, Cons. 1795.02.20, No. 18, 405-421; Hicky paid his staff between Rs 30 to Rs 100 a month as well as lodging. Hicky borrowed his money from Captain Price. According to Hicky, the brass rule, iron work and other equipment he made for the regulations were inapplicable to any other printing. NAI, Home Public, Body Sheet, 1793.02.01, No. 28, O.C. 1793.01.09.

86. These officers were Colonels Owen and Morgan. NAI, Home Public, Body Sheet, Cons. 1793.02.01, No. 28, O.C. 1793.01.09.

87. The artillerymen numbered 2,438. Pearse had pled his case to preserve his command directly to the Supreme Council. Despite Pearse's pleas, the Council ordered him to comply and disband his artillery corps. Wylly, *Eyre Coote*, 174-176; Parkes and Merivale, *Francis Memoirs, Vol. 2,* 174-175.

88. HBG 1781.01.27, 2; Hicky also recounted this conversation in a petition. NAI, Home Public, Body Sheet, Cons. 1793.02.01, No. 28, O.C. 1793.01.09.

89. Hicky printed five sheets, with 2,135 copies per sheet. With two pages per sheet that is 21,350 pages, plus the 384 pages of Coote's personal regulation book. He had composed and corrected the next three proof sheets, but the officers never returned the sixth and seventh sheets.

90. NAI, Home Public, Body Sheet, Cons. 1788.08.22, No. 26, Kyd's statement on Hicky's petition.

91. Specifically, Hicky lived in Hooda Taltolah, within the district of Colinga Muchipara. Nair, *Hicky and His Gazette*, 2-3. Hicky wrote

that Droz's visit was 'several days' before the publication of his first issue on January 29. HBG 1780.11.11, 2-3.

92. Nair, *Hicky and his Gazette*, 2; Iqtidar Hussain Siddiqi, 'Islamic Learning and Intellectual Thought in the Sultanate of Delhi During the Lodi Period,' *Indo-Iranica*, 43 (1990): 11. (Taltola).

93. See NAI, Home Public, O.C., No. 2, 1764.11.05, 692.

94. Droz started his career as secretary to the Mayor's Court, then as Calcutta's sheriff, before being appointed to the Patna Council. NAI, Home Public, O.C. 1772.02.06, 311-313; William Bolts, *Considerations on India affairs: particularly respecting the present state of Bengal and its dependencies*, (London: J. Almon, 1772), 49 and Anand A. Yang, *The Limited Raj: Agrarian Relations in Colonial India, Saran District, 1793-1920*, (Berkeley: University of California Press, 1989), 44. The Patna Council was notorious for its dark politics. In one instance, they blackmailed a woman named Bibi Sukun by claiming she had murdered her bastard child. In another, they received bribes to fabricate a trial and evict a woman, Nauderah Begum, from her land by supporting claims that she had committed forgery. Bishwa Nath Pandey, *The Introduction of English Law into India: The Career of Elijah Impey in Bengal, 1774-1783*, (London: Asia Publishing House, 1967), 141.

95. HBG 1780.06.17, 1.

96. Although *The North Briton* was written anonymously, Wilkes was closely affiliated with it. Cash, *John Wilkes*, 223–230.

97. H. E. Busteed, *Echoes from Old Calcutta, Being Chiefly Reminiscences from the Day of Warren Hastings, Francis, and Impey*, 2nd ed. (Calcutta: W. Thacker & Co, 1908), 182.

98. Margarita Barns, *The Indian Press: a history of the growth of public opinion in India*, (London: G. Allen & Unwin, 1940), 45; Norman Leslie Hallward, *William Bolts, a Dutch Adventurer Under John Company*, (Cambridge: Cambridge University Press, 1920), 49. Bolts made good on his threats, but only after being deported to Europe, printing a book called *Considerations on India Affairs* in 1772, where he accused the Company of rampant corruption.

99. It appears Hastings gave Hicky sanction to print a newspaper, although I can find no record of this authorisation. 'The G—r has given his sanction to a Mr Hickey to print a Newspaper weekly, for the entertainment of the Settlement. I am almost persuaded that it will never answer in a place like Calcutta for many Reasons; we shall see however very soon.' BL, Mss Eur E 9, f. 10, K. Lacam to

Margaret Fowke, Undated 1779. See also BL, Add MS 29148, f. 418, Pearse to Hastings, 1781.04.29.

100. Prospectus, date unknown, found in the University of Melbourne's copy of *Hicky's Bengal Gazette*.

101. HBG 1780.08.05, 2.

102. HBG 1780.11.11, 2. (mostly illegible, bottom left).

103. Kiernander arrived in Cuddalore with fellow missionaries Johann Philipp Fabricius and Daniel Zeglin on August 8; Zeglin and Fabricius left to Tranquebar the next month. H. Sandegren, *Johann Zachariah Kiernander, The First Swedish Missionary in India*, trans. E. Wimmercranz, (Madras: Missionary Society Press, 1928), 6; AFSt/M 2 K 10 : 1a.

104. AFSt/M 1 B 37: 32, Kiernander to Gotthilf August Francke, 1747.04.29; AFSt/M 2 K 12: 30, Kiernander to Gotthilf August Francke, 1745.01.14. Kiernander became desperate many times in his early career. 'The remaining money in our cash seemeth to be hardly enough for our expenses, till we can expect a supply from Europe. We will manage it with all possible frugality, and leave the rest to Providence,' he once wrote. AFSt/M 2 L 2: 1, Diary of Johann Ernst Geister and Kiernander, 1741.01.18 to 1741.12.28, entry dated in February.

105. AFSt/M 2 E 47: 7, Kiernander to David Brown, 1788.04.21.

106. Sandegren, *Swedish Missionary*, 2.

107. Andreas Gross, 'Some Aspects of English-Halle Mission in Cuddalore (1739–1829),' in *Halle and the beginning of Protestant Christianity in India: The Danish-Halle and the English-Halle Mission*, Vol. 1, (Halle: Franckesche Stiftungen, 2006), 386; AFSt/M 2 K 6: 6, Gotthilf August Francke to Kiernander, 1739.11.14; AFSt/M 2 K 6: 10, Appointment from Christian VI, King of Denmark and Norway for Kiernander, 1739.12.03.

108. AFSt/M 2 K 6: 1, Jean Kiernander and Catharina Behm to Kiernander, 1739.09.29; AFSt/M 2 K 6: 2, Petrus Regneer to Kiernander, 1739.09.29.

109. Derozario, *The Complete Monumental Register, Containing All the Epitaphs, Inscriptions, &c &c &c*, (Calcutta: Paul Ferris, 1815), 109.

110. Gross, *Christianity in India*, Vol. 1, 386-7.

111. Many scholars have claimed that it was originally Kiernander who walked door to door explaining theology, but Geister seems to have begun this practice. Geister wrote in his journal

on 10 January 1740 (before Kiernander arrived): 'Finding myself tolerably well advanced in the study of the Malabar language, I resolved to go abroad, and converse with the natives without doors. Therefore I visited today all the schools in this place, enquiring ... if they had a mind to know the ways, customs and Religion of the Europeans, they might give me an opportunity of conversing with them ... I chose the visiting of the schools chiefly for that reason, because I knew, the children would tell their parents, and relations, what an unusual thing that had happened at school, and that consequently I would be sooner known among them.' AFSt/M 2 L 1 : 2, Diary of Johann Ernst Geister and Kiernander, 1740.01.01 to 1740.12.29.

112. Sandegren, *Swedish Missionary*, 17-19.
113. AFSt/M 2 E 47 : 8, Kiernander to David Brown, 1788.08.18; Johannes Ferdinand Fenger, *History of the Tranquebar mission worked out from the original papers*, (Tranquebar: Evangelical Lutheran Press, 1863), 240-241.
114. Isaac's family stripped him of his inheritance, nor would acknowledge his presence when his father died later that year. Sandegren, *Swedish Missionary*, 22-25.
115. AFSt/M 2 L 1 : 2, Diary of Johann Ernst Geister and Kiernander, 1740.01.01 to 1740.12.29.
116. AFSt/M 2 E 47 : 8, Kiernander to David Brown, 1788.08.18.
117. Ibid.
118. AFSt/M 2 G 16 : 37, Johann Philipp Fabricius to Kiernander, 1745.12.23; AFSt/M 2 G 16 : 55, Gotthilf August Francke to Friedrich Michael Ziegenhagen, 1747.01.12.
119. Erika Pabst, 'The Wives of Missionaries: Their Experiences in India,' in Andreas Gross, *Halle and the beginning of Protestant Christianity in India, Christian mission in the Indian context*, Vol. 2. (Halle: Franckesche Stiftungen, 2006), 693-694.
120. Gross, *Christianity in India*, Vol. 1, 386-7; Sandegren, *Swedish Missionary*, 14-15.
121. AFSt/M 1 B 36: 31, Kiernander to Gotthilf August Francke, 1747.01.18.
122. Derozario, *Monumental Register*, 109; AFSt/M 2 K 13 : 34, Kiernander to Gotthilf August Francke, 1749.02.17; AFSt/M 2 K 13: 19, Kiernander to Gotthilf August Francke, 1749.10.26.
123. Furber, 'Asia and the West as Partners,' 715; Furber, *Rival Empires*, 289.

124. AFSt/M 1 B 59: 55, Johann Georg Knapp to Kiernander, 1771.01.26. I am indebted to Andrew Zonderman for this reference; T. Fisher, 'Memoir of the Rev. John Zachariah Kiernander,' *The Gentleman's Magazine: And Historical Chronicle,* (Dec. to June 1824), 105.

125. Gross, *Christianity in India,* Vol. 1, 391.

126. AFSt/M 2 E 47: 7, Kiernander to David Brown, 1788.04.21.

127. SPCK.MS E2/4, Journal of the Mission at Cuddalore by Kiernander and Hüttemann, Jul-Dec, 1757.

128. AFSt/M 2 E 47: 10, Kiernander to David Brown, 1789.11.12.

129. AFSt/M 1 H 4: 46, Kiernander to David Brown, 1780.10.16.

130. AFSt/M 2 E 47: 7, Kiernander to David Brown, 1788.04.21.

131. AFSt/M 1 B 75: 42, Kiernander to Friedrich Wilhelm Pasche, 1784.10.12.

132. There are two competing dates for when Kiernander arrived in Calcutta. Sandegren, in *Swedish Missionary,* 34, claims September 18; Derozario in *Monumental Register,* 110, claims September 29, and that Kiernander left Tranquebar September 11.

133. Kiernander appears to have established the first Protestant Mission in Bengal, although the Society had a presence in Bengal since 1700, when members began preaching and established a parish library. See Abulfazal M. Fazle Kabir, 'English Libraries in Eighteenth-Century Bengal,' *The Journal of Library History* 14, No. 4 (Fall, 1979): 438-439. Kiernander spent his first Rs 100 immediately to find shelter, and his last Rs 300 on a year's rent. AFSt/M 1 H 4: 46, Kiernander to Society, 1780.10.16.

134. Fisher, 'Memoir of Kiernander,' 106; Derozario, *Monumental Register,* 111. AFSt/M 2 E 47: 7, Kiernander to David Brown, 1788.04.21; The next Governor, John Zephaniah Holwell, gave the Portuguese their chapel back; Kiernander returned to preaching from his house. Sandegren, *Swedish Missionary,* 38.

135. AFSt/M 1 B 74: 53, Kiernander to Hallings, 1783.10.27.

136. Gross, *Halle and the beginning of Protestant Christianity in India, Vol. 3, Communication between India and Europe,* (Halle: Franckesche Stiftungen, 2006), 1508. Stephen Neill, *A History of Christianity in India: 1707-1858,* (Cambridge: Cambridge University Press, 2002), 108.

137. John Carne, *Lives of Eminent Missionaries, Vol. 1,* (London: Fisher, Son & Jackson, 1832), 307; Parker, *A Sermon Preached in the Parish-church of Christ-church, London...,* (London: John Rivington Jr., printer to the SPCK, 1781), 93. Kiernander

converted a 28 year old Jew, Aaron Levi, who was renamed
John Charles, originally from Izmir, Turkey. AFSt/M1 B 56 : 40,
Kiernander to Thomas Broughton, 1766.12.31. I am indebted to
Andrew Zonderman for this reference. Kiernander was also proud
of his convert, Gunnesam Das, a Hindu from Delhi who joined
the English army at fifteen, became a Persian interpreter for the
Supreme Court, worked as Impey's personal munshi (See Impey,
Memoirs, 237), and travelled to England in 1770. Sandegren,
Swedish Missionary, 51-52. Gross, *Christianity in India, Vol. 1*,
426-429; Derozario, *Monumental Register*, 111.

138. Robert Travers, 'Death and the Nabob: Imperialism and
Commemoration in Eighteenth-Century India,' *Past & Present*
196 (Aug. 2007): 112; Peter James Marshall, 'British Society in
India under the East India Company,' *Modern Asian Studies* 31,
No. 1 (Feb. 1997): 104.

139. Kiernander's Mission was relatively unsupported; in comparison,
the Tranquebar Mission had six missionaries and local assistants.
Gross, *Christianity in India, Vol. 1*, 424.

140. Wendela Kiernander died on 9 May 1761. Kiernander married Ann
Woolley on 10 February 1762. Prabhakar, *Mission in the Past and
Present*, 20-22; *Selections from the Calcutta Review, Vol. 2*, 514.
Kiernander sent his son Robert, and his godson Andreas Moos,
to England in October 1764. AFSt/M 1 B 53 : 34, Kiernander to
Friedrich Michael Ziegenhagen, 1764.10.14.

141. AFSt/M 2 E 47 : 7, Kiernander to David Brown. 1788.04.21.

142. AFSt/M 2 H 4 : 46, Kiernander to the Society, 1780.10.16.

143. AFSt/M 2 E 47 : 7, Kiernander to David Brown. 1788.04.21.

144. The Calcutta Council awarded Kiernander the contract on 25
April 1768. Walter Kelley Firminger, 'Leaves from the Editor's
Note Book,' *BP&P* 1, No. 1 (July – Dec. 1907): 74. The Company's
Directors later censured the Council for the Hospital's great
cost, which totaled Rs 98,000. BL, IOR 354.541, Letter from
the Court of Directors to the Calcutta Council, 1770.03.23, No.
169, 47.

145. According to Kiernander, the loss of life was greatest between
Patna and Murshidabad. SPCK.MS A33/5 (1770-1788), Indian
Missions Committee Meeting, 1772.05.05.

146. Atis Dasgupta, 'Early Trends of Anti-Colonial Peasant Resistance
in Bengal,' *Social Scientist* 14, No. 4 (Apr., 1986): 22.

147. BL, IOR/P/2/1: Bengal Proceedings, Cons. 1772.05.04.

148. Kiernander estimated that he moved 300 maunds of brick from his church to the hospital. One maund roughly equaled 37 kilograms. See Roy, *An Economic History of Early Modern India*, 133, for maund to kg conversion.

149. BL, IOR/P/2/1: Bengal Proceedings, Cons. 1772.05.04; BL, IOR/P/1/51: Bengal Proceedings, Cons. 1772.04.23.

150. Only Rs 1,817 came from donations to construct Kiernander's church. This included a Rs 186 gift from Captain John Griffin, a Rs 237 gift from Gottleib Anastasius Francke, and Rs 1221 from Kiernander's balance with the Society. AFSt/M 1 B 59 : 35f. I am indebted to Andrew Zonderman for this reference. When Kiernander finished his church in 1771, he wrote to the Society that he had consecrated it under their care. Despite his claim, he never transferred ownership to the Society. SPCK.MS A33/5 (1770-1788), 1771.11.26.

151. AFSt/M 2 B 3 : 24, Ground plan of the church Beth Tephilla Calcutta. The other building known to have glass windows was Hastings' mansion. Wylly, *Eyre Coote*, 157. Kiernander's name for his church, Beth Tephilla, meaning house of prayer in Hebrew, never stuck. British called it the Mission Church, Bengalis, Lal Girja, the Red Church, because of its colour. Government of Bengal Public Works Department, *List of Ancient Monuments in the Presidency Division*, (Calcutta: Bengal Secretariat Press, 1896), 20.

152. AFSt/M 1 B 59 : 55, Johann Georg Knapp to Kiernander. 1771.01.26. I am indebted to Andrew Zonderman for this reference; AFSt/M 1 B 53 : 51, Gotthilf August Francke to Kiernander. 1764.06.23.

153. AFSt/M 2 E 47 : 11, Kiernander to David Brown. 1788.08.24.

154. Stanhope, *Asiaticus*, 26.

155. AFSt/M 1 B 74 : 53, Kiernander to Michael Hallings, 1783.10.27.

156. *Swedish Missionary*, 62. Kiernander laid the foundation for his school on 7 July 1773, though it is unclear when he actually finished it. SPCK.MS A33/5 (1770-1788), see meetings on 1774.11.08, 1774.11.15, and 1774.11.30; Gross, *Christianity in India, Vol. 1*, 423; Kiernander called his personal houses Beth Saron and Saron Grove. Kathleen Blechynden, *Calcutta Past and Present*, (London: W. Thacker & Co., 1905), 80-82.

157. They were Clarinda, enslaved by his deceased wife Ann Wolley, and Rebekah, enslaved by his deceased catechist Marcellino Joseph Ramalhete. See Henry Barry Hyde, *Parochial Annals*:

Being a history of the Bengal ecclesiastical establishment of the Honourable East India Company in the 17th and 18th centuries, (Calcutta: Bengal Secretariat Book Depot, 1901), 156 and 'Burials in Calcutta,' *BP&P* 6, No. 2 (July – Dec 1910): 100.

158. Sometime after Kiernander talked to Hicky about printing almanacs, his son Robert purchased a small printing press and an old, incomplete, worn out Portuguese typeset. Around the same time, Kiernander and his son advertised they would be printing an almanac for the year 1778 themselves, which Robert printed sometime before 7 January 1778. It is uncertain where Robert Kiernander got this equipment from, but he may have requested it from Tranquebar in South India. See Gerald Duverdier, 'Deux imprimeurs en proces a Calcutta: Hicky contre Kiernander,' *Moyen Orient & Ocean Indien* 2, (1985): 63.

159. AFSt/M 1 B 56 : 40e, Kiernander to Thomas Broughton. Calcutta, 1766.12.31. I am indebted to Andrew Zonderman for this reference.

160. Kiernander deposited 400 Riechsthalers for Diemer's passage. AFSt/M 1 B 74 : 53, Kiernander to Michael Hallings, 1783.10.23. See also SPCK.MS A33/5 (1770-1788), 1770.08.14.

161. Society for the Promotion of Christian Knowledge, *An Account of the Society for Promoting Christian Knowledge,* (London: J. and W. Oliver, Printers to the SPCK, 1774), 93-94.

162. AFSt/M 1 H 4: 46, Kiernander to the Society, 1780.10.16; SPCK. MS A33/5 (1770-1788), 1776.01.16.

163. AFSt/M 2 E 47: 13 K, Kiernander to David Brown, 1789.11.23.

164. Diemer had to find his own living accommodations, as it was not until March 1777 that Kiernander finished renovations on the Mission House. AFSt/M 1 H 4 : 46; AFSt/M 1 B 73: 40, Kiernander to Gottleib Anastasius Freylinghausen, 1783.05.23; AFSt/M 1 C 29b: 90, Diemer to Johann Ludwig Schulze, 1788.10.28. I am indebted to Markus Berger for this translation. AFSt/M 1 B 74: 53, Kiernander to Michael Hallings, 1783.10.27; AFSt/M 1 B 73: 32, Kiernander to the Society, 1782.10.30.

165. Diemer frequently visited Serampore and Chinsurah. AFSt/M 1 B 68: 52, Kiernander to Thomas Broughton, 1776.12.31; AFSt/M 1 B 68: 49, Kiernander to Thomas Broughton, 1776.10.14.

166. AFSt/M 1 B 68: 48, Diemer to Thomas Broughton. 1776.12.19.

167. Diemer left Calcutta on January 24, 1777 and returned on January 30. AFSt/M 1 B 73: 40, Kiernander to Gottleib Anastasius

Freylinghausen, 1783.03.25. Kiernander wrote that Diemer tried to force Charles Weston to give him money promised to his wife, but failed. 'This money being refused, as not given for that purpose, he still thought he could force the matter; resolved at the beginning of the 1777 to go with a Danish Ship.' AFSt/M 1 H 4 : 46, Kiernander to the Society, 1780.10.16.

168. AFSt/M 1 H 4: 46, Kiernander to the Society, 1780.10.16.

169. James Hough, *The history of Christianity in India from the Commencement of the Christian Era*, *Vol. 4*, (London: Church Missionary House, 1845), 34-35.

170. Griffin had a number of run-ins with the Company. At one point, the Directors accused Griffin of 'very gross neglect of Duty' after he was found with three boxes of gold and silver lace, buttons, and thread, knowingly shipped without license. Griffin commanded the Lapwing until 1765, the Admiral Stevens from 1765 to 1767 and the Admiral Watson thereafter. BL, E/4/617, 550; BL, E/4/618, 731; BL, E/4/619, 209. Griffin died on May 28, 1770. AFSt/M 1 B 60 : 25 Kiernander to Johann Georg Knapp, 1770.08.09.

171. AFSt/M 1 B 73: 26, Kiernander to Pasche, 28.10.1782.

172. Kiernander gave Diemer charge of the school on 29 March 1777. See AFSt/M 1 B 73: 31, Kiernander to Michael Hallings, 1782.10.29, and AFSt/M 1 B 73 : 40, Kiernander to Gottleib Anastasius Freylinghausen, 1783.03.25; AFSt/M 1 H 4: 47, Kiernander to Michael Hallings, 1780.11.28. AFSt/M 1 B 70: 52.

173. The town charity paid the superintendent a Rs 100 a month salary to oversee the charity children's education and another Rs 462 a month for their schooling expenses. In a bit of internal accounting, Kiernander then charged the Mission school Rs 100 in rent. AFSt/M 1 B 73 : 40, Kiernander to Gottleib Anastasius Freylinghausen, 1783.03.25; BL, IOR/P/2/22: Bengal Proceedings, Cons. 1778.01.19, No. 17-19. The town charity had been established after the Company recaptured Calcutta in 1757 and forced Calcutta's Muslims to pay reparations for when the Nawab of Bengal sacked the city. These reparations formed the base of the town charity, which was supplemented by donations from rich merchants and by the profits of a building the Company's priests rented to the Supreme Court, which was used as the Court House. Hough, *Christianity in India*, *Vol. 4*, 37-38.

174. For instance, one teacher, John Mate, quit to become a Company writer in 1765 for a higher salary. See AFSt/M 1 B 55: 22,

Kiernander to Gotthilf August Francke, 1765.12.31, AFSt/M 1 B 55 : 24, 1766.02.15, and AFSt/M 1 B 59 : 35, 1769.12.07; SPCK. MS B1/1776, 83-84.

175. Kiernander made his request on 30 July 1777. The Council exempted other religious institutions, like the Armenian and Portuguese churches, from taxation. BL, IOR/P/2/20: Bengal Proceedings, Cons. 1777.09.01, No. 15.

176. The exemption from 'ground rent' and police tax for his church and burying ground amounted to Rs 42, 6 anna, 4 pice per year. BL, OIR, 354.541, Letter from Supreme Council to Court of Directors, 1777.11.21, No. 36, 357.

177. BL, IOR/P/2/22: Bengal Proceedings, Cons. 1778.01.19, No. 17-19.

178. AFSt/M 1 H 4 : 37a, Kiernander to Diemer, 1780.09.15.

179. AFSt/M 1 H 4 : 47, Kiernander to Hallings, 1780.11.28.

180. AFSt/M 1 B 72 : 81, Diemer to Hallings, 1780.12.01.

181. AFSt/M 1 B 69 : 55, Diemer, Gerlach and Kiernander to Michael Hallings, 1779.02.16; AFSt/M 1 B 72 : 81, Diemer to Hallings, 1780.12.01.

182. AFSt/M 1 B 73 : 40, Kiernander to Gottleib Anastasius Freylinghausen, 1783.03.25.

183. George Robert Gleig, *Memoirs of the Life of the Right Hon. Warren Hastings, First Governor-General of Bengal, Compiled from original papers*, Vol. 2, (London: Richard Bentley, 1841), 139.

184. Alfred Mervyn Davies, *Strange Destiny: A Biography of Warren Hastings*, (New York: Putnam, 1935), 11; Lyall, *Warren Hastings*, (London: Macmillan & Co., 1894), 2.

185. Lyall. *Hastings*, 8.

186. George Robert Gleig, *Memoirs of the Life of the Right Hon. Warren Hastings, First Governor-General of Bengal, Compiled from original papers*, Vol. 1, (London: Richard Bentley, 1841), 37, 42-43.

187. Lyall, *Hastings*, 11, 23. Hastings' wife, Mary Buchanon, died on 11 July 1759 and was buried in the Murshidabad British Cemetery. Fay, *Original Letters*, 231.

188. Clive forged admiral Charles Wilson's signature after Wilson refused to sign the deceptive copy.

189. Jafar also made Clive a mansabdar, putting him in charge of 6,000 infantry and 5,000 cavalry. Chatterjee, *Black Hole*, 42; George Bruce Malleson, *Lord Clive*, (Oxford: Clarendon Press, 1898), 118.

190. Nitish K. Sengupta, *Land of Two Rivers: A History of Bengal from the Mahabharata to Mujib*, (New Delhi: Penguin Books India, 2011) 173-185.

191. Nicholas B. Dirks, *The Scandal of Empire*, (Cambridge: Harvard University Press, 2006), 51. Sengupta, *Land of Two Rivers*, 173-195.

192. Hallward, *William Bolts A Dutch Adventurer*, 7-8; Lyall, *Warren Hastings*, 15-17; See also Hastings and Vansittart's letter to the Calcutta Council, reprinted in Parliament, House of Commons, 'Third Report on the East India Company,' *Reports from Committees of the House of Commons, Vol. 3: A Report from the Committee Appointed to Examine into the Several Facts and Circumstances Relative to the Late Obstructions To the Execution of the Orders of this House, Reported on the Thirtieth Day of April, 1771*, (London: 1773), 340.

193. Parliament, House of Commons, 'Fourth Report on the East India Company,' *Reports from Committees of the House of Commons, Vol. 3: A Report from the Committee Appointed to Examine into the Several Facts and Circumstances Relative to the Late Obstructions To the Execution of the Orders of this House, Reported on the Thirtieth Day of April, 1771*, (London: 1773), 486.

194. G. J. Bryant, *The Emergence of British Power in India, 1600-1784: A Grand Strategic Interpretation*, (Woodbridge: Boydell & Brewer Ltd, 2013), 170.

195. On 7 July 1763, the Council declared war against Mir Qasim. Henry Dodwell, *Dupleix and Clive: Beginning of Empire*, (London: F. Cass and Co, 1967. Reprint, London: Routledge, 2013), 224-225.

196. Dirks, *Scandal of Empire*, 51.

197. Mary Evelyn Monckton Jones, *Warren Hastings in Bengal 1772-1774*, (Oxford: Clarendon Press, 1918), 228.

198. Marshall, *East India Fortunes*, 116-120.

199. Willem G. J. Kuiters, *The British in Bengal, 1756-1773: A Society in Transition Seen Through the Biography of a Rebel: William Bolts (1739-1808)*, (Paris: Indes savantes, 2002), 83.

200. Jones, *Hastings in Bengal*, 102.

201. Penderel Moon, *Warren Hastings and British India*, (London: Hodder & Stoughton, 1947), 59; Gleig, *Hastings Memoirs Vol. 1*, 135.

202. Henry Beveridge, *A Comprehensive History of India, Civil, Military and Social: From the First Landing of the English, to the Suppression of the Sepoy Revolt; Including an Outline of the Early History of Hindoostan, Vol. 2*, (London: Blackie and Son, 1862), 302.

203. Lyall, *Warren Hastings*, 24.

204. Bryant, *British Power in India*, 224.

205. On 28 April 1772, Hastings formally took his seat as Governor. Gleig *Hastings Memoirs, Vol. 1*, 176.

206. Abdul Majed Khan, *The Transition in Bengal, 1756-75: A Study of Saiyid Muhammad Reza Khan*, (Cambridge: Cambridge University Press, 2007), 217.

207. Rice tripled in price in Calcutta from Rs 0.73 in 1754 to Rs 3.33 per maund in 1771, and increased ten times in price outside Calcutta. Dasgupta and Chakraborti 'Growth of Calcutta,' 45.

208. Khan, *Saiyid Muhammad Reza Khan*, 218-220; See also Ainslie Thomas Embree, *Charles Grant and British Rule in India*, (London: George Allen & Unwin, 1962), 36.

209. Report from Ujagger Mull, amil of Jessore. Jones, *Hastings in Bengal*, 91.

210. Jones, *Hastings in Bengal*, 92.

211. Dasgupta, 'Peasant Resistance in Bengal,' 22; Amartya Sen, *Poverty and Famines: An Essay on Entitlement and Deprivation*, (Oxford: Oxford University Press, 1981), 39.

212. Jones, *Hastings in Bengal*, 63-64. Khan, *Saiyid Muhammad Reza Khan*, 221-223. Sayyid Reza Khan, the deputy diwan to the Nawab of Bengal, was reported to throw defaulting amils into a pit filled with human excrement to extract payments. For further examples, see John R. McLane, *Land and Local Kingship in Eighteenth-Century Bengal*, (Cambridge: Cambridge University Press, 2002), 61-95.

213. For a discussion of the Fakir-Sanyasi rebellions see William R. Pinch, *Warrior Ascetics and Indian Empires*, (Cambridge: Cambridge University Press, 2006).

214. Jones, *Hastings in Bengal*, 257.

215. Ibid., 331.

216. Hastings placed his council in charge of the *Sadr Diwani Adalat*, the Central Civil Court, and the *Nizamat Adalat*, the Central Criminal Court. Jones, *Hastings in Bengal*, 324.

217. Although it is certain Hastings made more than his official salary,

Munni Begum's present to Hastings is one of the few proven instances of Hastings' corruption during this time. According to P. J. Marshall, Hastings remitted £122,000 to England after his first four years in office, while his official salary totaled £97,500. Even if Hastings had saved the entirety of his salary, by January 1776, he had remitted about £25,000 more than he was officially permitted to earn. Marshall, *Impeachment of Warren Hastings*, 131, 145, 147.

218. Jones, *Hastings in Bengal*, 233-235.

219. Even before Hastings signed a treaty in which Cooch Behar would pay for the Company's intervention against Bhutan, Hastings sent in Company troops. The treaty, signed on 5 April 1773, stipulated that Cooch Behar's Maharaja Dharendra Narayan would pay the Company's military expenses and give the Company half of Cooch Behar's annual revenue. Pinch, Warrior Ascetics and Indian Empires, 90-91; Jones, *Hastings in Bengal*, 212; Karma Phuntsho, 'The Opportunistic EIC,' *The History of Bhutan*, (Noida: Random House India, 2013), unpaginated.

220. Sanjay Upadhya, *Nepal and the Geo-Strategic Rivalry between China and India*, (New York: Routledge, 2012), 18.

221. Parliament, House of Commons, 'Fifth Report from the Committee of Secrecy,' *Reports from Committees of the House of Commons: Re-printed by Order of the House, Vol. 7, East Indies, Carnatic War, 1781-1782*. 901-943. According to the translator of the treaty, William Redfearn, the original Persian word was 'istesaul,' which had been variously translated as 'exterminate' or 'extirpate.' The original treaty in Persian is no longer existent. C. Collin Davies, *Warren Hastings and Oudh*, (Oxford University Press, 1939), 60 and J. Strachey, *Hastings and the Rohilla War*, (Oxford: Clarendon Press, 1892), vii, both argued that Hastings had no intent to exterminate the Rohillas and that extirpate was a better translation.

222. House of Commons, 'Fifth Report from the Committee of Secrecy,' 1015-1023.

223. Ibid., 882, 985-987, 1013-1018, 1031.

224. Nuwab Moost'ujab Khan Buhadoor, *The life of Hafiz ool-Moolk, Hafiz Rehmut Khan*, trans. Charles Elliott, (London: Oriental Translation Fund, 1831), 110-117.

225. House of Commons, 'Fifth Report from the Committee of Secrecy,' 924.

226. Charles Hamilton, *An Historical Relation of the Origin, Progress*

and Final Dissolution of the Rohilla Afghans, (London: J. Debrett, 1783), 241; House of Commons, Fifth Report from the Committee of Secrecy, 924.

227. *The Origin and Authentic Narrative of the Present Maratha War; and also, the Late Rohilla War in 1773 and 1774*, (London: J. Almon and J. Debrett, 1781), 6.

228. House of Commons, 'Fifth Report from the Committee of Secrecy,' 1061, 1067.

229. Ibid., 927.

230. Strachey, *Hastings and the Rohilla War,* 149. Morale was further lowered when Hastings refused the prize money because the newly arrived Regulating Act forbade all presents. *India Courier Extraordinary Vol 2*, (1786), 9-19, and *Appendix Vol. 1*, (1786), 1-3.

231. Gleig, *Hastings' Memoirs, Vol. 1*, 421; House of Commons, 'Fifth Report from the Committee of Secrecy,' 1005.

232. House of Commons, 'Fifth Report from the Committee of Secrecy,' 1031, 1041.

233. The fate of these of Rohillas has been debated fiercely. Some claimed that the Rohillas were forced into hostile territory and likely perished. 'Rohilla War,' *Authentic Narrative*, 12. Others, like Charles Hamilton, who wrote his book to defend Hastings, claimed they passed peacefully into neighbouring territory. Hamilton, *An Historical Relation*, 293-297. J. Strachey claimed that mostly they were 'unmolested, and either remained in their former homes or settled in the Rampur State.' Strachey, *Hastings and the Rohilla War*, 151.

234. Parkes and Merivale, *Francis Memoirs, Vol. 2*, 18.

235. Busteed, *Echoes*, 67.

236. H. V. Bowen, *Revenue and Reform: The Indian Problem in British Politics 1757-1773*, (Cambridge: Cambridge University Press, 2002), 118-128, 153, 186.

237. Francis was ever suspicious of Hastings' motivations for the Rohilla War. 'We had reason to believe that Hastings had not gone up to Benares, nor engaged in so dangerous and unwarrantable a measure as the extirpation of a nation allied to the Company, without taking ample care of his own fortune,' Francis wrote in a private memo. Parkes and Merivale, *Francis Memoirs, Vol. 2*, 49-51.

238. House of Commons, 'Fifth Report from the Committee of Secrecy,' 991.

239. Ibid., 1007. Hastings was surprised to find the new councillors

so opposed to a war that he thought clearly benefitted both the Company and the British Empire. 'To me the whole proceedings in this business carries the air of an inquisition,' he wrote. House of Commons, 'Fifth Report from the Committee of Secrecy,' 986.

240. Sophia Weitzman, *Warren Hastings and Philip Francis*, (Manchester University Press, 1929), 84.

241. Ibid., 74.

242. Ibid., 55.

243. Pandey, *Impey*, 51-59. Hastings and Nanda Kumar's animosity dated back to 1758 when Nanda Kumar replaced Hastings as the Company's revenue collector for Burdwan, a lucrative post. See Gleig, *Hastings, Vol. 1*, 62-68. Hastings denied corruption allegations, and with Barwell, walked out of the Council, declaring its meetings void. See also James Fitzjames Stephen, *The Story of Nuncomar and the Impeachment of Sir Elijah Impey, Vol 1*, (London: Macmillan and Co., 1885).

244. It is still unknown to what extent Hastings was involved in Nanda Kumar's trial. But it is certain that his aide, George Vansittart, kept Hastings closely informed as he gathered evidence and witnesses. See Lucy S. Sutherland, 'New Evidence on the NandaKuma Trial,' *The English Historical Review* 72, No. 284 (Jul., 1957): 438-465.

245. Weitzman, *Hastings and Francis*, 114-117.

246. Sailendra Nath Sen, *Anglo-Maratha Relations During the Administration of Warren Hastings, 1772-1785*, (Calcutta: Firma K. L. Mukhopadhyay, 1961), 143-147.

247. BL, Mss EUR E 14, Francis to Andrew Ross, 1780.02.12., 362.

248. HBG 1781.04.21, 2. See also 1781.06.09, 3.

249. Since *Hicky's Bengal Gazette* was still the only newspaper printed in Calcutta as of August 1780, Fay must have meant it by writing 'Calcutta Gazettes.' Fay, *Letters*, 142. Eliza Fay to Unknown, 1780.08.31.

250. HBG 1780.04.22, 2.

251. The cemetery was 600 square yards. HBG 1780.03.25, 2 Philantropos.

252. HBG 1780.05.06, 2 Publicus.

253. HBG 1780.04.08, 2 Homo.

254. Hill, *Women's History: Eighteenth-century Women: An Anthology*; Jones, *World and Word: Women in the Eighteenth Century: Constructions of Femininity*.

255. HBG 1781.10.20, 2.

256. HBG 1781.11.17, 2, quoting Thomas Pollen, *The Fatal Consequences of Adultery ... With a Defence of the Bill, Passed in the House of Lords in the Year 1771, Intitled 'An Act to Restrain Persons Who Shall Be Divorced for ... Adultery from Marrying,'* (London: Printed for and sold by the author, 1772).

257. Iona Italia, *The Rise of Literary Journalism in the Eighteenth Century: Anxious Employment,* (New York: Routledge, 2005), 4.

258. HBG 1781.09.29, 1, Old Nell.

259. HBG 1782.02.02, 2-3, Bon Ton Intelligence. One of Hicky's most promising female correspondents was a woman who penned her name Lavinia Languish. She promised that she could write satire as witty, if not wittier than any man in *Hicky's Gazette*. 'Amidst the great Number of Correspondents who have rais'd your paper to a superiority over the other, I do not remember to have observed any of the *Female Sex* ... I cannot bear to see the Men have it all to themselves,' she wrote. Hicky's newspaper was shuttered before she could bring her talents to bear. HBG 1782.03.02, 1, Lavina Languish.

260. Her words were: 'झूठी बात,' (Jhūṭhī bāta), roughly meaning 'fable or lie'.

261. HBG 1781.08.04, 1-2, An Extraordinary Anecdote.

262. HBG 1780.05.27, 1; 1780.06.10, 1; Hicky also discussed man eating tigers, including an instance where a tiger ate a crewmember of a capsized boat. See HBG 1780.04.01, 2; HBG 1780.03.18, 1.

263. The accident occurred in the Shobhabazar. HBG 1780.06.10, 2.

264. Gilchrist and Williamson, *East India Vadecum*, 232-233.

265. HBG 1780.04.01, 1.

266. The fire even reached Hicky's house. 'To compleat the distresses of the printer it set fire to the little out Houses in his Garden and also to his Bungalo, and consumed the whole with the furniture contained therein,' he wrote. HBG 1780.03.25, 2.

267. HBG 1780.04.01, 2.

268. HBG 1780.04.15, 1.

269. HBG 1780.04.15, Thomas Motte.

270. BL, IOR/P/2/37, Bengal Proceedings, Cons. 1780.06.26; Letter from Supreme Council to Company's Directors, 1780.11.29, No. 53, 54; Letter to Directors, 1781.04.30, No. 41, reprinted in *Fort William-India House Correspondence, and other Contemporary Papers Relating Thereto, 1777-1781, Vol. 8,* ed. Hira Lal Gupta, (Delhi: National Archives of India, 1981), 520 and 540 respectively.

271. This masthead first appeared in HBG 1780.05.01, 1. 'Open to all parties, but influenced by none', was first the slogan of *The Massachusetts Spy* in 1771, a paper that argued for independence from Britain. A copy is on view at the Newseum in Washington D.C. The *Virginia Gazette* also used the slogan in 1775, a year before the American Revolution.

272. For some writing in *Hicky's Gazette* from a pro-British perspective on America, see, for instance, HBG 1780.07.08, 1; HBG 1780.07.15, 4, Bellario; and 1780.08.05, 2.

273. HBG 1780.04.01, 4. This poem was first printed in James Rivington's *Royal Gazette*, 1778, found in Edmund Clarence Steadman, *A Library of American Literature: Literature of the revolutionary period, 1765-1787 Vol. 3*, (New York: Charles L. Webster & Co., 1888), 353-354.

274. Rumbold left for England on April 9. HBG 1780.04.29.

275. For instance, prize money was given out on 19 June 1780 for the capture of Chandernagore. See letter from Supreme Council to Company's Directors, 1780.11.29, No. 42, reprinted in *Fort William-India House Correspondence, 1777-1781, Vol. 8*, 518.

276. HBG 1780.06.24, 2, Phico Miles.

277. Callahan, *Army Reform*, 130-135.

278. HBG 1780.07.15, 3.

279. HBG 1780.06.10, 1.

280. Paul Cowan, Scottish Military Disasters, (Glasgow: Neil Wilson Publishing, 2011) Chapter 14 (no pagination); HBG 1780.10.21, 2; an account of the battle written by a British officer in chains in Bangalore can be read in HBG 1781.10.27, 1. For a full account of the battle, see Alan Tritton, *When the Tiger Fought the Thistle: The Tragedy of Colonel William Baillie of the Madras Army*, (New York: The Radcliffe Press, 2013), 238-270.

281. HBG 1780.10.07, 1; HBG 1781.04.07, 2.

282. HBG 1780.10.21, 2.

283. HBG 1780.12.02, 1.

284. Compared to Hicky, the *India Gazette* portrayed Hyder Ali as the devil incarnate. A writer for the *India Gazette* even called him a 'demon in human shape,' who was 'insatiably thirsting after the Blood and Wealth of Neighbours.' IG 1781.01.06, 1 Pericles.

285. HBG 1780.12.02, 2. Hicky printed an account of the siege of Arcot in HBG 1780.12.16, 3.

286. Elijah Barwell Impey, *Memoirs of Sir Elijah Impey: Knt., First Chief Justice of the Supreme Court of Judicature, at Fort William, Bengal, etc,* (London: Simpkin, Marshall, and Co., 1846), 213.

287. The displaced were estimated to number 200,000. William Hodges, *Travels in India during the years 1780, 1781, 1782 and 1783,* (London: Printed for the author, 1783), 5-6.

288. HBG, 1780.08.26, 1.

289. The Madras Council forbid anyone from buying more than one bag of rice at a time to prevent hoarding. In Spring 1780, rice retailed for between 14 – 18 Sicca Rupees per maund (37kg) at Madras. By the late spring of 1781, rice was being sold at 120 Pagodas per maund in South India. (One Pagoda equaled 3.7 Arcot Rupees, which were slightly weaker than Sicca Rupees). HBG 1781.05.27; HBG 1781.06.09.

290. HBG 1781.05.05, 2.

291. HBG 1781.06.09, 2.

292. The following newspaper and journals are known to have reprinted or quoted Hicky's articles: *St James's Chronicle or the British Evening Post,* No. 3142 (London: 19 April 1781 – 21 April 1781): 1, *London Chronicle,* No. 3976 (London: 23 May 1782 – 25 May 1782), *London Courant and Westminster Chronicle* (London: 20 April 1781), The *Whitehall Evening-Post,* No. 5463, (London: 1781.04.19): 3. and the *Providence Gazette; And country Journal,* Vol. 18, No. 916, (Providence, 1781.07.21): 3, which contains reference to Hicky under 'East India News.'

  a. A few of Hicky's articles were widely reprinted, such as his *Hicky's Bengal Gazette Extraordinary* for 6 August 1781, recounting a battle with Tipu Sultan, as seen in the *Public Advertiser* (London: May 24, 1782) and *The Remembrancer, Or Impartial Repository of Public Events, For the Year 1782* 14 (London: J. Debrett, 1782): 26.

  b. Hicky's coverage of Baillie's defeat at Pollilur was his most reprinted story (HBG 1780.10.07, 1, 'By the Nymph Sloop of War,') as seen in the *New-Jersey Gazette* Vol. 4, No. 190, (Trenton, 1781.08.15): 2, *The Lady's Magazine; or, Entertaining Companion for the Fair Sex, Appropriated Solely to their Use and Amusement* 12 (London: G. Robinson, April 1781): 221. *The Remembrancer; Or, Impartial Repository of Public Events. For the Year 1781* 11, (London: J. Almon and J. Debrett, 1780): 290 and *The New Annual Register, Or,*

General Repository of History, Politics, and Literature for the Year 1781, (London: G. Robinson, 1782): 41.

293. *Journal politique: ou Gazette des Gazettes,* (April 1781): 55; *Mercure de France,* 7 April 1781, (Paris: Chez Panckoucke): 2.

294. *Politisches journal: nebst Anzeige von gelehrten und andern Sachen Ersten Jahrgangs Erster Band Erstes bis 6tes Monats Stück 1781,* (Hamburg: Gesellschaft von Gelehrten, 1781): 472-473.

295. AFSt/M 1 B 72 : 81, Diemer to Hallings, 1780.12.01.

296. AFSt/M 1 B 71 : 51, Kiernander and Gerlach, New School Advertisement, 1780.01.27.

297. AFSt/M 1 B 72 : 81, Diemer to Hallings, 1780.12.01.

298. AFSt/M 1 B 73 : 31, Kiernander to Michael Hallings, 1782.10.29.

299. AFSt/M 1 H 4 : 36, Diemer to Kiernander, 1780.09.08.

300. AFSt/M 1 H 4 : 37, Kiernander to Diemer, 1780.09.15.

301. Gleig, *Hastings' Memoirs, Vol. 2,* 330.

302. BL, Add MS 39878, f. 18.

303. John Stockdale, *Minutes of Warren Hastings and Philip Francis, Esquires,* (London: John Stockdale, 1783), 7-11.

304. Sen, *Anglo-Maratha Relations,* 161-162.

305. Supreme Council, Secret Cons. 29 May 1780. No. 7; Supreme Council, 1780.06.20. Secret Cons reprinted in Parliament, 'Sixth Report from the Committee of Secrecy', 901-912.

306. Sydney C. Grier, *The Letters of Warren Hastings to His Wife,* (London: William Blackwood and Sons, 1905), 64.

307. Hastings and Francis had slightly different recollections of Francis' words. I have chosen Francis' recollection since he recorded it on the same and they were his words. BL, MSS Eur E 23, f. 318; See Hastings' recollection in BL, Add MS 39878, f. 24.

308. Busteed, *Echoes,* 107.

309. In theory, Hastings would not be immune to a murder indictment had he killed Francis. The Supreme Court had earlier indicted another man for murder in a duel. See the trial of *Rex v. Thomas Frisby Hare,* in Hyde, *Hyde's Notebooks,* 1780.06.28.

310. HBG 1780.07.15, 2; Busteed, *Echoes,* 109.

311. Fay, *Letters from India,* 142.

312. I have retold the duel using three accounts: Francis' account in Parkes and Merivale, *Francis Memoirs, Vol. 2,* 198, Hastings' account in BL, Add MS 39878, f. 18-36. (Partially reprinted in George Nathaniel of Curzon, *British Government in India: the story of the Viceroys and Government Houses, Vol. 2,* (London:

Cassell and Co., 1925), 153-154, and Moon, *Warren Hastings*, 247-248), and Pearse's account printed in Samuel Parlby, 'Memoir of Colonel T. D. Pearse,' *The British Indian Military Repository*, No. 2, (Calcutta: Church Mission Press, July 1822): 164-169. There are some minor differences between the three accounts but all three largely coincide. Further information taken from Busteed, *Echoes*, 107-116.

313. See for instance, the perspective in Seid Gholam Hossein Khan, *Sëir Mutaqharin; Or View of Modern Times: Being an History of India...*, Vol. 2, (Calcutta: Printed for the translator, 1789), 518.

314. Gleig, *Hastings' Memoirs*, Vol. 2, 330.

315. For more on the case of *Nauderah Begum v. Bahadur Beg, Qazi Saudi, Mufti Barracktoola, and Mufti Ghulam Mackdown*, commonly known as the Patna Case, see James Fitzjames Stephen, *The Story of Nuncomar and the Impeachment of Sir Elijah Impey*, Vol. 2, (London: Macmillan and Co., 1885), 163-198, Pandey, *Impey*, 131-147, and Thomas M. Curley, *Sir Robert Chambers Law, Literature, and Empire in the Age of Johnson*, (Madison: University of Wisconsin Press, 1998), 278-288.

316. For more on the case of *Kashinath Babu v. Raja Sunder Narayan and the East India Company*, commonly known as Kashijora Case, see Stephen, *Nuncomar and Impey*, Vol. 2, 209-220; Pandey, *Impey*, 176-195, and Curley, *Chambers*, 298-305. For both cases, see also the *Report from the Committee to whom the petition of John Touchet and John Irving, agents for the British subjects residing in the provinces of Bengal, Bahar, and Orissa* ... (London: 1781), known as the 'Touchet Report.'

317. Hastings proposed the salary on 24 October 1780, but waited until after Francis left to carry it through. Hastings gave Impey the salary on 22 December 1780. Stephen, *Nuncomar and Impey*, Vol. 2, 230.

318. The vote was Hastings and Coote against Francis and Wheler. Impey accepted his appointment on October 19. See BL, Mss Eur E 14, f. 381, Francis to George Shee, 1780.10.10.

319. BL, Add MS 16262 f. 35, f. 37, and f. 122. In particular, letter f. 35, Hastings to Impey, November 1780, is indicative of the importance of Francis leaving on Impey and Hastings' relationship. Hastings wrote: 'Dear Sir E, Mr Fr is come to Council. I have thought it best to keep back your papers till Mr Wheler has privately seen you, or till Mr F. leave us for good. I

have a much better office in reserve for Wilkes & have therefore not proposed his apt. WH'.

320. Hastings appointed Rider to the Board of Trade on 2 November 1780. In addition to having his salary backdated, Rider received it for nine more months before he actually began serving on the Board, in July 1781. BL, Mss Eur E 23, f. 342; NAI, Home Public, No. 63, O.C. 1783.12.18, and No. 16, O.C. 1781.07.16.

321. Impey, *Memoirs*, 215, quoting Hastings' minute to the Council on 29 September 1780.

322. Ibid.; Gleig, *Hastings Memoirs, Vol. 2*, 38, 332.

323. Curley, *Chambers*, 327; Hyde, *Hyde's Notebooks*, 1784.12.24.

324. William Chambers was paid £900 a year as the Sadr Diwani Adalat's Persian interpreter. Curley, *Chambers*, 196, 603 footnote No. 5.

325. Hyde, *Hyde's Notebooks*, 1780.12.21, in which Hyde recorded in shorthand Hastings' oblique attempt to probe his willingness to change his behaviour on the bench through Hastings' agent, the Police Superintendent, Thomas Motte. 'Mr Motte told me he was sent by the Governor General Mr Hastings to tell me that great application was made on behalf of Ramnarain who was convicted of a conspiracy against Gopee Nasir and that Mr Hastings was willing that Gopee should do anything that might be thought proper by me and the court; that the punishment should be made as slight as the court thought proper,' Hyde stubbornly refused.

326. Hicky announced Messink and Reed's plans to the public: 'some secretive and scheming Persons in Calcutta, are preparing materials for establishing a Newspaper, and that they have already, both themselves and their Friends, privately Solicited the Subscribers to Mr HICKY's Paper, requesting them to withdraw their Names from the said Mr HICKY's Subscription Paper, and to place them upon theirs.' HBG 1780.06.24.

327. Wilhelm David Becker in Vepery had made a copy of a press. Becker then wrote to Gottlieb Anastasius Freylinghausen on 25 October 1780 that he would soon send the copy to Kiernander. Duverdier, 'Hicky contre Kiernander,' 65.

328. Only Hastings and Wheler were present for this vote, thus giving Hastings the casting vote. The original terms for free postage were six months, but the Supreme Council appears to have granted the *India Gazette* free postage until at least 11 March 1782, when Messink wrote that it had expired and requested it to be

reinstated. The Council's reply to Messink's letter is not recorded. NAI, Home Public, Cons. 1780.10.09, No. 41. Reprinted in S. C. Sanial, 'More echoes from old Calcutta,' *Calcutta Keepsake*, ed. Alok Ray (Calcutta: Ṛddhi-India, 1978), 291-293.

329. Messink arrived in Calcutta in 1774 or 1775. His theatre was built in Lyon's Range, near the Writer's Building. The military also patronised his theatre. Colonel Gilbert Ironside, Hastings' friend, had watched Messink's theatre, and wrote to a friend that he 'would do anything he could to advance the young man's fortune.' Derek Forbes, 'Our Theatrical Attempts in This Distant Quarter:' The British Stage in Eighteenth Century Calcutta,' *Theatre Notebook* 61, No. 2, (January 2007): 67-68.

330. From 1768 to 1780, private merchants could sell salt. Roy Moxham, 'Salt Starvation in British India: Consequences of High Salt Taxation in Bengal Presidency, 1765 to 1878,' *Economic and Political Weekly* 36, No. 25 (Jun. 23-29, 2001): 2270.

331. See *William Bolts v. Peter Reed*, 1771.10.22 and *Thomas Gibson v. Peter Reed*, 1771.10.22, High Court of Calcutta, Mayor's Court archives; NAI, Home Public, Cons. 1770.02.13, No. 1b and No. 4; NAI, Home Public, Cons. 1770.01.23, No. 6; NAI, Home Public, Cons. 1771.04.16, No. 1a.

332. HBG 1781.05.05, 2-3.

333. Wildmore later reconsidered beating his munshi, realising 'I employed him to speak Persian, not English.' IG 1780.12.23, 1 and 1780.12.30, 1 Hy. Wildmore.

334. IG 1781.03.17, 1 Harry Bawberry.

335. IG 1780.12.02, 1.

336. IG 1780.12.09, 1; IG 1781.01.20, 1 W. Friendly.

337. IG 1781.02.17, 1 Censor.

338. IG 1781.03.03, 1 Dick Wingate. Messink and Reed published another article eulogising Calcutta's 'good old merry days ... when the whole circle of society was confined to the old Fort; and our evening amusements ... was playing Cards and Backgammon, chewing Beetle, and smoking Cherutes.' IG 1781.02.24, 1 An Old Country Captain.

339. IG 1780.12.30, 2.

340. See for instance, IG 1780.12.16, 2 Rejection of Plain Truth.

341. For examples of their opinion letters see, IG 1781.08, 18 Philantropos, IG 1780.12.09, 2 Sam Smack and IG 1781.06.23 Publicus.

342. In comparison, the police and the Supreme Council were the only Company entities to continue advertising in *Hicky's Gazette* after the postal ban. The police to advertise for wanted criminals, and Council to print proclamations that they were deporting all Frenchmen, and would send any vagrant Europeans who did not enlist in the army to England as prisoners. HBG 1780.12.30, 2.

343. See, for instance, IG 1780.12.30, 4; IG 1781.03.17, 4; and IG 1781.03.24, 4.

344. See IG 1780.12.23, 4; IG 1781.01.13, 4; IG 1781.02.10, 4; IG 1781.02.17, 4; and IG 1781.02.24, 4.

345. For instance, Hastings sent £69,466 of his £218,000 total known remittances in the form of diamonds. Peter James Marshall, 'The Personal Fortune of Warren Hastings,' *The Economic History Review, New Series* 17, No. 2 (1964): 288.

346. See IG 1780.12.12 Pericles; IG 1781.02.10 A Friend to Magna Charta; IG 1781.02.24 Anti Pasquin; IG 1781.06.09, 1 J.L.; IG 1781.06.30 Amicus.

347. IG 1780.12.02, 1-2 Pericles.

348. IG 1781.02.10, 1 A Friend to Magna Charta.

349. Ibid.

350. IG 1782.03.23, 1 Logan.

351. HBG 1780.11.04, 3.

352. HBG 1781.11.11, 3. Hicky later wrote that, 'seeing the drift of such Order, that it might succeed,' and might draw away his subscribers, he decided to match them by paying his subscribers' postage, to put it on the 'same footing as the India Gazette.' HBG 1781.05.05, 2.

353. See HBG 1780.11.11, 2.

354. Hicky placed most of his blame on Droz for coercing Messink and Reed into printing, reprinting a second-hand conversation a friend had with Messink. 'I was led on by a leading Man, one of the Members of the Board of Trade,' Messink reportedly said. 'He insists on my doing of it, should I refuse, it might prove my ruin.' HBG 1781.11.11, 2.

355. HBG 1781.11.11, 2.

356. HBG 1780.11.18, 2. The Council wrote that they 'highly disapprove' of Hicky's 'illiberal attack'. For further action, they suggested Droz pursue his claims to the 'proper and Legal authority,' perhaps meaning the Supreme Court. This order was passed when the Board met on November 13, but was written

in the consultation for November 23. NAI, Home Public, Body Sheet, Cons. 1780.11.23, No. 1a. Impey wrote that Hastings prepared and carried the order. BL, Add MS 16260, f. 81.

357. HBG 1780.11.18, 1. Originally printed in the *London Magazine, Or, Gentleman's Monthly Intelligencer* 48, (Jan. 1779): 24-26.

358. HBG 1780.11.18. Hicky's claim appears to have been optimistic. He later reported the ban cost him Rs 1,000 a month. HBG 1781.05.05, 2-3. Despite his newspaper's popularity, Hicky had realised less than Rs 2,000 from his Gazette for its first ten months, with many subscriptions in arrears. 'Every realistic Man will think that he must at this present moment be much embarrassed in his affairs,' he wrote. HBG 1780.11.04. Nevertheless, *Hicky's Gazette* appears to have been quite profitable. At Rs 1 per issue, printing about four issues a month, Hicky claimed to earn about Rs 2,000 a month, or £2,400 a year. In contrast, the famous English printer Samuel Richardson a generation earlier made £600 on his best years. John Brewer, *The pleasures of the imagination: English culture in the eighteenth century,* (London: Routledge, 2013), 111.

359. HBG 1780.12.09, 3.

360. HBG 1780.12.09, 3.

361. HBG 1780.11.18, 3, Many Subscribers.

362. HBG 1780.11.18, 2-3.

363. HBG 1780.11.18, Genuine Effusions.

364. HBG 1780.11.25, 2 'A Friend to good Men.'

365. HBG 1780.11.18, 2.

366. HBG 1780.11.25, 2. I have formatted Hicky's editorial to make it more readable to the modern reader.

367. HBG 1780.11.25, 3.

368. Hyde, *Hyde's Notebooks*, 1780.11.23.

369. Hicky printed only fourteen opinion articles before the Council forbade his paper from the post. Five of these talked of the poor or subalterns, two talked about corruption, and only one talked about freedom of the Press, and that was a republication of Charles Fox's speech in Parliament in support of Wilkes. Not a single article discussed tyranny or oppression. After their order, for the same number of issues, Hicky printed 141 opinion articles. Of these, 44 discussed tyranny, 22 mentioned corruption, 21 discussed freedom of the Press, and 11 talked about the poor and subalterns.

370. Hicky was not alone in writing about these ideals. See, for instance,

the virulent pamphlet debate during the American Revolution. Gordon S. Wood, *The American Revolution: Writings from the Pamphlet Debate 1773-1776*, (New York: Library of America, 2015).

371. Colonel Campbell, and the chief engineers before him, for instance, gave contracts to themselves using Indians as proxies, and the actual value for their work accounted for only one-third of the total value of the contracts. They also certified their own work and accounts. Hyde, *Hyde's Notebooks*, 1778.02.17.

372. Marshall, *Impeachment of Warren Hastings,* 166. Despite Hastings' noncompliance, the directors had ordered on 23 March 1770 that contracts must be given to outside contractors, not to Company servants, and that they had to be to the lowest bidder. The Regulating Act made the directors' orders legally binding. The Regulating Act (13 G. 3. C. 63, Section 9.) Reprinted in *The Statutes, Second Revised Edition: From the Twentieth Year of the Reign of Henry III ... to the Second Session of the Sixty-Fourth Year of Queen Victoria, Vol. 2* (London: Stationery office, 1889), 430.

373. HBG 1781.03.10, 2 Crito.

374. In August 1779, over Francis and Wheler's dissent. Parliament, House of Commons, 'Ninth Report from the Select Committee,' 442. *Reports from committees of the House of Commons: which have been printed by order of the House, and are not inserted in the journals; reprinted by order of the House, Vol 6, East Indies – 1783,* (London: 1806). Who exactly Croftes' friends were remains unknown. 'The Letters of Richard Barwell – XIV,' *BP&P 16*, No. 31, (1918): 82.

375. HBG 1781.03.10, 2 Crito.

376. HBG 1781.08.25.3, Daran Ghur.

377. Hicky's correspondent's estimate was £125,000. My conversion is reckoning the sicca rupee at two shillings in 1779, making £1 equal to 8.62 sicca rupees. HBG 1781.08.25.3, Daran Ghur, and HBG 1781.03.10. For the conversion, see *Fort William-India House correspondence and other contemporary papers relating thereto Vol. 9 1782-5,* eds. K. D. Bhargava, B. A. Saletore, (Delhi: National Archives of India, 1959), 341. Under the old contract, the Company paid between Rs 2.9 to Rs 5 per month per bullock for 3,053 bullocks (this averaged to Rs 177,883.5 per year), and Rs 60 to feed each European soldier per year (averaging

Rs 212,820 per year to feed their 3,547 European soldiers). Under the new contract, the Company would pay Croftes between Rs 8 to Rs 12 per month per bullock for 6,700 bullocks (estimated to average Rs 703,548 per year), and Rs 77.15.6 per year (estimated at Rs 292,626 per year) to feed their European soldiers. Parliament, 'Ninth Report from the Select Committee,' 437-453. In 1780, Hastings reassigned the contract from Croftes to John Fergusson, but this was a change in name only, as Fergusson and Croftes were partners in the same firm. The contractor in 1775, when the conditions were less lucrative, wrote that he made Rs 43,901 in profit over a three-month period. Marshall, *Impeachment of Warren Hastings*, 165, 174.

378. Hastings and Barwell gave the contract (over Francis' objections) to Fraser on 13 February 1778. The contract was worth Rs 120,000 the first year and Rs 80,000 per year for the next four years. The officials of the Rana of Burdwan had previously maintained the Poolbundy. Fraser, who had no experience in dike repair or engineering, immediately subcontracted his contract, appears to have never visited Burdwan, and in fact left India midway through his contract despite still being the official contractor. *An Authentic Copy of the Correspondence in India: Between the Country Powers and the Honourable the East India Company's Servants ... which Were Laid Before Parliament in the Session of 1786*, Vol. 6, (London: J. Debrett, 1787), 75-76. BL, IOR/P/2/54, Bengal Proceedings, Cons. 1782.08.19, No. 16-19.

379. HBG 1781.04.14, 2, Philanthropos.

380. Hicky sarcastically stated Impey's new position was the reward 'the Great Mogul bears him for his long, faithful and disinterested services.' HBG 1781.03.17, 2.

381. HBG 1781.05.26, 4, Urbanus.

382. Hicky's contributors were disheartened that few in Calcutta shared their outrage about Impey's appointment. 'Would your friend Lord Poolbundy be allowed notoriously to violate an act of the Charter, by accepting an additional Salary from the Company,' wrote one, 'while not one has the resolution to expose the Act?' HBG 1781.06.09, 2.

383. BL, IOR/P/2/37, Bengal Proceedings, Cons. 1780.06.26; Letter from Supreme Council to Company's directors, 1780.11.29, No. 53, 54; Letter to Directors, 1781.04.30, No. 41, reprinted in *Fort William-India House Correspondence, 1777-1781*, Vol. 8, 520 and

540 respectively. It appears the tax came in under expectations. Impey wrote that the amount raised 'would not amount to Rs 140,000 ... which is not adequate to the work proposed,' and that the 'the sum raised by the ordinance will I have no doubt be exaggerated.' BL, Add MS 16260 f. 50.

384. The Bye-Law's detractors believed it was illegal taxation without representation. Europeans assembled at the Harmonic tavern and drafted two petitions. One argued it was unjust to allow the police to inflict corporal punishment or imprison those unable to pay the tax. The other demanded more police commissioners to oversee the tax. Indian merchants drew their own petition, protesting that the poor would be forced out of the city if the police tore down all the straw houses and that many would be put out of business because of the exorbitant cost of building brick silos. BL, IOR/P/2/40: Bengal Proceedings, Cons. No. 2-5, 1780.11.23.

385. The Supreme Council appointed Chambers head commissioner in 1778. He resigned from this position in May 1783. The Bye-Law changed the terms of Chamber's appointment and let him pay himself for his labour as head commissioner, whereas before the position of head police commissioner was an unpaid volunteer position. The Bye-Law had been considered by the Supreme Court in October and November before the judges approved it. Hyde, *Hyde's Notebooks*, 1780.10.23, 1780.11.23, 1781.01.11, and 1781.04.02.

386. HBG 1781.04.07, 2-3, Anti Poolbundy.

387. HBG 1781.03.17, 1, An Enemy to Bribery.

388. HBG 1781.05.19, 2, Caledoneus.

389. HBG 1781.04.21, 3, Hicky.

390. Ibid.

391. Hicky's correspondent, Magna Charta, wrote fictitious reports from Japan where a cruel and power hungry tyrant ruled. In this faraway land, the tyrant gained control by appointing 'tools and sycophants' to all important positions. The tyrant and his cronies had embezzled enormous sums from the country, and presided over a regime marked by 'barefaced corruption,' 'public plunder,' and 'illegal taxation,' much like in Bengal. See HBG 1781.01.27, 1-2; HBG 1781.02.10, 3; HBG.02.17, 1.

392. HBG 1781.03.03, 2.

393. BL, Add MS 29147, f. 316, Pearse to Hastings, 1781.02.04.

394. On 7 October 1779, Mudhaji Bhonsle sent his son Chimnaji to the

southern border of Bengal, at Cuttack. They arrived at Cuttack in May 1780. In October, Hastings had proposed an alliance, secretly sending Chimnaji Rs 3 lakh and promising Rs 13 lakh more. This money reached Chimnaji's army on December 28, 1780. HBG 1781.01.27, 1 Plain Truth.

395. BL, Add MS 29147, f. 235, Hastings to Pearse, 1781.01.29.
396. BL, Add MS 29147, f. 253, Pearse to Hastings, 1781.01.30.
397. BL, Add MS 29147, f. 294, Pearse to Hastings, 1781.02.03.
398. 'A Memoir of Colonel Thomas Deane Pearse of the Bengal Artillery: Part 2,' *BP&P* 3, No. 7 (Jan. – Mar. 1909): 68, 70-71; NAI, Home Public, Cons. 1781.02.08, No. 18.
399. BL, Add MS 29147, f. 316, Pearse to Hastings, 1781.02.04.
400. Pearse is known to have had a Hindu mistress, Murtee, and a Muslim wife, Punna Purree. For more on Punna Purree, the mother of Deane's son, Tommy, see Durba Ghosh, *Sex and the Family in Colonial India: The Making of Empire*, (Cambridge: Cambridge University Press, 2006), 107 and William Dalrymple, *White Mughals: Love and Betrayal in Eighteenth-Century India*, (New York: Penguin, 2004), 295-296.
401. HBG 1781.01.13, 2.
402. HBG 1787.05.05, 2.
403. Hicky implied that this ostentation was insensitive at the time when the Company's treasury was nearly empty from the expense of war. 'To think that in such times as these, when the heavy Hand of universal War presses hard on the state ... He is squeezing from the Vitals of the *consumptive state*,' he wrote. HBG 1781.02.10, 3.
404. HBG 1781.01.27, 2.
405. HBG 1781.04.07, 3.
406. Ibid.
407. See for instance HBG 1781.05.05, 2.
408. See HBG 1780.12.16, 3 Intelligence from the Coast; HBG 1781.05.19, 1, Crito.
409. HBG 1781.02.17, 2
410. HBG 1781.02.03, 2.
411. HBG 1781.06.16, 3, Letter dated Peddapore 11 May 1781. Pearse, who valued these goods at Rs 15,000, claimed he was taking a loss by taking the gifts. 'Had I taken the money it would ... have been about 15,000 Rupees, but an Elephant &c. you know the actual value of and the expense of keeping them,' Pearse wrote to Hastings. Parlby, 'Memoir of Colonel T. D. Pearse,' 247-248.

412. HBG 1781.06.16, 3, letter dated Peddapore, 11 May 1781.

413. HBG 1781.02.17, 2.

414. Mirza Najaf Khan, a Shia from Persia, was the Shah Alam's top general. For more on Najaf Khan, see Julia Keay, *Farzana: The Woman Who Saved an Empire*, (London: I. B. Tauris, 2014), 110.

415. The Supreme Council later issued orders to deliver Gwalior to Chhatar Singh on 2 April 1781. Sen, *Anglo-Maratha Relations*, 192.

416. HBG 1781.02.03, 3. सौदागर (Saudagar) means merchant in Hindi and Marathi.

417. See letters from Thomas Calvert to John Peiarce, Collector of Midnapore, 11 March 1781, D. Anderson to Major Allan Macpherson, 16 March 1781, and Allan Macpherson to John Peiarce, 20 March 1781. *West Bengal District Records, New Series: Midnapore: letters received, 1777-1800*, eds. J. C. Sengupta and Sanat Kumar Bose (Kolkata: Sree Saraswaty Press, 1962), 63-65.

418. HBG 1781.03.17, 2, Extract of a Letter from Midnapore.

419. HBG 1781.04.28, 3.

420. HBG 1781.03.24, 2. I believe this letter was written by William Young, a member of the Company's Council at Patna. Hicky stated that Young was one of his correspondents on which he was indicted for libel. Furthermore, after having read many of Young's letters in the British Library and elsewhere, the writing style is, subjectively, strikingly similar. See Shaw, 'A Letter from James Augustus Hicky,' 395-397.

421. The treaty was signed on April 6, on which Rs 13 lakh was paid. Rs 3 lakh was already paid in October and Rs 10 lakh given as a loan. James Talboys Wheeler, *Summary of Affairs of the Mahratta States, 1627 to 1856*, (Calcutta: Office of the Superintendant of Government Printing, 1878), 347-349.

422. HBG 1781.04.07, 3.

423. BL, Add MS 29148, f. 179-185, Pearse to Hastings, 1781.03.25.

424. BL, Add MS 29147, f. 366, Pearse to Hastings, 1781.02.10.

425. BL, Add MS 29148, f. 140-141, Pearse to Hastings, 1781.03.18, from Ganjam. Pearse also alluded to a shadow government initiated by Hastings' enemies, formed on February 13. 'Wretches indeed they must be who could dare to act in the manner you describe but such I know there are in Calcutta ... I know you despise them as much as I do from my soul.' BL, Add MS 29148, f. 179-185, Pearse to Hastings, 1781.03.25. Hastings named

the conspirators in another letter: George Livius, Murray and Gerard Ducarel, stating their plan was to 'reform the state … They endeavoured to convince Mr Wheler that I was engaged in a policy which would lead to certain ruin, and that nothing could prevent it but the recall of Carnac and Pearse, and the offer of Peace to the Mahrattas.' Gleig, *Hastings Memoirs, Vol. 2,* 384. Livius was also the source for one of the remaining copies of *Hicky's Bengal Gazette.* See HBG 1781.03.17, 1. University of Heidelberg version.

426. Ibid.
427. BL, Add MS 29148, f. 223.
428. Parlby, 'Memoir of Colonel T. D. Pearse,' 212-213.
429. BL, Add MS 29148, f. 169, Pearse to Hastings, 1781.03.23.
430. Pearse, who started with 4,860 men, had only 3,955 left by April 5. Parlby, 'Memoir of Colonel T. D. Pearse,' 226.
431. BL, Add MS 29148, f. 179-185, Pearse to Hastings, 1781.03.25.
432. Ibid., f. 418, Pearse to Hastings, 1781.04.29.
433. AFSt/M 1 B 73 : 31, Kiernander to Hallings, 1782.10.29.
434. Kiernander advertised in the *India Gazette.* See IG 1781.01.13, 3 and 1781.01.20, 4.
435. The *India Gazette* issued a rebuttal the next week, writing that Kiernander had lent them types, but did not know why they were wanted. Messink added that Kiernander later converted the loan to a gift. Hicky was incredulous. 'Every person in Town knew of this proposal … is it to be supposed therefore that Mr Kiernander could be ignorant of this, above all the Men in the Settlement?' Hicky wrote. IG 1781.04.07, 3; HBG 1781.04.21, 3.
436. Capias were arrest warrants.
437. HBG 1781.03.31, 1-2. Hicky cited Job 15:6, Matthew 7:15, Philippians 3:19, Matthew 18:7, and 2 Samuel 12:7 from the Bible.
438. HBG 1781.03.31, 1-2.
439. AFSt/M 1 B 74 : 53, Kiernander to Hallings, 1783.10.27.
440. AFSt/M 1 B 73 : 31, Kiernander to Hallings, 1782.10.29.
441. Kiernander immediately suspected Diemer was behind Hicky's article. Kiernander contacted the Chief Agent of Serampore, who told him that a man named Watts had been given the article by some German. 'It is well known at [Serampore] that this German is none other than Diemer,' Kiernander wrote. AFSt/M 1 B 73 : 31, Kiernander to Hallings, 1782.10.29.

442. AFSt/M 1 B 73: 40, Kiernander to Freylinghausen, 1783.03.25.
443. AFSt/M 1 B 72: 87, Kiernander to Pasche, 1781.05.02.
444. William Vincent, *A Sermon Preached in the Cathedral Church of St Paul, London: On Thursday, June the 10th, 1784 etc,* (London: John Rivington, Printer to the Society, 1784), 89; AFSt/M 1 B 72: 85, Kiernander to Freylinghausen, 1781.04.05.
445. AFSt/M 1 B 72: 87, Kiernander to Pasche, 1781.05.02.
446. HBG 1781.05.05, 3.
447. Vincent, *Account of the SPCK*, 91.
448. Hugh Pearson, *Memoirs of the life and correspondence of the Reverend Christian Frederick Swartz, to which is prefixed a Sketch of the history of Christianity in India,* (Philadelphia: Perkins, Marvin, & Co., 1835), 224.
449. John Zachariah Kiernander, *The Tryal and Conviction of James Augustus Hicky, Printer of the Bengal Gazette before the Supreme Court of Judicature at Calcutta in Bengal,* (Calcutta: Office of the Mission, 1782), Kiernander's testimony (no pagination).
450. HBG 1781.04.14, 3, Hicky.
451. 'For Cutting Disposing and curing an Abscess on his back.' High Court of Calcutta, Archives, *James Augustus Hicky v. Frederick Charles*, 1773.06.24,
452. HBG 1781.04.14, 3, Hicky.
453. Ibid. Hicky borrowed his language from 'Editor's Remarks,' *An English Green Box,* (London: Printed for G. Kearsly, 1779), 79.
454. HBG 1781.04.28, 1-2, Cassius.
455. Junior officers had also mutinied in 1766 in Bengal for better pay and promotion opportunities. Tritton, *When the Tiger Fought the Thistle*, 73; Callahan, *Army Reform*, xi-xii. A sepoy revolt could cause extreme chaos, as it did in the famous 1857 rebellion, when Indian soldiers nearly overthrew the entire British government in India.
456. The mutineers at Vizag then released a European officer who was in jail and marched off into the countryside with him at their head. They apparently dispersed as I can find no further record of them. BL, P/A/56: Secret Cons., 1780.10.26, No. 8-17; BL, MS Eur E 23, p. 333.
457. HBG 1781.06.16, 1-2, Cato.
458. HBG 1781.06.16, 1, Marsorio.
459. HBG 1781.05.26, 2-3, Loyal Subject. See also HBG 1781.05.26, 1-2, Vindex.

460. HBG 1781.06.02, 2, Britannicus.

461. 'Indifferent is my Choice to live or die,' is an allusion to the line 'Indifferent in his choice to sleep or die,' by Joseph Addison, *Cato: A Tragedy and Selected Essays [1710]*, Act 5, Scene 1, ed. by Christine Dunn Henderson and Mark E. Yellin, with a Foreword by Forrest McDonald (Indianapolis: Liberty Fund, 2004). 6/23/2017. <http://oll.libertyfund.org/titles/1229>

462. HBGE 1781.06.25, 2, Britannicus.

463. For the confusion over whether they were the Calcutta Police or the Company's Pike, see Hyde, *Hyde's Notebooks*, 1780.12.18.

464. The account of Hicky's arrest is taken from HBG 1781.06.16, 2 and BL, Add MS 16260 f. 52. Articles 4 & 5, undated [appears to be written 24 September 1781 to Masterman, Harrington and Dunning].

465. BL, Add MS 16260, f. 81.

466. HBG 1781.06.23, 3.

467. Ibid.

468. The two petitions can be found in Hyde, *Hyde's Notebooks*, 1781.06.19, and HBG 1781.06.23, 3.

469. HBG 1781.06.23, 1. I found Curley's interpretation of this satiric playbill largely accurate, with the exception that the playbill was printed on June 23, not June 16. Curley, *Chambers*, 334-335.

470. Hyde, *Hyde's Notebooks*, 1781.06.26.

471. The area outside the Supreme Court would have been treeless as seen in paintings from the period, and Henry W. Lawrence, *City Trees: A Historical Geography from the Renaissance Through the Nineteenth Century*, (Charlottesville: University of Virginia Press, 2008), 105.

472. Hicky recited his 'Extraordinary Gazette' to the court. HBGE 1781.06.25, 2.

473. HBGE 1781.06.25, 1.

474. See Fay, *Letters*, 136, for a description of Impey's pride on heading an independent judiciary; According to the unreliable William Hickey, Impey had a reputation for being vindictive, refusing to interact with lawyers he disliked, even barring those from practicing who crossed him. When William Hickey returned to Calcutta after bringing Touchet's petition to Parliament, he claimed Impey stripped him of his right to practice law in Bengal. 'This extraordinary measure was evidently levelled at me in revenge for my having been instrumental in forwarding the

petition to Parliament soliciting for trial by jury in all civil as well as criminal cases.' Hickey wrote. Hickey, *Memoirs, Vol. 3*, 142. See also Hickey's petition to be reinstated on June 29, 1783, BL, Add MS 16264, ff. 113-114.

475.   Ghosh, *Sex and the Family in Colonial India*, 61.

476.   BL, Add MS 16260, f. 52.

477.   After the defence and prosecution could only agree on eight jurors, Hicky had to drop his objections. William Smoult officiated as clerk in place of William Johnson. Smoult was also Robert Chambers' clerk.

478.   Philip Harling, 'The Law of Libel and the Limits of Repression, 1790-1832,' *The Historical Journal* 44, No. 1 (Mar., 2001): 110.

479.   William Hawkins, *Pleas of the Crown A Treatise of the Pleas of the Crown: Or, A System of the Principal Matters Relating to that Subject, Digested Under Their Proper Heads ...*, Vol. 1, (Printed by Eliz. Nutt, 1716), 196. Under former Chief Justice of the Court of King's Bench, John Holt's rulings, juries lost their ability to decide the defendant's 'intent'—whether the writer meant malice. Judges now decided if content was malicious. Philip Hamburger, 'The Development of the Law of Seditious Libel and the Control of the Press,' *Stanford Law Review* 37, No. 3, (Feb., 1985): 754-757. C. R. Kropf, 'Libel and Satire in the Eighteenth Century,' *Eighteenth-Century Studies* 8, No. 2 (Winter, 1974-1975): 153-168. See also Charles Viner, *A General Abridgement of Law and Equity: Alphabetically Digested Under Proper Titles, with Notes and References to the Whole, Vol. 12*, (Aldershot in Surrey: Printed for the Author: 1751), 228-229.

480.   The letter was published in the *Public Advertiser* on 19 December 1769, and was written by Philip Francis under the pseudonym, Junius. The article can be read in John Wade, *The Letters of Junius, Vol. 1*, (London: Henry G. Bohn, 1850), 255-270, and the verdict and deliberation on 470-473. See also Lance Bertelsen, 'The Education of Henry Sampson Woodfall, Newspaperman,' *Mentoring in Eighteenth-century British Literature and Culture*, ed. Anthony W. Lee, (Farnham, England: Ashgate Publishing, 2010), 163. Hicky was not alone in using Woodfall as precedent. In the case of *The King v. Rev. William Davies Shipley, 1783-1784*, Shipley was accused of seditious libel for reprinting a pamphlet in support of electoral reform. Shipley won the case, being found guilty of 'publishing only.' See T. B. Holwell, *A Complete*

Collection of State Trials and Proceedings for High Treason and Other Crimes and Misdemeanors from the Earliest Period to the Year 1783, with Notes and Other Illustrations, Vol. 21, (London: T. C. Hansard, 1816), 848-1046.

481. To reinforce Hicky's argument, half of HBG 1781.07.07 displayed the trial of Henry Sampson Woodfall.

482. William Oldys, John Malham, *The Harleian Miscellany: A Collection of Scarce, Curious, and Entertaining Pamphlets and Tracts, as Well in Manuscript as in Print, Vol. 7*, (London: Printed for Robert Dutton, 1810), 261.

483. Future editors and newspapers also attempted to use *Fox's Book of Martyrs* for their defense, including, for instance, in defense of the Boston Globe in 1893. See *The Fundamental Holmes: A Free Speech Chronicle and Reader – Selections from the Opinions, Books, Articles, Speeches, Letters and Other Writings by and about Oliver Wendell Holmes, Jr*, ed. Ronald K. L. Collins, (Cambridge: Cambridge University Press, 2010), 119.

484. Like Hicky, Impey also cited *Rex v. Woodfall*, reading from his own notebook, as well as from Hawkins, *Pleas of the Crown, Vol. 1*, 194 and Blackstone's *Commentaries, Vol. 4*, 151-153. Hyde, *Hyde's Notebooks*, 1781.06.26.

485. Sources for this trial have been taken from Hickey, *Memoirs, Vol. 3*, 160-163 and Hyde, *Hyde's Notebooks*, 1781.06.26 and 1781.06.27. There are some inconsistencies in Hickey's account. Although Hickey wrote that Thomas Lyon, an architect, was the foreman, he does not appear as one of the twelve jurors in Hyde's notebook for this trial, nor any other trial concerning Hicky. Hickey's *Memoirs* are often unreliable and sensationalized. Therefore, when in doubt, I have relied on Hyde's version of events.

486. Despite my best efforts to locate records for this trial in the archives of the High Court of Calcutta and elsewhere, I was unable to find further references to it besides *Hyde's Notebooks* on 1781.06.27 and those printed in the *India Gazette* on 1781.06.30. Hyde's notebooks appear sadly lacking in information in this trial and going forward. It appears that once Impey told Hyde that Hicky's trial were going to be transcribed and printed in England (an event that never occurred) Hyde stopped actively recording. Thus, we lose one of the most detailed and elucidating sources of Hicky's trials.

487. AFSt/M 1 B 72 : 95, Kiernander to Pasche, 1782.02.05.

488. Hickey, *Memoirs, Vol. 3*, 163. Hickey did not specify at which trial Hicky made these objections. However, they come within the same paragraph in his memoirs as Hicky's objection to John Rider, so I have placed them with Kiernander's trial.

489. It appears that Hicky was successful in his argument to prevent Rider from joining the jury as Rider was not one of the members sworn. See *Hyde's Notebooks*, 1781.06.28.

490. Chambers came in before indictment was begun to be read. See *Hyde's Notebooks*, 1781.06.28.

491. Kiernander mentioned two other legacies, Mary Handell and Edward Sutton's, both small. 'Of these I know but of two small legacies, the one of Mrs. Mary Handell, and the other of Mr Edward Sutton. These two legacies are brought to the mission account, and I have acquainted the Society of it.' Kiernander, *Tryal*, Kiernander's testimony (no pagination).

492. AFSt/M 1 B 73 : 26, Kiernander to Pasche, 1782.10.28; AFSt/M 1 C 31a : 40, Kiernander to David Brown, 1790.01.30.

493. Hyde noted that, 'The second count differed from the first only in ending with the words "Pious Samaritan", leaving out the latter paragraphs, which were inserted in the First Count. And it seems to me the jury were right in acquitting the defendant of the charge in the first count, because I believe the reproaches in the latter part of the paper, copied into the first count, were intended for the Rev. Mr William Johnson and not for the Rev. Mr Kiernander.' Details of this chapter taken from Kiernander, *The Tryal and Conviction of James Augustus Hicky*, Hickey, *Memoirs, Vol. 3*, 160-165, and Hyde, *Hyde's Notebooks*, 1781.06.28.

494. HBG 1781.06.30, 2, Emilius.

495. HBG 1781.04.28, 2. Cassius.

496. Davies cited Michael Foster, *A Report of Some Proceedings on the Commission of Oyer and Terminer, and Gaol Delivery for the Trial of the Rebels in the Year 1746 in the County of Surrey, and of other Crown Cases etc.*, (Dublin: Printed by Sarah Cotter, 1766), 256-257, on the word 'malice'.

497. The source for this chapter is Hyde, *Hyde's Notebooks*, 1781.06.29.

498. Davies also read Hicky's newspaper from 16 June 1781 in aggravation of his charge. I have been unable to determine which article in it caused Davies to ask for aggravation. See Hyde, *Hyde's Notebooks*, 1781.07.02 to 1781.07.09.

499. 'You can have no adequate idea of their Arrogance and Presumption, such is their Return for the Lenity of our Government, they should in future be ruled with a rod of Iron,' Young added. BL, Add MS 45434, f. 251, Young to David Anderson.

500. Parliament, *Minutes of the evidence taken at the trial of Warren Hastings esquire, late governor general of Bengal, at the bar of the House of Lords, in Westminster Hall, upon an impeachment against him for high crimes and misdemeanors etc*, (Place of publication unidentified: publisher unidentified, 1794), 1698. Hereafter known as 'Minutes'.

501. Ibid., 1757.

502. Ibid., 1697.

503. Ibid.

504. Ibid., 678-681, 1696.

505. Warren Hastings, *A Narrative of the Late Transactions at Benares*, (London: J. Debrett, 1782), 40. The bodies of the European officers were later found 'mangled in a most shocking manner,' while over eighty sepoys were found dead and ninety more wounded. Parliament, *Minutes*, 1773.

506. IG 1781.09.08, 2.

507. HBG 1781.09.15, 2.

508. Hastings, *A Narrative of the Late Transactions at Benares*, 42-50; Parliament, *Minutes*, 194; IG 1781.09.08, 2.

509. Parliament, *Minutes*,1757-1758; HBG 1781.09.08, 3.

510. A howdah is the seat on an elephant's back. Impey, *Memoirs*, 234.

511. Parliament, *Minutes*, 188-189.

512. Ibid., 674, Hurdeaul Singh's affidavit.

513. Ibid., 684, Lieutenant Gordon's letter.

514. Ibid., 669, Mahommed Moraud and Doond Singh's affidavits.

515. IG 1781.10.27, 1-2.

516. Weitzman, *Hastings and Francis*, 360.

517. BL, Add MS 16260, f. 48b.

518. At this time, Hastings was sending letters rolled up in quills carried in hircarrahs' ears to avoid detection. See Gleig, *Hastings Memoirs, Vol. 2*, 412.

519. BL, Add MS 16262, f. 147-148.

520. Impey documented his increasing health problems over many letters in BL, Add MS 16260 and 16263, for instance Add MS 16263 f. 36, Impey to Fleming, 1780.05.06, and Add MS 16260

f. 44, Impey to Michael Impey, 1780.09.14 in which he expresses his desire to return to England as well as f. 47 and f. 48.

521. For Impey's entourage, see BL, Add MS 16260, f. 105 and Government of Bengal, *Press List of Ancient Documents relating to the Governor-General of Bengal in Council preserved in the secretariat record room of the government of Bengal, Vol. 9, 6 March to 18 December 1781*, (Alipore: Bengal Government Press, 1942). Revenue Cons. 1781.07.17, No. 61, and Revenue Cons. 1781.07.27, No. 1, consulted in the West Bengal State Archives. For his family's illnesses, see BL, Add MS 16260, f. 25, f. 110, and f. 133.

522. *Masterpieces from the Department of Islamic Art in the Metropolitan Museum*, eds. Maryam D. Ekhtiar, Priscilla P. Soucek, Sheila R. Canby, and Navina Najat Haidar, (New York: Metropolitan Museum of Art, 2011), 401; Clemency Fisher and Janet Kear, 'The taxonomic importance of two early paintings of the Pink-headed Duck Rhodonessa caryophyllacea (Latham 1790)' *Bulletin of the British Ornithologists' Club* 122, No. 4 (2002): 244.

523. BL, Add MS 16260, f. 25, Impey to Michael Impey, April 1781.

524. Ibid., f. 46, Impey to Masterman, 1781.09.14. Impey is replying to news that arrived in August that a petition for trial by jury from European inhabitants was being discussed in Parliament. See HBG 1781.08.04.

525. BL, Add MS 16260, f. 17.

526. Ibid.

527. Ibid., f. 42, Impey to Thurlow, date unknown.

528. BL, Add MS 16260, f. 52. Articles 4 & 5, undated, [appears to be written September 24, 1781 to Masterman, Harrington and Dunning]. Impey later claimed he sent Hicky's trials to England in February 1782, yet I have been unable to track down the trial transcripts. BL, Add MS 16260, f. 102, Impey to Sir Richard Sutton, Under Secretary of State for the Southern Department, 1782.02.07.

529. Hastings proposed the chief judgeship of Chinsurah to Chambers on July 7, 1781. Chambers accepted two days later. Curley, *Chambers*, 326-328, 603. Unlike Chambers, Impey never touched his salary, instead borrowing an equal sum and remitting it home in at least two parts, first Rs 27,000 and then Rs 16,800, via China. See BL, Add MS 16260, f. 169, 1782.10.18 and f. 262, 1783.03.22.

530. BL, Add MS 16260, f. 52. Article 6, undated.
531. Ibid., f. 81, which is an alternate version of f. 52.
532. Impey sent this money home to his brother in England to help him find a parliamentary borough for the next election. BL, Add MS 16260, f. 44, Impey to Michael Impey, September 1781, and f. 46 Impey to Masterman 1781.09.14.
533. BL, Add MS 16260, f. 95. As Chambers was in Chinsurah, Hyde was alone at the Court. Chambers joined him on October 29.
534. Pandey, *Impey*, 224.
535. Parliament, *Minutes*, 635.
536. Ibid., 625-633, 838-843, 1969.
537. Marshall, *Impeachment*, 127.
538. HBG 1781.11.24, 2.
539. The judges sentenced Hicky to six months in jail and fined him Rs 1,000 for his article insinuating Hastings had erectile dysfunction, four months and Rs 500 for his article, 'The Good of the Mission,' and six months and Rs 1,000 for his article calling on the Company army to mutiny, making for a total sentence of sixteen months in jail and a fine of Rs 2,500. Hyde and Chambers then deducted four months to account for the four months Hicky had already spent in prison. Hyde, *Hyde's Notebooks*, 1781.10.29.
540. Hyde, *Hyde's Notebooks*, 1781.11.02.
541. HBG 1781.07.21, 1-2.
542. HBG 1781.12.29, 2-3, Originally published in John Trenchard and Thomas Gordon's *Cato's Letters*, on 22 July 1781. See John Trenchard and Thomas Gordon, *Cato's letters, or, Essays on liberty, civil and religious, and other important subjects*, Vol. 2. (London: Printed for J. Walthoe, T. and T. Longman, etc, 1755), 34-50.
543. HBG 1781.10.20, 3. Hicky claimed that this article was a reprint from an English paper. I have been unable to track down the original paper or publication.
544. HBG 1781.12.08, 1-2, Aristides.
545. One correspondent pointed out that the Company resident at Oudh, Middleton, had so much control over the young Nawab that he even dictated household expenses. 'Every thing ... is solely in the hands of the Resident.' The Resident might 'without impropriety be called the Nabob himself.' HBG 1781.09.29, 2.
546. HBG 1781.09.15, 2, Plain Truth.
547. HBG 1781.10.20, 1.

548. HBG 1781.09.29, 2, Ingenuous.
549. HBG 1781.12.08, 1-2, Aristides.
550. HBG 1781.10.20, 1.
551. HBG 1781.09.29, 2, Ingenuous.
552. HBG 1781.09.22, 1, Hicky.
553. HBG 1781.08.25, 3, Daran Ghur.
554. HBG 1781.10.06, 1, Spectator.
555. HBG 1782.10.06, 1, Spectator.
556. HBG 1781.08.25, 3, Daran Ghur.
557. HBG 1782.02.23, 2, A well-wisher to the Company.
558. HBG 1782.02.16, 1-2, Aristides.
559. HBG 1781.11.24, 3. One officer who had served in the Rohilla War wrote to Hicky that the plunder was like a long overdue recompense, writing 'I had Relinquished in my own mind all hope of ever getting any part of the late Nabob's donation.' HBG 1782.01.26, 2-3, A. B.
560. Popham himself took nearly Rs 3 lakh in the first division of it. Hicky reported that Popham ignored Hastings' repeated orders to hand over the treasure. HBG 1781.12.01, 3.
561. HBG 1782.01.05, 3, Berhampore. Hicky later issued a retraction for this article after Hastings declared it was a rumour. HBG 1782.02.02, 3.
562. Sanial, *Calcutta Keepsake*, 285-288. Hastings also wrote to Impey about the libel. 'I have been employed this Morning in writing to the Board to assist me in detecting the Author of an infamous Libel published by Hicky against Colonel Blair. Mr Wheler will shew it to you, if you wish to see it.' Add MS 16260, f. 180, Hastings to Impey, 1782.01.16, 'Below Buxar.'
563. HBG 1781.06.23, 3.
564. Hicky claimed one lawyer had offered to help but had incurred the 'displeasure of some great men in power in this settlement' and no longer wanted to be 'concerned' with him. He claimed three others worked for the Company. Two of those had actually assisted the earlier prosecution against him. Another had agreed to be his counsel, but quit, publicly declaring that he 'would not, nor could not be concerned against Mr Hastings.' The last, Hicky claimed, was not even in Calcutta, nor could honestly act as his counsel because Hastings had given him 'a very lucrative salt agency,' and could 'deprive him of it in an instant.' Hyde, *Hyde's Notebooks*, 1782.01.12.

565. These lawyers were Christian Frederick Brix and John Hare.

566. Details and quotes from this chapter taken from Hyde, *Hyde's Notebooks*, 12, 23 and 24 January 1782. Hyde seemed to agree that this second trial was not double jeopardy. 'Damages in a civil Action are not at all in the nature of a fine; they are not for punishment, but a recompence to the plaintiff for an injury received, and when proved the damages are so a civil right in him, as a debt would be if he brought an action for it,' he noted. Hyde, *Hyde's Notebooks*, 1782.01.24.

567. Curley, *Chambers*, 337.

568. John Vanbrugh and Colley Cibber, *The Provok'd Husband, Or a Journey to London, a Comedy*, (London: J. Watts, 1728).

569. HBG 1782.02.09, 2-3, Ambulator.

570. HBG 1782.02.16, 2-3.

571. HBG 1782.03.09, 2.

572. HBG 1782.03.23, 3.

573. 'To be sold by public auction: On Wednesday the 10th day of April inst. Between the hours of 10 and 11 in the Forenoon, at the Old Court-House, by virtue of two Writs of Execution in the hands of the Sheriff; a quantity of Furniture, Plate, Silk, the apparatus of a Printing Press, and about 100,000 Types: the property of James Augustus Hicky.' IG, 1782.04.06, 3.

574. NAI, Home Public, Body Sheet, Cons. 1793.02.01. No. 28, O.C. 1793.01.09.

575. HBG, 1780.11.25, 3.

576. BL, MSS Eur E 19, f. 11, Francis to Edward Wheler, 1781.11.24.

577. BL, MSS Eur E 14, f. 513, Francis to Lord North, 1780.08.30.

578. BL, MSS Eur E 19, No. 1, Francis to Wellbore Ellis, 1781.11.06.

579. Parkes and Merivale, *Francis Memoirs, Vol. 2*, 204-205.

580. Parliament, *Select Committee's First Report*, 439-440.

581. Mackingtosh, *Travels in Europe, Asia, and America ... delineating, in particular, a new system for the government and improvement of the British settlements in the East Indies ...* (London: J. Murray, 1782), 397.

582. Parkes and Merivale, *Francis Memoirs, Vol. 2*, 206.

583. BL, MSS Eur E. 19, f. 6, Francis to Mackenzie, 1782.11.24.

584. Ibid., f. 13, Francis to Livius, 1782.01.14.

585. Ibid., f. 19, Francis to Ducarel, 1782.01.17.

586. Parkes and Merivale, *Francis Memoirs, Vol. 2*, 213, Francis to Sir John Day, 1781.11.24. I have been unable to find the original

letter. While it is unlikely any of Francis' letters would have reached Hicky before his newspaper was shut down, one letter signed Horatio, which Hicky printed on 25 November 1780, is remarkably similar to Francis' Junius. I suspect Francis wrote this letter to Hicky on the eve of his departure to England: 'The Case of Mr Hicky, is exactly similar to that of Mr Wilkes. – The one standing up for the liberty of the press. The other for that of the Subject. – Junius makes the following Just and elegant remark on the Oppression of Mr Wilkes—That the Rays of Royal Indignation tended 'rather to illumine than to destroy the persecuted object of it &c. &c.

  a. 'The Author of these Lines hopes the generosity of the Settlement will verify this, position of Junius, in the case of Mr Hicky, who I dare venture to say will never disgrace the name of an Englishman, or Relinquish his Birth right, by tamely submitting to Arbitrary and illegal Oppressions.' HBG 1780.11.25, 3, Horatio.

587. BL, MSS Eur E 19, f. 4, Francis to Ducarel, 1781.11.24. Francis was determined no one would know that he was contributing to the press. He sent home newsletters on politics concerning India in London and then made clear that he did not want it known they came from him. 'You need not proclaim that you have received them from me,' he wrote. BL, MSS Eur E. 19, f. 12, Francis to Mackenzie, 1782.01.14. See also, for instance, E 19, f. 10, Francis to Andrew Ross, 1782.01.10.

588. Marshall, *Impeachment*, 16.

589. Parliament, *Select Committee's First Report*, 390.

590. BL, MSS Eur E 19, f. 7, Francis to Chambers, 1781.11.24.

591. Ibid., f. 12, Francis to Mackenzie, 1782.01.14.

592. Ibid., f. 9, Francis to Ducarel, 1781.12.25.

593. Ibid., f. 11, Francis to Burke, 1781.01.11.

594. Parliament, *Select Committee's First Report*, 413-415.

595. The conversation took place on Tuesday, 5 February 1782. BL, Add MS 29153, f. 67, Scott to Hastings, 6 February 1782.

596. Parkes and Merivale, *Francis Memoirs Vol 2*, 214, citing Francis to Sir Robert Chambers, 1781.12.27.

597. Ibid., 215, citing Francis to Gerard Ducarel, 1782.01.17.

598. BL, MSS Eur E 19, f. 28, Francis to Wheler, 1782.02.12.

599. Weitzman, *Hastings and Francis*, 146.

600. A vote of no confidence forced Prime Minister Lord North out

of office. His successor, Rockingham, died only two months later. The next Prime Minister, Shelburne, was removed from office. Lord North came back in a coalition with Charles Fox, but that collapsed eight months later. Only finally, at the end of 1783, was there stability, and a new Prime Minister, William Pitt.

601. Holden Furber and Peter James Marshall eds. *The correspondence of Edmund Burke: July 1782-June 1789, Vol. 5*, (Cambridge: Cambridge University Press, 1965), 245, citing Burke to Francis, 1785.12.23.

602. Ibid., 241-244, citing Burke to Francis, 1785.12.10.

603. AFSt/M 1 B 72 : 95, Kiernander to Pasche, 1782.02.05

604. Neill, *History of Christianity in India*, 440.

605. AFSt/M 1 B 72 : 95, Kiernander to Pasche, 1782.02.05.

606. AFSt/M 1 B 73 : 31, Kiernander to Hallings, 1782.10.29. A common case at the Supreme Court cost around Rs 500, while the most complicated cases could cost upwards of Rs 40,000. In a city where a day labourer earned Rs 4 a day, and the literate earned around Rs 100 to 300 a month, these were sums beyond what most could afford. *The Parliamentary Register; Or, History of the Proceedings and Debates of the [House of Lords and House of Commons Vol. 2*, (London: J. Debrett, 1781), 512-514.

607. Kiernander, *Tryal*, preface (no pagination).

608. Kiernander accused Johnson of not having the courage to defend himself, writing, 'Hicky had indeed published many and most abominable things against him, in which, he has silently pleaded guilty, and has not had the courage to defend himself.' AFSt/M 1 B 73 : 40, Kiernander to Gottlieb Anastasius Freylinghausen, 1783.03.25. Johnson had built godowns on the south-east corner of the church yard and rented them to the Superintendent of the Khalsa [Treasury] for Rs 600 per month. See BL, IOR/P/2/35: Bengal Proceedings, Cons. No. 10. 1780.01.30, IOR/P/3/32: Bengal Proceedings, Cons. 1788.01.23 No. 24 and IOR/P/4/4: Bengal Proceedings, Cons. 1791.07.08, No. 8.

609. Kiernander, *Tryal*, Preface (no pagination).

610. AFSt/M 1 B 74 : 53, Kiernander to Hallings, 1783.10.27.

611. Kiernander, *Tryal*, citing Revelation 21:8 (no pagination).

612. AFSt/M 1 B 73 : 26. Kiernander to Hallings, 1782.10.28.

613. Ibid.

614. Sandegren, *Swedish Missionary*, 55. Kiernander sent 50 Pagodas to Cuddalore. SPCK.MS A33/6 (1788-1796), 1788.11.06.

615. AFSt/M 1 C 37a : 93, Bernard Philip Berkemeyer to Kiernander, 1786.06.25; AFSt/M 1 C 37a : 94, Berkemeyer to Kiernander, 1786.01.26.

616. Kiernander's Mission Printing Office sold Rs 4,000 worth of almanacs for 1781. Duverdier, 'Hicky contre Kiernander,' 63.

617. See, for example, AFSt/M 1 C 24 : 37, AFSt/M 4 E 2 : 27, AFSt/M 1 B 75 : 40, AFSt/M 1 C 25 : 29 and AFSt/M 4 E 2 : 45. It was so commonly known in Calcutta that Kiernander sold his types that a person once indicted for theft claimed that he had bought his stolen type from Kiernander. See Hyde, *Hyde's Notebooks, Rex v. Jacob Thomas and Gabriel Manuel*, 1789.11.17.

618. Kiernander's Mission had first suffered in 1780, when the Supreme Council passed the Bye-Law. The poor, including the elderly who lived in straw huts Kiernander built, had to move out of the city's limits, reducing Kiernander's congregation. As well, Anglo-Indians were increasingly shut out of English society, 'On account of their dark complexion, [they] were laughed at, when they went to the English Chapel,' Kiernander wrote. Gross, *Christianity in India, Vol. 1*, 425.

619. See the report in AFSt/M 1 C 29b: 73a, Brown to Gaskin, 1788.03.07. See also AFSt/M 1 C 27: 22, Kiernander to Hallings, 1786.12.31; AFSt/M 1 C 29b: 67, Kiernander to George Gaskin, 1788.02.25.

620. Official reports indicated his salary was paid from 1782 to 1787 when it actually was not. See SPCK.MS B1/1781 to 1788.

621. AFSt/M 1 B 73: 32, 1782.10.30.

622. AFSt/M 1 B 75: 45. Gerlach to Freylinghausen, 1784.11.26. I am indebted to Markus Berger for translating this letter.

623. AFSt/M 1 B 74: 52, Kiernander to Gottleib Anastasius Freylinghausen, 1783.08.14.

624. AFSt/M 1 B 74: 57, Kiernander to Gottleib Anastasius Freylinghausen, 1783.01.14.

625. AFSt/M 1 B 75: 45. Gerlach to Freylinghausen, 1784.11.26.

626. AFSt/M 1 C 27: 29, Kiernander to Sebastian Andreas Fabricius, 1787.03.05.

627. AFSt/M 1 B 75: 42, Kiernander to Pasche 1784.10.12.

628. 'No salaries neither for me nor Mr Bento de Souza have been remitted for these 5 now almost 6 years. Only a Chest of Stationary and a Cheese,' Kiernander wrote. AFSt/M 1 C 27 : 20, Kiernander to Sebastian Andreas Fabricius, 1786.11.10. Unfortunately, the

records of the Society's Indian Missions Committee between 17 February 1778 and 26 April 1787 have gone missing, shedding no light on why Kiernander had not received any letters.

629. Kiernander wrote. AFSt/M 2 E 47 : 13, Kiernander to David Brown, 1789.11.23.

630. AFSt/M 1 B 4 : 4, Kiernander to Michael Hallings, 1783.10.27.

631. AFSt/M 1 C 29b : 44, Kiernander to Hagelund, Kohloff and others at Tranquebar, 1787.10.12.

632. AFSt/M 1 B 75 : 44, Kiernander to Friederich Wilhelm Pasche, 1785.01.27.

633. AFSt/M 1 C 27 : 20, Kiernander to Sebastian Andreas Fabricius, 1786.11.10.

634. AFSt/M 1 B 75 : 44, Kiernander to Friederich Wilhelm Pasche, 1785.01.27.

635. AFSt/M 1 C 27 : 23, Kiernander to Michael Hallings, 1787.01.29.

636. AFSt/M 1 C 29b : 27, Kiernander to George Gaskin, 1787.09.17.

637. AFSt/M 1 C 27 : 20, Kiernander to Sebastian Andreas Fabricius, 1786.11.10.

638. BL, Add MS 16260, f. 100.

639. BL, IOR/P/2/54, Bengal Proceedings, Cons. 1782.08.19, No. 16. O.C. 1782.08.08.

640. BL, Add MS 16260, f. 169, Impey to Shelburne, 1782.10.18.

641. Pandey, *Impey*, 228.

642. Stephen, *Nuncomar and Impey, Vol. 2,* 245, quoting Impey to Dunning, 1782.11.01.

643. BL, Add MS 16260, f. 216, Impey to unknown, 1782.11.08.

644. Impey, *Memoirs*, 270.

645. Pandey, *Impey*, 229. Despite his departure, Impey kept drawing his salary until officially resigning as Chief Justice in November 1787.

646. BL, Add MS 16264, f. 5, Hicky to Impey. 1783.01.17.

647. William Hickey moved into his new house in Calcutta on 1 September 1783, so his meeting with Hicky must have occurred sometime soon after. He said Hicky's letter was 'dated from his old quarters, the gaol of Calcutta,' however, by that time Hicky had moved to the new Birjee Jail, so Hickey either confused the two jails in his *Memoirs*, or read Hicky's letter after Hicky had moved to the new Birjee jail. Hickey, *Memoirs, Vol. 3,* 159-160.

648. BL, IOR/P/2/51: Bengal Proceedings, Cons. 1782.05.02, No. 29.

649. Hickey, *Memoirs, Vol. 3,* 160-163.

650. BL, Add MS 16264, f. 5 Hicky to Impey. 1783.01.17. Lieutenant

Gould was confined again in 1784 for 'assaulting and injuring' a servant of Elijah Impey in a 'fit of insanity.' Impey promised leniency as long as Gould promised to 'prevent similar conduct in the future' and to 'prevent his improper use of strong licquor.' NAI, Home Public, O.C. 1784.09.08, No. 35.

651. BL, Add MS 16264, f. 201.

652. Ibid., f. 202-209.

653. Forbes' first name found in NAI, Home Public, O.C. 1780.02.29, No. 10.

654. BL, Add MS 16264, f. 206.

655. It appears the judges did not help Hicky. Impey sent this letter to Chambers. Chambers wrote at the foot of Impey's note, 'The improprieties in Mr Hicky's letter may well be pardoned on account of his distress, but I do not see how we can relieve his distress. As to his request that he may be informed of all the demands that can be made upon him relative to this business, the Clerk of the Crown will undoubtedly inform him if he applies to that officer.' Hicky sent one more letter on August 22, saying he had gotten no response, to which he again appears to have received no response. See BL, Add MS 16264, f. 204-209.

656. Hickey, *Memoirs, Vol. 3*, 160-163. Quotes in this chapter from Hickey have been modified slightly for readability.

657. Gleig, *Hastings' Memoirs, Vol. 3*, 304, Hastings to Anderson, 1786.09.13.

658. Fox's India Bill of 1783 was drafted by Edmund Burke, who took many ideas from Francis. Although this bill was defeated, it was, in part, an impetus for Pitt's India Act of 1784.

659. Hastings to Scott, 1784.12.26 cited in Gleig, *Hastings' Memoirs, Vol. 3*, 224, 227.

660. Grier, *Letters of Hastings to his Wife*, 251. Hastings had indicated his desire to resign on 20 March 1783, when he received the directors' letter of 28 August 1782, criticising his treatment of Chait Singh. Gleig, *Hastings' Memoirs, Vol. 3*, 87.

661. Hastings to the directors, January 1785, cited in Gleig, *Hastings' Memoirs, Vol. 3*, 232.

662. Hickey, *Memoirs, Vol. 3*, 262. It is possible Hicky may have been released from jail in September 1783, not near Christmas 1784, based on Hicky's claim to the Supreme Council in 1793 that he had been confined in jail for 'two long years and three months.' Given that Hicky's imprisonment started in June 1781, two years

and three months of imprisonment would mean he was released in September 1783. NAI, Home Public, Body Sheet, 1793.02.01. I have chosen Hickey's recollection, despite his unreliability, because he is specific in his details in this instance, and because I have no further information corroborating Hicky's claim.

663. See, for instance, Hastings thoughts in Gleig, *Hastings' Memoirs, Vol. 3*, 241.

664. Parkes and Merivale, *Francis Memoirs, Vol. 2*, 251.

665. Warren Hastings, *The Defence of Warren Hastings, Esq. (Late Governor General of Bengal,) At the Bar of the House of Commons, etc*, (London: John Stockdale, 1786), 24.

666. Ibid., 121.

667. Ibid., 134.

668. Ibid., 143.

669. Ibid., 245, 28.

670. Gleig, *Hastings Memoirs, Vol. 3*, 287.

671. Marshall, *Impeachment*, xiv-xv.

672. BL, IOR/L/PARL/2/8/71 : 1787, 1-40.

673. Stephen, *Nuncomar and Impey, Vol. 2*, 6-7.

674. Peter Burke, *The public and domestic Life of the right hon. Edmund Burke*, (London: Nathaniel Cooke, 1854), 195-224, and 'Account of the Trial of Warren Hastings, Esq. (late Governor-General of Bengal), before the High Court of Parliament, for High Crimes and Misdemeanors,' *The European Magazine*, and *London Review* 13, No. 2, (Feb. 1788, 124-133. A colourful account of the first day can be found in Fanny Burney, *The Diary and Letters of Madame D'Arblay, Vol. 2*, (London: Vizetelly & Co, 1891), 96 and on.

675. E. A. Bond, ed., *Speeches of the Managers and Counsel in the Trial of Warren Hastings, Vol. 1*, (London: Longman, Brown, Green, Longmans, & Roberts, 1859), 182.

676. Hastings' diary is full of entries beginning like, 'London. Impeachment. 1794. April 9. Westminster Hall, 126th day, 1.30 – 5.05,' and 'Westminster Hall, 127th day, 1.53 – 5.20.' See, for instance, BL, Add MS 39882, f. 159-160.

677. Burke, *Life of the right hon. Edmund Burke*, 220-222.

678. Marshall, *Impeachment*, 189-190. For the drain on Hastings' finances, see Peter James Marshall, 'The Personal Fortune of Warren Hastings in Retirement,' *Bulletin of the School of Oriental and African Studies* 28, No. 3 (1965): 541-552.

679. *Calcutta Gazette*, 1797.03.30, 1.

680. Hastings bought Daylesford on 26 August 1788. Elisabeth Lenckos, 'Daylesford,' East India Company At Home, last modified 20 August 2014, accessed 27 June 2017, http://blogs.ucl.ac.uk/eicah/daylesford-case-study/; Lindsay Boynton, 'The Furniture of Warren Hastings,' *The Burlington Magazine* 112, No. 809, (Aug., 1970): 508.

681. Gleig, *Hastings' Memoirs, Vol. 1*, 8-9.

682. AFSt/M 1 B 74 : 59, Diemer to Gottlieb Anastasius Freylinghausen, 1782.12.26.

683. AFSt/M 1 C 30c : 40a, Christian Wilhelm Gericke to Friedrich Wilhelm Pasche, 1789.04.06.

684. Gross, *Christianity in India, Vol. 1*, 433.

685. AFSt/M 1 C 29b : 73a, David Brown to George Gaskin, 1788.03.06.

686. The Calcutta housing bubble collapse also seems to have resulted from an order by the Company directors reducing salaries and funds for house rent for many Company servants. See BL, Add MS 29169, f. 302. Rev. William Johnson to Warren Hastings, 1786.01.10, and letter from the Company's directors to the Supreme Council, 1785.04.11, printed in *Fort William-India House Correspondence, 1782-1785, Vol. 9*, 204-313,

687. AFSt/M 1 C 29b : 47, Kiernander to Johann Ludwig Schulze, 1788.01.12.

688. Diemer attended the Society's meetings many times in October, November, and December 1787. SPCK.MS A1/30. 1787-1791.

689. Recorded in SPCK.MS A33/6 (1788-1796), Indian Missions Committee Meeting, 1788.10.30; and AFSt/M 1 C 29b : 73a, David Brown to George Gaskin, 1788.03.07.

690. SPCK.MS A33/5 (1770-1788), 1788.02.26.

691. They chose Abraham Clarke, a Cambridge educated Anglican priest, to replace Kiernander. SPCK.MS A33/6 (1788-1796), 1788.11.06. On 6 May 1790, the Society received another letter from Brown, Chambers, and Grant explaining that because they had bought the mission themselves and were not going to transfer it to the Society. SPCK.MS A33/6 (1788-1796), 1790.05.06.

692. AFSt/M 1 C 30a : 31, George Gaskin to Kiernander, 1789.17.03. Kiernander denied that he had ever had mortgaged this woman's property. 'It never was intrusted to my Care, nor have

I administered to that Estate,' he wrote. AFSt/M 1 C 31a : 15, Kiernander to Gaskin, 1790.01.15.

693. Cinsurensis, 'Remarks on the Memoir of Kiernander,' *The Calcutta Christian Observer* 6, (July 1837): 374. Diemer's father-in-law, Charles Weston, also supported Kiernander. AFSt/M 1 C 33b : 4b-d, Christian Wilhelm Gericke to Johann Ludwig Schulze, 1792.05.04. I am indebted to Andrew Zonderman for this reference.

694. AFSt/M 2 E 47 : 12 Kiernander to Johann Ludwig Schulze. 1789.12.12.

695. AFSt/M 2 E 47 : 7, Kiernander to David Brown. 1788.04.21; AFSt/M 1 H 4 : 46, Kiernander to Society.

696. AFSt/M 2 E 47 : 7, Kiernander to David Brown, 1788.04.21.

697. AFSt/M 2 E 47 : 10, Kiernander to David Brown, 1789.11.12.

698. Ibid; Despite years of searching, Brown and Clarke found no remaining legacies. When the Society received Clarke's inconclusive report, they thanked him 'for the trouble he had in this investigation,' but recorded in their minutes that, 'The Society do not wish to countenance any further [negotiations] with Mr Kiernander.' SPCK. MS A33/6 (1788-1796), 1791.03.10. 'Efforts had in vain been used, to explore, and recover Legacies said to have been received by Mr Kiernander, for the support of the Mission,' the Society recorded. SPCK.MS A33/6 (1788-1796), 1791.02.17.

699. AFSt/M 2 E 47 : 13, Kiernander to David Brown, 1789.11.23.

700. AFSt/M 1 C 31a : 40, Kiernander to David Brown, 1790.01.30.

701. AFSt/M 2 E 47 : 10, Kiernander to David Brown, 1789.11.12.

702. Brown suggested the Society send Kiernander a pension for his long years of service, 'I cannot but lament his destitution, in the 84th year of his age,' Brown wrote. SPCK.MS A33/6 (1788-1796), Indian Missions Committee Meeting, 1795.02.05. The Society complied, sending Kiernander £40 a year. Sandegren, *Swedish Missionary*, 56.

703. AFSt/M 1 C 37b : 1 Kiernander to Johann Christian Christoph Ubele, 1796.02.25.

704. 'The first Protestant Missionary to Bengal,' *The Calcutta Review* 7, (January – June 1847): 184.

705. BL, Add MS 29173, f. 116.

706. Hicky appears to have restarted his newspaper on 22 October 1785. It lasted at least until 21 January 1786, although it is unclear how many issues were printed before it shut down. I have been unable to trace any surviving issues. See BL, Mss Eur E 6, f. 76, Joseph Fowke to Francis Fowke, 1785.10.11, in which Joseph

wrote: 'Our old friend Hicky is to appear again the 22nd instant, and as he is likely to afford some amusement I shall subscribe in my own name for you...' See also *Hyde's Notebooks, Thomas Jones v. Constantine Parthenio,* 1787.11.15, in which Hicky is noted to have printed his new gazette at least nine times. And see 'Further Extracts from Hicky's Bengal Gazette of January 21. &c. 1786,' *General Advertiser* (London) 1786.09.03 cited in Nigel Little, *Transoceanic Radical, William Duane: National Identity and Empire 1760-1835,* (New York: Routledge, 2008), 81-82. This same article was also featured in the *Columbian Herald,* (South Carolina) 1786.12.14, 2. Furthermore, the *Times of London* also printed an odd note about the new *Hicky's Bengal Gazette,* further indicating that Hicky had reopened his newspaper. 'The following advertisement is prefixed at the head of Hicky's Bengal Gazette: N. B. "A lion's head is fixed near the gate of the printing-office, which has all the proper qualities of a printer's lion. He has eyes which cannot see, ears which cannot hear, and a mouth which is capacious and convenient."' *Times of London* (London) 1786.09.14, 2.

707. Shaw, 'A Letter from James Augustus Hicky,' 397-398.

708. NAI, Home Public, Cons. 1788.07.28, No. 26, Hicky's petition, O.C. 1788.05.28.

709. Ibid., Cons. 1788.08.22, No. 27, Report of Secretary on Hicky's petition.

710. Ibid., Cons. 1792.11.02, No. 30, Hicky to E Hay, Secretary, O.C. 1792.10.30.

711. Ibid., Cons. 1793.02.25, No. 22, Hicky to E. Hay, Secretary.

712. Ibid., Cons. 1793.07.26, No. 14A, Hicky to E. Hay, Secretary.

713. Ibid., Cons. 1793.06.28, No. 12, Hicky to E. Hay, Secretary.

714. Hicky reserved special ire for Mr Morris, who had been a public advocate in 1779, secretary to the Supreme Council in 1795, and had advised the decision to grant Hicky only 6,711 Rupees. Hicky wrote that Morris was 'the one needy dependent of Sir Elijah Impey,' who, 'aided and assisted by the said Sir Elijah Impey was the ruin of your Memorialist's family.' NAI, Home Public, Cons. 1795.02.20, No. 18. Interestingly, Morris' daughter, T. L. Morris, married Kiernander's son, Robert. Cinsurensis, *The Calcutta Christian Observer, Vol. 6, Remarks on the Memoir of Kiernander,* 374.

715. NAI, Home Public, Body Sheet, Cons. 1793.02.01, O.C. 1793.01.08, No. 28. Hicky claimed that he was cheaper than Halhed and Wilkins. His claim is bolstered by evidence that

Halhed and Wilkins had charged Rs 5 for every double-sided page, whereas Hicky had charged only Rs 2. NAI, Home Public, O.C, 1779.01.28, No.10.

716. BL, Add MS 29173, Hicky to Hastings, 1793.11.13.

717. In his petition, Hicky also mentioned a deed he had done for the Company when he was young. 'Know then Gentlemen that he your Humble petitioner did many years ago render the Hon'ble Company no less a service than the saving them upwards of seventy three thousand pounds in one day at the Hazard of his life, and that in hard Cash, for which he received great applause, and was advised to apply to the Directors, who he was assured would reward him, this application he never made, being then young with an independent fortune, and very great expectations in life, he therefore looked for no reward.' I have been unable to uncover more information about his claim. NAI, Home Public, Cons. 1795.02.20, No. 18. Hicky to E. Hay, Secretary.

718. NAI, Home Public, Cons. 1795.03.06, No. 9, Hicky to W. Jackson, Company's Attorney.

719. Ibid., Cons. 1795.03.06, No. 10, W. Jackson, Company's Attorney, to Hicky.

720. Ibid., Cons. 1795.03.13, No. 23, Hicky to W. Jackson, Company's Attorney.

721. Chambers, *Hyde's Notebooks*, 1797.06.21; *Oracle and Public Advertiser*, No. 19855, (London, 1798.02.13): 3. *The Whitehall Evening Post*, No. 7996, (London, 1798.02.13): 2.

722. BL, Add MS 29177, f. 165 Hicky to Hastings, 1799.12.26.

723. Gross, *Christianity in India, Vol. 1*, 435. See also Lambeth Palace Library, VG 1/12 p 99;100.

724. Impey, *Memoirs*, 354.

725. 'IMPEY, Sir Elijah (1732-1809), of Newick Park, Suss.,' The History of Parliament,' accessed 27 June 2017, http://www.historyofparliamentonline.org/volume/1790-1820/member/impey-sir-elijah-1732-1809.

726. BL, IOR/D/151, f. 195-196, IOR/D/152, f. 289-292, 295-302 and IOR/D/161, f. 157-60.

727. A. F. Salahuddin Ahmed, *Social Ideas and Social Change in Bengal 1818-1835*, Leiden: E. J. Brill, 1965), 84-85; Anindita Ghosh, *Power in Print: Popular Publishing and the Politics of Language and Culture in a Colonial Society, 1778-1905*, (Oxford: Oxford University Press, 2006), 142.

728. Shaw, *Printing in Calcutta*, 42-71.

729. Little, *Transoceanic Radical*, 57.

730. Ibid., 57-65.

731. Ibid., 387.

732. Little, *Transoceanic Radical*, 72-85.

733. A dramatised account can be read in John Wood, *The History of the Administration of John Adams, late President of the United States*, (New York: Printed by Denniston and Cheetham, 1802), 110-112. Duane afterward emigrated to America and became editor of the paper, the *Aurora*. Even in America his writing was considered libelous and he was arrested in July 1799 and charged with seditious libel. Little, *Transoceanic Radical*, 86-95.

734. Little, *Transoceanic Radical*, 95.

735. Ibid., 97. See also Mrinal Kanti Chanda, *History of the English press in Bengal, 1780-1857*, (Calcutta: K.P. Bagchi, 1987), 362-363, 482 and Robert Rouiere Pearce, *Wellesley Memoirs, Vol. 1*, (London: Richard Bentley, 1846), 278-282.

736. 'On the Effect of the Native Press in India,' Friend of India, No. 1, (September 1820): 125; Ahmed, *Social Change in Bengal*, 95.

737. Ahmed, *Social Change in Bengal*, 81-85.

738. Chatterjee, *Black Hole of Empire*, 117.

739. 'Debate at the East India House: The Press in India. – Banishment of Mr Buckingham,' *The Oriental Herald and Colonial Review*, 3, (September to December 1824): 109-110; Nancy Gardner Cassels, *Social Legislation of the East India Company: Public Justice versus Public Instruction*, (New Delhi: SAGE Publications India, 2010), 370-372.

740. S. N. Mukherjee, 'Class, Caste and Politics in Calcutta, 1815-1838,' 65 in *Elites in South Asia*, eds. Edmund Leach and S. N. Mukherjee, (London: Cambridge University Press, 1970); Cassels, *Social Legislation*, 372.

741. Figures as of 2014, the most recent data I can find. 'Shri Prakash Javadekar releases 'Press in India 2013-14,' Press Information Bureau, Government of India Ministry of Information & Broadcasting, last updated November 5, 2014, accessed June 27, 2017. http://pib.nic.in/newsite/PrintRelease.aspx?relid=111100.

742. 'Freedom of the Press 2017: India Profile,' Freedom House, accessed 27 June 2017. https://freedomhouse.org/report/freedom-press/2017/india.